WORKPLACE PSYCHOLOGY

THE SCIENCE AND PRACTICE OF HUMAN RESOURCES

FIRST EDITION

By Oriel Strickland, Ph.D., PHR
California State University, Sacramento

cognella™

Bassim Hamadeh, CEO and Publisher
Michael Simpson, Vice President of Acquisitions
Jamie Giganti, Managing Editor
Jess Busch, Graphic Design Supervisor
Sarah Wheeler, Senior Project Editor
Stephanie Sandler, Licensing Associate
Sean Adams, Editorial Assistant

First published in the United States of America in 2013 by Cognella, Inc.

Trademark Notice: Product or corporate names may be trademarks or registered trademarks, and are used only for identification and explanation without intent to infringe.

File licensed by www.depositphotos.com

Printed in the United States of America

ISBN: 978-1-62131-354-0 (pbk)

www.cognella.com 800.200.3908

CONTENTS

Introduction
Workplace Psychology: Theory and Practice

1 Chapter Outline

Learning Objectives

The list of objectives below is your guide for organizing the content of this chapter. After you have read the chapter, you can test your proficiency by ensuring that you can address each of the objectives. Place a check in each box ☐ once you feel confident about your knowledge.

☐ Define workplace psychology and identify the various fields related to it

☐ Explain why workplace psychology is important to employees and organizations

☐ Describe the historical influences on the philosophy of workplace psychology

☐ Identify major trends in the field of workplace psychology

☐ Identify the six areas of study for the Human Resources (HR) Certification Exam

☐ Describe key ethical areas for the HR profession

☐ Explain some of the educational and career options in workplace psychology

☐ Define the scientist-practitioner gap and potential reasons for it

☐ Explain the components of the Scientific Method and the importance of each

☐ Identify and define the four major components of an APA-style paper

☐ Identify considerations for ensuring ethics in research

☐ Define basic considerations in methods: types of data; external and internal validity

☐ Explain major methodological approaches and their relative strengths and weaknesses

☐ Define different types of variables and how they relate to hypotheses

Chapter Overview

There are several fields of psychology and business that are dedicated to the study of workplace psychology. Psychology is generally defined as the emotions, behavior, and cognitions of individuals interacting with their environments. Contrary to popular misconception, workplace psychology does not involve counseling. Instead, the mission of workplace psychology is twofold: (1) to improve organizational outcomes such as efficiency and productivity, and (2) to improve the working lives of employees.

Several fields address the study of psychology as it occurs at work. Industrial/Organizational Psychology (I/O Psychology) is the fourteenth division of the American Psychological Association (APA). It covers issues such as performance management, hiring, training, motivation, negotiation, and occupational health. There are other formal fields of study of workplace psychology that are typically positioned in business schools. Human Resource Management (HRM) emphasizes the coordination of overall business strategy with short- and long-term planning in the daily management of employees. Another related field in business is Organizational Behavior, which focuses on the individual, group, and company-level influences on behavior and organizational effectiveness. An important feature of all of these fields is that they follow a Scientist-Practitioner Model, meaning that professional training is based on the scientific method. The information gained from science can then be practiced within organizations.

Workplace psychology has been influenced by many historical developments, and follows (and influences) important trends in the business and academic worlds. One of these trends is the increased reliance on professional certifications. For Human Resources practice in the United States, the national certification is the Professional Human Resources (PHR). Achieving this certification demonstrates professional competence and is often used as a requirement in hiring. There are many employment opportunities for people that achieve advanced training in workplace psychology.

It is important for everyone (whether working in an applied or academic setting) to understand the fundamentals of research. This knowledge enables one to find and correctly apply the most effective techniques. Research is guided by the scientific method, which allows for a data-based approach to decision-making. Research and its practical applications are influenced by a set of professional considerations and ethics that will be addressed in this chapter.

Misconceptions about Workplace Psychology...

Philosophies of Workplace Psychology (a few Historical Influences)

Several philosophies have shaped the research and practice that affect employment principles. This topic is covered extensively in other sources (e.g., Zickar & Gibby, 2007; Vinchur & Koppes, 2011) and will be re-visited in Chapter 7 (Labor and Employee Relations). The following section briefly highlights some of the enduring historical and philosophical influences on workplace psychology.

Scientific Management. **Scientific Management** emphasized the observation and measurement of job-related behaviors, with an over-arching goal of increasing efficiency and productivity. It is often associated with the work of Frederick Taylor in the late 1800s, and is sometimes referred to as Taylorism. Some of the principles of scientific management involved a highly specialized workforce with a clear division of labor. Scientific Management addressed how people differ in terms of their skills and abilities, and this practice is still fundamental to hiring and training employees. Consistent with the emphasis on efficiency, studies of workflow were conducted with time-and-motion studies in terms of the actual movements required to complete a task. The purpose of these studies was to maximize the efficiency of the workspace and to minimize injuries. This is still an important emphasis in the field of Ergonomics today.

Human Relations Movement. The essence of the **Human Relations Movement** is that social psychology operates at the workplace. The empirical studies that are often credited with first documenting the recognition of social influences at the workplace were published by Roethlisberger and Dickson in 1939. These authors reported the results of a series of studies conducted at the Hawthorne Works of the Western Electric Company. The original goals of the studies were to identify optimal working conditions (e.g., pay rates, illumination of the workspace). However, the results showed that humans are not machines who respond in predictable ways to these conditions; rather, they are complex social beings who construe meaning from their environments and behave accordingly. For instance, social norms were often the most important influence on workers' behavior. These studies are also credited with the origination of the term **Hawthorne effect** which means that any observed changes in a behavior being studied may be due simply to the novelty of the situation. In other words, the process of studying a behavior may change that behavior. Today, workplace psychologists recognize the complexities of conducting research within organizations, and are very aware of the role of social influences at work.

The Civil Rights Movement. The United States saw major societal changes in the 1960s and 1970s that emphasized the establishment and protection of individual rights. The social movement was bolstered by significant federal legislation that attempted to mandate the fair treatment of protected classes of workers, and specified employment practices that would be deemed unlawful. The Civil Rights Movement was important in raising attention to fairness and justice at the workplace, and psychologists emphasized these topics as well. Important terms related to perceptions of fairness at work include the **Psychological Contract** and the **Social Exchange** Relationship inherent at the workplace. Many policies in Human Resources are founded on the recognition of this exchange relationship. In other words, employees exchange their inputs (such as time, energy, and productivity) for outcomes (such as pay, opportunities, and recognition). Today it is well known that employees generally expect a fair exchange relationship at work and are more content when they receive one.

Cross-cultural Psychology. In the relatively brief history of workplace psychology, the vast majority of studies and theories have been conducted with "western values," particularly those of the United States (Arnett, 2008). However, many findings in psychology depend upon the culture in which they exist (Gelfand,

Erez, & Aycan, 2007). Research in the 1980s and 1990s documented a variety of cultural influences, and developed theories about the ways in which different national cultures affect various work processes (for a review, see Hofstede, 1996). Workplace psychologists now recognize the role of culture and have begun to chart cross-cultural similarities and differences.

The Scientific Method. Throughout its history, enduring practices in workplace psychology have been established via the scientific method (Zickar & Gibby, 2007). This is a rigorous and systematic means of collecting data to address a question of interest. Workplace psychology relies on the scientific method to establish theories and best practices. The scientific method is so fundamental to the field of workplace psychology that the latter part of this chapter is dedicated to its description. In applying the scientific method, psychologists have recognized the many different **levels of analysis** at the workplace. This means that any topic can be studied in terms of the smallest unit of analysis (typically considered as the individual employee) or larger units (such as the work group, organization, or society). Many research models and practical applications now acknowledge the impact of these different levels (e.g., Bliese, Chan, & Ployhart, 2007). ⌸

Levels of Analysis = the recognition that workplace psychology can be studied in terms of individual, work team, or organizational variables

Current & Future Trends in Workplace Psychology

It is not possible to foresee all the changes to the future workplace, but several trends to the workplace have gained momentum over the past few years and appear likely to continue. A brief description of some of these trends follows.

Technology. There are seemingly continuous changes to technology that affect the workplace. **Automation** has replaced the need for manufacturing jobs and online search engines have replaced the need for workers in various information services. Another major technological change has been the increased expectations for communication availability. One advantage to these types of communication technologies is that they allow employees to work off-site, and can increase flexible working arrangements such as **flextime** and **flex place**. A potential bonus of technology for HR is the increased use of **Human Resources Information Systems (HRIS)**. These can be used for a wide variety of purposes such as applicant tracking, performance data, compensation, and training.

Automation = use of robotics, computers, and other machinery to provide goods and services

Flextime = providing a flexible working arrangement such that employees must be on-site for certain hours, but can make their own schedules for the remaining hours in the work week

Cost-cutting Measures. The workplace is strongly affected by local and global economies. Changes to the U.S. economy since the economic collapse beginning in 2007 have brought about emphases on streamlining the workforce and cutting back on expenses. As the graphs in the sidebar shows, unemployment statistics doubled in the resultant recession (Bureau of Labor Statistics, 2011). Many employees experienced the resultant layoffs and overall lack of business growth, and those who remained were often required to pick up additional job responsibilities.

Flexplace = providing a flexible working arrangement such that employees are free to work the regular working hours at off-site locations

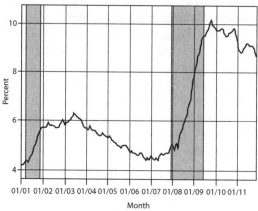

Unemployment in the U.S.

Unemployment rate (seasonally adjusted)

Month

Note: Cross-hatched area represents recession.

Source: Bureau of Labor Statistics.

Outsourcing. Another trend related to cutting costs is to contract services that used to be part of regular organizational operations. These can occur throughout the organization; within Human Resources, examples include administration of payroll, benefits, and employee training. A Business Process Outsourcer (BPO) may in fact take over the entire Human Resource department for an organization.

To outsource a business function means that the function will be controlled by third-party contractors who are paid according to project specifications and do not receive employee benefits such as health care. To outsource an organizational function, there is typically a bidding process that starts with a **Request for Proposal (RFP)**. This includes all the details of the job to be done, timelines, and related specifications. The third-party contractor, or vendor, is then chosen based on ability to successfully do the job and price. **Outsourcing** should not be confused with **offshoring**, which is another cost-cutting approach wherein operations are actually moved to another country. This trend particularly influenced manufacturing and telecommunications industries, where corporations moved to acquire less costly labor in other regions.

Globalization. Offshoring, international mergers, and the Internet have expanded the network of businesses across the globe. For workplace psychology, this means that there is an increasing need for understanding of other countries laws and customs. Cross-cultural psychology has established some understanding of the laws and customs typical of particular cultures. This information can provide useful education and training for **expatriates**, whose companies send them to offshored locations to work.

Changing Demographics of the U.S. Workforce. Within the United States, there is increasing diversity of the workforce in terms of age, ethnicity, and gender (Department of Labor, 2011). The retirement age for most citizens is

Outsourcing = replacing in-house permanent employees with those who work on a contractual basis

Offshoring = moving a job from within the US to another location, either within the same company or another company

Expatriates = employees from one country who are sent to another and must adapt to the culture of the hosting country

increasing, and many seniors find themselves needing to stay or return to the workplace due to losses in retirement accounts. Women are increasingly represented at various levels of the workplace, as are people of varying ethnic backgrounds. The implications for the workplace include the need for diversity training and increased tolerance for individual differences.

Earnings and Demographics in U.S.

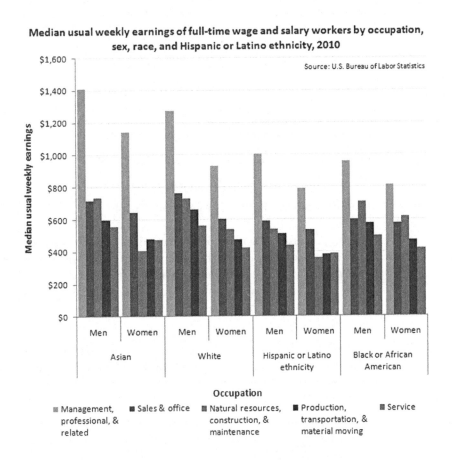

Median usual weekly earnings of full-time wage and salary workers by occupation, sex, race, and Hispanic or Latino ethnicity, 2010

Source: U.S. Bureau of Labor Statistics

Occupation

■ Management, professional, & related   ■ Sales & office   ■ Natural resources, construction, & maintenance   ■ Production, transportation, & material moving   ■ Service

Source: Bureau of Labor Statistics

Legislation. A trend that has existed over the past several decades has been the increased involvement of the government in employment law. This trend has evolved to help raise the standardization of employment principles, but it has also resulted in a large number of costly lawsuits. It is probable that the trend toward legislation of the employment arena will continue.

Professional Issues in Workplace Psychology

Human Resources Certification

As trends in the workplace have led to increased competition, there are increasing demands for professional certification. Professional certification is a voluntary process wherein a governing body issues a credential to those who have demonstrated competence in experience, knowledge, and lifelong learning through ongoing education. The Human Resources Certification Institute, established in 1976, is the organization responsible for professional human resources certification. This institute designates several types of professional certifications (see hrci.org for details), listed below:

- Professional in Human Resources (PHR)
- Senior Professional in Human Resources (SPHR)
- Global Professional in Human Resources (GPHR)
- California Certification (PHR-CA and SPHR-CA)
- Human Resource Management Professional (HRMP)
- Human Resource Business Professional (HRBP)

For each professional certification, a candidate must successfully complete three components: (1) educational attainment, (2) documentation of years of applied experience; and (3) passage of a national examination.

The list below identifies the content areas of the national PHR examination, as well as the relative weight for each topic.

- *Workforce Planning and Employment (24%).* Workforce planning is the "nuts and bolts" of HR, consisting of identifying job requirements, necessary job competencies, hiring practices, and equal employment opportunity law.

- *Employee and Labor Relations (20%).* This area concerns the details involved with union workforces and managing the processes of union formation and development. It also includes strategies for maintaining positive working relations, negotiations, and dispute resolution.

- *Compensation and Benefits (19%).* This content area covers compensation packages and benefit options. This content area also covers nonfinancial ways in which employees might be rewarded.

- *Human Resource Development (18%).* It is important to ensure that employees are prepared for the needs of the workplace. This content area consists of ongoing training, development opportunities, establishing a learning culture, and managing change throughout the organization.

- *Business Management and Strategy (11%).* Human Resources should be part of the "big picture" planning of the organization. This area covers basic business functioning and interactions with the external environ-

---

Types of HR Certifications and Years Experience Required with a Bachelors Degree

1. Professional in Human Resources (PHR)

  - 2 years professional HR experience

2. Senior Professional in Human Resources (SPHR)

  - 5 years of professional HR experience

3. Global Professional in Human Resources (GPHR)

  - 3 years of professional HR experience, with 2/3 years being global experience

---

Content Areas for the HR Certification Examination

Compensation and Benefits	Workforce Planning and Employment
Human Resource Development	Employee and LaborRelations
Business Management and Strategy	Risk Management

ment. It also includes proactive planning and assessing the effectiveness of various programs.

- *Risk Management (8%).* Risk management concerns the identification and management of potential risks to the organization and its employees. These include workplace safety issues, employee physical and mental health, security, and privacy.

There are many uses and advantages of professional certification, for both job candidates and employers (see table).

Candidates	Employers
• Quest for knowledge and personal satisfaction • Sense of achievement and knowledge verification • Desire to challenge oneself • Enhanced self-image • Acceptance by peers and colleagues • Competitive edge when seeking a job • Job promotion • Higher compensation	• Improved quality of products and services • Improved corporate image • Increased competitive advantage • Improved operating efficiency • Increased employee productivity • Increased profitability

Source: Knapp and Knapp (ASAE and the Center for Association Leadership, 2002). *The Business of Certification.* Used with permission.

Ethics for the HR Profession

The previous section focused on the body of knowledge necessary for national HR Certification. To further define the profession, the Society for Human Resource Management has identified ethical dimensions for maintaining professionalism. To make certain that they uphold these ethical principles while at work, practitioners should seek out ongoing training and should also incorporate a reminder system for day-to-day responsibilities.

Use of Information and Privacy. Those in HR are privy to a lot of personal information about employees. As a rule, this information should never be discussed with others except for clearly business-related reasons. Examples of ethically risky information include employee identification numbers, compensation, drug test results, performance, or conflict allegations. Although this may make for exciting gossip in some circles, it is a major ethical violation for someone in HR to talk about this information, including discussions that occur away from the work-site. A key distinction should be made between anonymity and confidentiality. Anonymity is relatively rare, and means that there is literally no way to link the information to a specific person because names are never collected. Confidentiality is clearly more common at the workplace, and it means that the link between a person and their information will not be disclosed. In addition, all employee records and data must be kept in highly secure physical and digital locations. The most important guideline is to *not talk about employee information* at the workplace, unless for a clear business necessity.

One way to set an expectation for personal privacy is to implement an organizational policy such as that described in the sidebar. Although it may be controversial, privacy can be addressed by enforcing consequences for gossiping at work. Given the frequency of gossip and its potential negative effects, it is worthwhile for organizations to consider such approaches to foster an ethical environment.

Fairness and Trust. This dimension of workplace ethics requires that those in HR treat other people with respect, and provide them with a voice on work-related matters. HR deals frequently with Equal Employment Opportunity Law issues and so fairness is a legal requirement (this will be covered more in the next chapter). In terms of an ethical stance, it is wise to simply treat others as one would like to be treated.

Professional Accountability. Many things that happen within Human Resources have potentially long-term consequences. An HR Professional needs to be prepared to stand by decisions made, and the reasoning behind those. This requires good record keeping and a strong attention to detail.

Conflicts of Interest. HR Professionals must recognize situations that create conflicts of interest. An example would be if an executive insisted upon cutting corners on safety procedures. This policy creates conflict because of the professional mandate to improve the well-being of employees. Another situation occurs when an HR professional stands to gain in any financial or personal capacity about a business matter (such as choice of vendor). In this case, the ethical choice is to acknowledge the potential conflict of interest.

Professional Development. Changes in the field require **continuing education**. This includes networking with others and staying current on employment practices. The Society for Human Resource Management has many local chapters to stay involved with the profession. There are many conferences and courses to meet the professional development challenge.

Ethical Leadership. By meeting the ethical responsibilities described above, those in HR can lead by example. In this regard, practitioners are responsible for serving as role models and helping to set the ethical culture for the organization.

Careers in Workplace Psychology

At the most fundamental level, a person can have a career as an **HR Generalist**, meaning that the job responsibilities cover the gamut of departmental functions. The major sections of the HR Certification exam correspond to areas of specialty and consulting opportunities. Those who receive specialized training in Human Resources may work as a practitioner within a private organization or government agency. They also may work as an educator within a college setting or as a trainer. Other job opportunities arise as a researcher at a university, in marketing, or for public agencies.

The Society for Industrial and Organizational Psychology conducts periodic salary surveys to identify professional trends in careers. Results indicate that a majority of respondents work in academic settings, followed by HR positions in

---

Continuing Education Opportunities for the PHR

- Professional Memberships

- University Coursework; E-learning

- Teaching/Instructional Workshops

- Conducting Primary Research in HR

- Leadership Roles in Local Organizations

- On-the-Job Experiences that involve research and implementation

---

Human Resources Generalist = A job title which requires job responsibilities in all basic Human Resources functions

private organizations and consulting firms. The percentage of respondents in each of these settings is represented in the piechart, which shows a variety of options for those with advanced training in Workplace Psychology.

Career Paths in Workplace Psychology

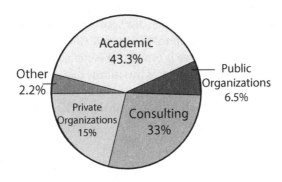

SOURCE: SIOP member survey (2011)

Education in Workplace Psychology

There are several different routes to formal training for a career in workplace psychology, depending upon the desired position. In the past, people in applied careers tended to use a combination of formal training and on-the-job training to rise up through a Human Resources Department. Recent trends in the labor market have resulted in an increased need for formal education to obtain a good job in Human Resources. Basically, as the labor pool increases relative to available jobs, organizations can be more selective in terms of the requirements they place on job applicants.

These requirements may include a college degree such as an Associates or Bachelors degree, which can be supplemented with the HR Certification described above. Most academic positions in colleges and universities require a Masters Degree (M.A. or M.S.) or Doctoral Degree (Ph.D.). The Society for Industrial/Organizational Psychology has developed guidelines for graduate level training in workplace psychology. The topics they deem important during this training are summarized in the sidebar. It is worth noting that there is a fair amount of overlap with the HRCI knowledge content areas. The graduate training guidelines, however, place a greater emphasis on knowledge geared towards conducting independent research, and on topics that may be considered "softer" (in the sense that they are more group-oriented and not subject to Equal Employment Opportunity Law).

Content Areas for Graduate Training in Workplace Psychology

History/ Fields of Psychology	Research Methodology
Statistical methods and Data Analysis	Ethical, Legal, and Professional Contexts
Measurement of Individual Differences	Criterion Theory and Development
Job and Task Analysis	Employee Selection and Classification
Performance Appraisal and Feedback	Training: Design and Evaluation
Work Motivation	Attitude Theory
Group Theory and Process	Organizational Development
Compensation and Benefits	Industrial and Labor Relations

SOURCE: SIOP Guidelines for Graduate Training (www.siop.org)

The Relationship between Science and Practice in Workplace Psychology

In an ideal world, there would be perfect overlap between the applied needs of the workplace and the answers generated through scientific inquiry. This is happening to a large extent (as evidenced earlier in the chapter), with a clear connection between knowledge gained and application to the workplace.

However, there are also discrepancies between science and practice, known as the 'translation problem' (Shapiro, Kirkman, & Courtney, 2007). These authors note that most universities have promotional systems that reward research that can be quickly conducted. Oftentimes this means that research is not conducted to address real, complex issues that require study over time. The lack of a connection between science and practice is further addressed below in terms of publication trends and a scientist-practitioner knowledge gap.

Publication Trends

As mentioned earlier in the chapter, improvements to technology have increased the availability of scientific research to those who do not work in academic settings. Scholarly journals publish studies that pertain to workplace psychology.

A recent analysis of some of these journals points to several trends in the nature and frequency of the topics that are being published (Cascio & Aguinas, 2008). These authors reported that the most frequently published topics in the 2000s included job attitudes, work groups, performance appraisal, test validation, and psychometrics. However, this stands in contrast to the topics that are of greatest "real world" importance, such as outsourcing, health care demands, compensation and benefits, work-life balance, and the aging population. The authors note that there will continue to be a gap between academicians and practitioners if the pressing needs of HR are not adequately studied.

Scientist-Practitioner Knowledge Gap

Research has documented a "scientist-practitioner gap" in the field of workplace psychology. Studies have compared and contrasted knowledge-based items for those working within academic institutions versus those who are working in HR departments. Comparisons indicate that there are statistically significant differences in these knowledge tests, with academically trained respondents generally outperforming people who are working in applied positions (Carless, Rasiah, & Irmer, 2009; Fleetwood & Hesketh, 2006; Rynes, Colbert, & Brown, 2002).

There are many potential reasons for this finding. Part of the explanation for these discrepancies is that practitioners often deal with real-life crises that must be addressed immediately. Time urgency can result in decision-making that is based upon practical demands rather than upon empirically demonstrated best practices. In addition, research is often written for (and reviewed by) those in university settings rather than those in applied settings. Finally, academic approaches tend to rely more often on the scientific method to inform their

---

Sample Items (true/false) from Knowledge-Based Tests

• "Poor performers are generally more realistic about their performance than good performers are."

• "Older adults learn more from training than younger adults."

• "The most important requirement for an effective leader is to have an outgoing, enthusiastic personality."

• "The most valid employment interviews are designed around each candidate's unique background."

• "Lecture-based training is generally superior to other forms of training delivery."

decisions. There is nothing mysterious about the scientific method. It is simply an organized set of steps for gathering information to address a question, with a view to minimizing bias and error. In fact, the scientific method can be thought of as 'project management' for any systematic inquiry. The following section describes the scientific method in more detail.

The Scientific Method

The scientific method is a systematic way to collect information to address a problem or question of interest. Relying on data to inform decisions is also known as the empirical approach to problem-solving. A related term that is often used in organization is to rely on best practices that have been demonstrated to work in other circumstances.

Many authors have written about the scientific method and its basic components. In fact, there are entire courses of graduate study that emphasize different aspects of the scientific method. The following list highlights some of the most important stages of this approach. Each stage requires a fair amount of time and effort, further highlighting a potential factor that contributes to the scientist-practitioner knowledge gap described above.

1. Identify the Problem or Question of Interest. The first component is generally considered to be to identify the problem or question of interest. This step can be driven by either an applied problem at work, such as "How should we evaluate performance?" or a more general scientific inquiry such as "What are the personality characteristics that make some people more likely to be late to work?" Ideas may be generated from either an **inductive** method such as noticing a certain trend based on observations, or from a **deductive** method, which involves deriving ideas from existing theoretical or empirical work.

2. Establish Expertise by Consulting Resources. Having identified the question of interest, it is important to develop one's expertise in the area. This can be established by conducting keyword searches of databases and reading relevant publications on the topics. There are a large number of research databases such as *PsycArticles* or Google Scholar, as well as books, conferences, and a wide host of other professional publications. During this stage it is a good idea to keep an **annotated bibliography** to document the sources that have been consulted and what you can draw from each.

3. Identify and Define important Terms. As you read the literature on a topic, you will find out what is known and considered to be important about it. Theories are often excellent resources. **Theories** are organizing frameworks for explaining any phenomenon. The more empirical support, the stronger the theory.

4. Design and Plan the Study. This stage of the scientific method consists of developing the "blueprint." During this stage the **population** of interest is

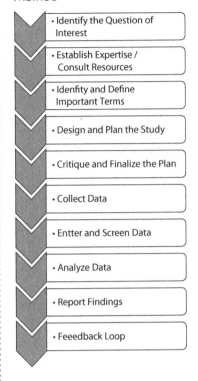

Steps in the Scientific Method

- Identify the Question of Interest
- Establish Expertise / Consult Resources
- Idenfity and Define Important Terms
- Design and Plan the Study
- Critique and Finalize the Plan
- Collect Data
- Entter and Screen Data
- Analyze Data
- Report Findings
- Feeedback Loop

Inductive method = ideas are generated based on observations of a particular topic or problem

Deductive method = ideas are generated based upon their logical derivation from existing theories

Annotated bibliography = a document that contains a summary of information and referencing material for all sources used during a literature review

defined, as well as the **sample** that will be representative of this population. All measurements will be defined with a view to maximizing validity of the measures. The timeline and associated budget will be drawn up, with major research milestones identified. Finally, the procedure for interacting with participants will be finalized.

5. Critique and Finalize the Plan. Data collection is a time-consuming process. It involves the valuable resources of research associates as well as participants. It is very important to anticipate and resolve any problems prior to conducting the actual study. This can be done by appointing a **devil's advocate**, who tries to identify flaws with any aspect of the research blueprint. Another essential step during this phase is called pilot testing, which consists of practice data sessions with all materials as well as the procedure, to ensure that everything functions as planned. Once the research plan is in order, it is necessary to obtain ethical approval from an **Institutional Review Board**. All organizations that sponsor research have a review process to ensure that participants will be treated ethically and that the anticipated benefits of the research outweigh the potential risks.

6. Collect Data. Once all the details about the procedure and measurement have been finalized and the IRB has approved the research plan, it is time to collect the data. This begins with **recruitment** of potential participants. Oftentimes people are too busy or uninterested, so the **response rate** for research can be a problem. It is a good idea to provide incentives for participation by highlighting the potential benefits of the study. Data collection must be conducted with persistence over time and a great deal of care to maintain the standardization of procedures. Ideally, the appropriate sample size will be chosen by conducting a **power analysis**, which will provide information about the necessary number of participants to be able to detect a significant relationship among variables. All data must be collected and stored to ensure the confidentiality of participants' responses.

7. Enter and Screen Data. When the data collection has been completed, it is important to ensure that it is coded and can be analyzed. Many researchers in workplace psychology use statistical software programs such as *SPSS* (IBM), *Excel*, or *SAS* (among others), all of which use a spreadsheet approach to storing data. During this stage it is a good idea to document the key for data entry so that this information is readily available to anyone who wishes to analyze the results. Screening the data means that entries are checked to ensure that they fall within a sensible range. This will catch errors that have been made either during the data collection and entry processes. It is also a good idea to check the shapes of distributions of variables in terms of **normality** or skewness. Some adjustments may need to be made to be consistent with the statistical assumptions required for data analysis (next step).

8. Analyze Data. One goal of analysis is to summarize the data to describe its basic nature. This goal is accomplished with **descriptive statistics**, which report overall characteristics of the data. Examples include averages and ranges of study variables, as well as the shape of the distributions for these

variables. Another major goal of data analysis is to address any hypotheses that have been specified. This is done using **inferential statistics** that are based on probability theory. Examples include comparisons between group means such as the t-test and ANOVA or the linear relationship between variables such as Pearson's correlation or linear regression.

9. Report Findings. An important stage of the scientific method is the **dissemination** of the findings. This can occur in a variety of forums, including lectures, presentations, professional conferences, or journals. Reporting the findings is the mechanism through which others can benefit from the conduct of a study.

10. Feedback Loop. Oftentimes the scientific method helps to address some aspects of a problem or question, but leaves other questions unanswered. An intriguing study usually creates additional questions as the phenomenon under study is better understood. Thus, the evolving nature of the Scientific Method depends upon the feedback loop component.

Dissemination (of findings) = sharing the findings of a study via written documents and/or professional presentations

Major sections of an APA-style Paper

The final stages of the scientific method highlight the importance of writing up and disseminating the findings of the work. There are essentially four major sections for accomplishing this, and are included in the "Spotlight on Research" sections of this textbook. Understanding these will help you to easily organize the information. APA stands for American Psychological Association, and the **APA-style** is a formal set of rules for writing technical reports.

1. *Introduction.* The Introduction section provides the basic purpose of the study, defines relevant terms and theories, and explains the research questions of interest.

2. *Method.* The Method section explains characteristics of the participants in the study (such as gender, age, and ethnicity), any measures or surveys that were used, and the procedure used in dealing with the participants.

3. *Results.* The Results section explains and summarizes the data for the reader. This includes a description of all the measurements taken and addresses the research questions.

4. *Discussion.* The Discussion section re-caps the major findings and integrates them with existing theory and research. It also provides a critique of the study and provides directions for future research on the topic.

Journal Outlets for Workplace Psychology

- Journal of Applied Psychology
- Leadership Quarterly
- Personnel Psychology
- Basic and Applied Social Psychology
- Journal of Organizational Behavior
- Academy of Management Journal
- Human Resource Management
- International Journal of Training
- Organizational Behavior and Human Decision-Processes

Ethics in Science: Mindset for Research

It is very important from an ethical perspective to have the correct mindset in conducting and reporting research. This approach involves trying to find the truth by carefully collecting and evaluating evidence. In all stages, it is necessary for the researcher to be **unbiased**. This means that there is no vested interest or hope for a particular outcome to be achieved. Another requirement is to be conscientious, meaning that the researchers pay careful attention to details. This is important to minimize errors and draw accurate conclusions.

There are several steps researchers can take to ensure that they are behaving ethically:

Unbiased = not having a vested interest or personal preference for a particular outcome

- Disclose any potential conflicts of interest. If a researcher has received any type of funding for conducting a study, these funding sources should be listed and described on any distribution of the findings. This will help the reader to interpret the findings in light of these potential influences on the study.

Blind research = a methodological feature in which any person handling the data is unaware of the purpose of the study or its hypotheses

- Conduct **blind research.** This term indicates that any person who interacts with study participants or collects information from them (or any other source) is unaware of the purpose of the study, variables under investigation, and/or hypotheses. This helps to ensure that the person gathering the data does not have a vested interest in its outcome.

- Be involved in all aspects of the study. A **conscientious** researcher demonstrates involvement in each stage of the scientific method. Neglecting any aspect of the study can lead to mistakes in terms of the collection of the information or conclusions drawn from it.

Basic Methodological Considerations

Qualitative = an approach based on narrative descriptions of the phenomenon of interest

Research methods have several ways that they differ, and these have inherent strengths and weaknesses. One of these ways is whether the information (data) gathered is qualitative or quantitative in nature. **Qualitative** information tends to rely upon descriptions of events or interviews of participants. As such, it is not summarized very easily but allows for a very detailed, open-ended view of the topic under study. **Quantitative** information, on the other hand, has been assigned a numerical value. Therefore, it is more readily summarized and can be run through statistical analyses based upon probability theory. Despite these advantages it has the disadvantage of potentially over-simplifying complicated events (such as performance, as described in the next chapter). Another way to state this point is that the use of numbers often gives an apparent objectivity that masks various types of measurement error.

Quantitative = an approach based on numerical assessments of the phenomenon of interest

Another major consideration is the extent to which the real-life phenomenon is captured versus control over extraneous and error variables. Clearly, it is desirable for a study to have **realism** so that its findings are more likely to **generalize** to other settings and organizations. The extent to which the results generalize is called **external validity**.

External validity = the degree of confidence that a study's findings can be applied to other settings

However, it is important to remember that approaches aimed at maximizing realism do not control all the variables that can influence the dependent variable. Failure to do so can lead to problems in reaching an accurate conclusion about the relationship between the independent and dependent variable(s). The extent to which these problems have been addressed is called **internal validity**. Essentially, internal validity refers to the confidence that one can infer that changes in the independent variable "caused" changes in the dependent variable.

Causation is a <u>very</u> tricky concept in terms of a research setting. In fact, it is not possible to have 100% confidence about causality from any single study, especially in fields such as workplace psychology. David Hume had identified the necessary conditions for inferring causation and these are described in the sidebar. The reason that causation may <u>never</u> be assured from a single study is that it is not possible to completely eliminate all alternative explanations within the context of one study.

Therefore, an accumulating body of research is needed to have confidence in any given finding. This confidence builds if a finding has been repeated over time, in different situations, by different people, using different methods. The major types of methods used in workplace psychology are described below.

The Classics: Major Methodological Approaches

Now that you have a solid grounding in some of the basic methodological considerations involved in the Scientific Method, it is important to consider the relative advantages and disadvantages to the major categories of research methods. These are the ways in which information is collected and can influence the conclusions that are drawn.

There are many approaches to conducting systematic research using the Scientific Method. Some of the more popular approaches in workplace psychology include the laboratory study, the case study, the survey study, and the field study. All of these approaches have in common the collection and analysis of information to address a question of interest.

The Laboratory Study

A lab study is one in which the researcher directly manipulates the independent variable(s) and assesses the effects on the dependent variables(s). As suggested by its name, this approach is typically conducted within a laboratory, often at a university or research institute. One of the best features of the lab study is the **experimental control**, meaning that the researcher attempts to hold all other extraneous and error variables constant. Individual differences in participants (such as age, gender, personality) are dealt with via **random assignment** to conditions based on the manipulation of the independent variable. Due to these experimental controls, the lab study is the strongest method in terms of internal validity.

Although the laboratory study has many good methodological features, it has a major disadvantage in that it is often low in terms of realism. Therefore, it is open to criticism for not being clearly related to the conditions that occur in the "real world."

Internal validity = the degree of confidence that extraneous variables have been controlled in a study

Necessary conditions for "Causation"

1. Temporal precedence = changes to the independent variable occur first in time (followed by changes in the D.V.)

2. Co-variation = changes to the independent variable are associated with changes to the dependent variable.

3. All alternative explanations are ruled out = experimental controls eliminate the influence of all extraneous factors and possible competing explanations for the co-variation.

Experimental control = the degree to which extraneous variables are held constant

Random assignment = a methods technique to reduce the impact of participant characteristics

Psychometrics = the study of measurement properties of psychological variables, with an emphasis on reliability and validity

Reliability = the consistency of a measure

Validity = the appropriateness of a measure

The Survey Study

A survey study is most often referred to as a questionnaire study, which relies on participants' opinions and experiences. A good study requires careful selection of questionnaire items to adequately measure these opinions. Some of the crucial **psychometric** issues with questionnaires are **reliability** and **validity**. Reliability typically refers to the consistency of the measure, which can be considered in terms of consistency over time or consistency of items on a measure. Validity is a complex characteristic that essentially refers to the appropriateness, or truth, of a measure. There are many ways that validity can be assessed, such as asking people their opinions about the measure (face validity), evaluating the extent to which the measure captures the full domain it is intending to (content validity), or considering the degree to which the measure can predict outcomes (criterion-related validity). We will re-visit the issues of reliability and validity, in detail, in Chapter 3 when discussing how to hire people.

The Case Study

A case study documents the development of a person or organization over time, identifying the important components of this development. It relies on a thorough compilation of information from different sources by an insightful researcher. The case study does not include any attempt to control extraneous variables or to address causation among variables; instead, its purpose is to document real-life occurrences. Thus, an advantage of this method is that it is realistic, but due to its low sample size it is not often used to generalize to a larger population. Fundamentally it has an advantage of being longitudinal and yielding in-depth, qualitative data.

The Field Study

A method that combines the best mixture of realism and experimental control is the field study, or quasi-experimental design. This type of research design is conducted within the context of the naturally occurring work environment, and also includes a manipulation of the independent variable of interest. As you can imagine, a disadvantage to this design is that many organizations are hesitant to sponsor this type of research. This research may also be more time-consuming than some of the others. These are only hurdles though, that should be cleared because the advantages of this method make it one of the strongest. All things considered, the field study provides the best blend of internal and external validity (for an excellent "classic" review, see Cook & Campbell, 1979).

The Meta-Analytic Study

A meta-analysis is a type of secondary research that is very helpful in drawing conclusions in workplace psychology. It is called "secondary" because it relies on previous studies that have already been conducted. In a meta-analysis, all published studies that have addressed the same basic topics are combined in a way that allows for a summary of them. In other words, the meta-analysis statistically combines findings to yield "average" effect sizes that represent the best integration of all of the studies. As such, it is extremely useful in workplace psychology.

Understanding Variables: Essential to Understanding Research

One of the most fundamental components of research is to fully understand the concept of variables and how they are used to guide the research process. This topic may at first seem jargon-filled, but once you have a grasp of these terms, you will be able to understand the purpose of the research and how the results can be applied to the workplace. The following section gives you an introduction to the types of variables studied in workplace psychology.

Variables: Independent and Dependent

As part of the attempt to study and explain, the majority of research endeavors involve the identification of important variables. A **variable** is simply a name given to anything that can take on different values (such as height, weight, job satisfaction, profit margins, and training-based knowledge). There are many types of variables in organizational research that you should become familiar with.

Two of the most important types of variables are the **independent (or predictor) variable** and the **dependent (or criterion) variable**. Whether a variable is independent or dependent is strictly a function of the hypothesis that a researcher makes.

A **hypothesis** is a statement of a potential relationship between any two variables. Typically a researcher proposes that an independent variable(s) leads to changes in the dependent variable(s). Examples of hypotheses below demonstrate the link between independent and dependent variables.

Use the hypotheses presented in the sidebar on the left to understand the link between the independent and dependent variables. The independent variables are those "on the left" indicating that they occur first, and lead to or influence changes in the variables "on the right," the dependent variables. Note the direction of the arrows in the graph define the respective variables by showing the motion of influence.

Use the Following Hypotheses to Practice Graphing:

What do you think is the I.V.? What is the D.V.?

Higher burnout will be associated with lower productivity at work.

There will be a gender difference on color preference, with women preferring the color pink over blue to a greater extent than men do.

There will be a positive link such that those with higher self-esteem will be more likely to seek out new challenges.

Ratings of support for the Obama administration will depend upon political party affiliation.

Relative to a placebo group and a group taking Prozac, a group that participates in regular exercise will display lower self-reported ratings of depression.

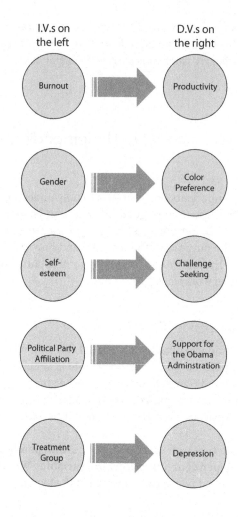

These graphs show the direction of influence of the variables themselves. Each variable is defined by having the levels, which are the values it can assume. For instance, in the third example the variable gender can take on values "male" or "female," and for this study the variable 'color preference' can take on values "blue" or "pink."

It is important to realize that most variables in workplace psychology can be either independent or dependent depending upon the hypotheses specified by the researcher. Graphing the flow of influence according to the hypothesis is the best way to understand the positioning of variables.

Variables: Mediator, Moderator, and Error

In the previous section you learned how to draw the link between variables. This is exactly how it is represented in research. There is more drawing to be done, however, because there are additional variables that are important to add.

Other important types of variables in workplace research include the mediator and moderator variables. These variables help to explain the <u>reason</u> and <u>circumstances</u> under which the independent variable affects the dependent variable. Many topics under research in workplace psychology have been developed to the point where these variables have been specified and a **model** has been established. A simple example including a mediator variable is given below:

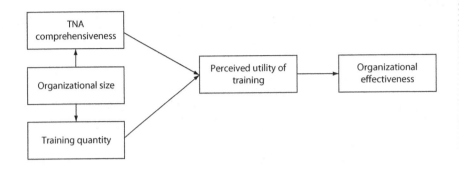

The **dependent variable** is the one on the right that reflects changes in other variables. So in this case, the D.V. is organizational effectiveness. The independent variables are the ones on the left. In this model, the authors hypothesize three I.V.s: Training needs assessment comprehensiveness, organizational size, and training quantity. Note that there is another variable in the middle.

In this case, the authors predict that the mechanism of influence is on the perceived utility of training, which in turn affects the D.V. (organizational effectiveness). This is the **mediator variable**, which explains how or why the independent variable influences the dependent variable.

A **moderator variable** often does not appear in the graphical model. These variables explain that the hypothesized effects will only occur in some situations or for some groups of people. For instance, perhaps only experienced employees will perceive the utility of training; younger employees will not be aware of it. In this case, age would function as a moderator variable.

Last (but not least), **extraneous variables** are all those that might affect the dependent variable but that are not of interest to the researcher. The extraneous variables that might influence organizational effectiveness are numerous, and may include market conditions, product desirability, and employee dedication. Because these variables have not been specified in the model, they introduce unaccounted variance, or **error variance**, into the dependent variable. To reduce this variance, a researcher often will include all the important variables in a model.

The previous section has given you an advanced "crash course" on how to specify the important variables for research. This is one of the most crucial hurdles to cross in understanding how studies are conducted. Once you understand these foundations in building models, you will be in a good position to understand much of the research in workplace psychology.

The next few sections of this chapter are important – don't miss them! The next page provides a "Spotlight on Research," which highlights a study of gender

Dependent variable (aka the criterion) = the one that is hypothesized to change as a function of changes to the independent variable

Mediator variable = a variable that explains how or why the independent variable affects the dependent variable

Moderator variable = a variable that explains the conditions that are necessary for the independent variable to affect the dependent variable

Error variance = effects on the dependent variable that are unaccounted for by the research; makes it difficult to address hypotheses

and persistence during a simulated negotiation. You will be able to view the study through the lens of your knowledge of research methods. The following page provides a conclusion page, "Putting it all Together," that re-caps the main points of the chapter in simplified language. The remainder of the chapter contains exercises that will allow you to check your knowledge and apply it to your own experiences. Remember to use the Learning Objectives to check your familiarity with each of the major topics of the chapter.

Putting it All Together

Considering the material in this chapter, here are a few "take home" ideas for making sure you have a good introductory understanding:

- Workplace psychology is the study of how to improve organizations and make things better for employees. There are many fields related to workplace psychology. The formal association is called Industrial/Organizational Psychology.

- Workplace psychology is based on principles that involve the use of data, and assumptions that people should be treated fairly and as major potential resources for the organization.

- The employment field is trending towards various cost-cutting measures including a leaner full-time workforce, and hiring/working in other countries with less expensive labor costs.

- Human resources in organizations are governed by a professional association that creates and manages an annual certification exam.

- Some HR professionals work their way up through the company, whereas others receive specialized training and advanced degrees in workplace psychology.

- Academically oriented HR professionals tend to outscore field-oriented HR professionals on knowledge exams, and those conducting research often don't address the needs of practitioners.

- The scientific method is the systematic process of data collection and analysis to address questions of interest.

- Scientific studies are written according to technical style (American Psychological Association) and published in peer-reviewed academic journals.

- There are a wide variety of ethical considerations for those conducting research and for those working in the field. These involve being careful with information, respecting privacy, and behaving conscientiously.

- Different methods can be used in research, each with advantages and disadvantages. The best way to resolve these pros and cons is to examine the same question of interest using different methods.

- To understand scientific research it is essential to understand the different types of variables and how they might relate to each other. Embrace these – they are not a drag!

Spotlight On Research

Babcock-Roberson, M., & Strickland, O. J. (2010). The Relationship between Charismatic Leadership, Work Engagement, and Organizational Citizenship Behaviors. Journal of Psychology, 144 (3), 313-326.

Participant Summary

▷ Undergraduate Students (N=102)

▷ 65 women, 36 men; 1 did not state

▷ Average age = 22 years (sd=5.6)

▷ Asian (12.1%), White (50.6%), Hispanic (17.6%, African American (9.9%)

Results

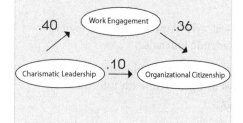

Leadership & Work Engagement

Introduction

Organizational Citizenship Behaviors = performance behaviors (such as helping) that are voluntary. They are typically not part of the job analysis.

Work Engagement = the dedication, vigor, and absorption that a person can have for their job.

Charismatic Leadership = a leadership process wherein a supervisor displays dynamic behaviors associated with charisma.

Research has documented positive effects of charismatic leadership, but has not fully demonstrated how these effects occur.

Research Questions:

Does charismatic leadership influence organizational citizenship behaviors? Does this influence operate through work engagement?

Method

Participants were recruited through a research website.

Design: Previously validated surveys were distributed to 102 undergraduate students. Measures were taken on a 1-7 scale, with participants indicating their level of agreement to each question. Measures are listed below.

• Charisma (Multifactor Leadership Questionnaire, 1999).
"My supervisor communicates expectations of high performance"

• Organizational Citizenship (OCB Scale, 1990).
"I help others who have been absent"

• Work Engagement (Work Engagement Scale, 2002).
"Time flies when I'm working"

• All participants were treated in accordance with APA Ethical Guidelines.

Results

There were significant positive correlations among all study variables.

The regression analysis showed that work engagement was a mediator variable of the effect of charismatic leadership on organizational citizenship (see graph).

Discussion: Directions for Future Research

Studies should assess other mechanisms by which charismatic leadership affects organizational citizenship.

Future research should identify whether certain people respond more favorably to charismatic behaviors.

Chapter Exercises

Science: Replication and Extension

<u>Instructions</u>: Consider the Spotlight on Research summarized in this chapter. Address each of the following items by using two or three complete sentences on a separate sheet of paper.

1. What do you think were the strengths of this research?

2. What were the weaknesses?

PROPOSAL: If you conducted a follow-up study, what you would include in terms of:

3. A sample of participants (who would you study?)

4. Variables you would include and hypotheses you would make (what would you test, specifically?)

Sequencing: Identify the Correct Order

<u>Instructions</u>: Consider the major steps of the scientific method presented below. Label each one with a number (next to the step), and describe why each step is important on a separate sheet of paper.

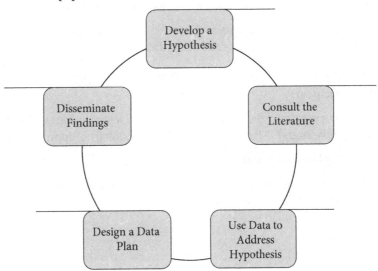

Short Essay Questions

<u>Instructions</u>: Please address the following essay questions concisely, writing in complete sentences on a separate sheet of paper.

1. Briefly describe any three content areas covered by the Human Resources Certification Exam.

2. List and briefly describe any 3 trends in workplace psychology.

3. What are the basic purposes of any 3 components of the scientific method?

4. Describe any 3 major types of studies, and a strength and weakness associated with each.

5. What is the Scientist-Practitioner Model, and why is there a knowledge gap between scientists and practitioners?

6. List and describe any two ethical positions that should be taken when conducting research.

Topics: Relate To Your Life

<u>Instructions</u>: Choose one or more of the topics below to write about a related experience from your own life.

- The changing nature of employment. What changes have you noticed in Human Resources during the course of your experience in the working world?

- Your educational/career goals. What are your long-term career goals? Explain your motivation for these goals? What are the educational requirements or paths most likely to lead you to your goals?

- What [skills/ knowledge?] do you hope to gain by taking this course?

- Research and the scientific method. Describe a research study you were part of, whether you read about it, participated as a subject, or conducted the study.

    If a participant:

    What do you suspect the dependent or independent variables were? Do you suspect it a qualitative or quantitative study? What did the study's methodological approach appear to be?

    If you read about or conducted:

    What was the study designed to investigate? Was the study qualitative or quantitative? What was the study's methodological approach?

Index

References and Recommended Readings

Arnett, J.J. (2008). The neglected 95%: Why American psychology needs to become less American. *American Psychologist, 63,* 602-614.

Baron, R. M., & Kenny, D. A. (1986). The moderator–mediator variable distinction in social psychological research: Conceptual, strategic, and statistical considerations. *Journal of Personality and Social Psychology, 51*(6), 1173-1182.

Bliese, P.D., Chan, D., & Ployhart, R.E. (2007). Multilevel methods: Future directions in measurement, longitudinal analyses, and non-normal outcomes. *Organizational Research Methods, 10,* 551-563.

Bowles, H., & Flynn, F. (2010). Gender and persistence in negotiation: A dyadic perspective. *Academy of Management Journal, 53*(4), 769-787.

Carless, S., Rasiah, J., & Irmer, B. (2009). Discrepancy between human resource research and practice: Comparison of industrial/organizational psychologists and human resource practitioners' beliefs. *Australian Psychologist, 44*(2), 105-111.

Cascio, W., & Aguinis, H. (2008). Research in industrial and organizational psychology from 1963 to 2007: Changes, choices, and trends. *Journal of Applied Psychology, 93*(5), 1062-1081.

Cook, T. D., & Campbell, D. T. (1979). Quasi experimentation. Boston, MA US: Houghton Mifflin Company

Fleetwood, S., & Hesketh, A. (2006). HRM-performance research: Under-theorized and lacking explanatory power. *The International Journal of Human Resource Management, 17*(12), 1977-1993.

Gelfand, M.J., Erez, M., & Aycan, Z. (2007). Cross-cultural organizational behavior. *Annual Review of Psychology, 58,* 479-514.

Hofstede, G. (1996). The cultural relativity of organizational practices and theories. In J. Billsberry, J. Billsberry (Eds.), *The effective manager: Perspectives and illustrations* (pp. 243-262). Thousand Oaks, CA; Sage Publications, Inc.

Laschinger, H., Leiter, M., Day, A., & Gilin, D. (2009). Workplace empowerment, incivility, and burnout: Impact on staff nurse recruitment and retention outcomes. *Journal of Nursing Management, 17*(3), 302-311.

McKersie, R., Sharpe, T., Kochan, T., Eaton, A., Strauss, G., & Morgenstern, M. (2008). Bargaining theory meets interest-based negotiations: A case study. *Industrial Relations: A Journal of Economy & Society, 47*(1), 66-96.

Publication manual of the American Psychological Association (6th ed.). (2010). Washington, DC US: American Psychological Association.

Roethlisberger, F. J., & Dickson, W. J. (1939). *Management and the worker.* Oxford England: Harvard Univ. Press.

Rogers, A., & Spitzmueller, C. (2009). Individualism—collectivism and the role of goal orientation in organizational training. *International Journal of Training and Development, 13*(3), 185-201.

Rynes, S.L., Colbert, A.E., & Brown, K.G. (2002). HR Professionals' beliefs about effective human resources practices: Correspondence between research and practice. *Human Resource Management, 41*, 149-174.

Sekerka, L. (2009). Organizational ethics education and training: A review of best practices and their application. *International Journal of Training and Development, 13*(2), 77-95.

Shapiro, D. L., Kirkman, B. L., & Courtney, H. G. (2007). Perceived causes and solutions of the translation problem in management research. *Academy of Management Journal, 50*, 249–266.

Vinchur, A. J., & Koppes, L. L. (2011). A historical survey of research and practice in industrial and organizational psychology. In S. Zedeck (Ed.) , *APA handbook of industrial and organizational psychology, Vol 1: Building and developing the organization* (pp. 3-36). Washington, DC US: American Psychological Association.

Zickar, M. J., & Gibby, R. E. (2007). Four Persistent Themes Throughout the History of I-O Psychology in the United States. In L. L. Koppes (Ed.) , *Historical perspectives in industrial and organizational psychology* (pp. 61-80). Mahwah, NJ US: Lawrence Erlbaum Associates Publishers.

Business Strategy
and Performance Management

2 Chapter Outline

Learning Objectives

The list of objectives below is your guide for organizing the content of this chapter. After you have read the chapter, you can test your proficiency by ensuring that you can address each of the objectives. Place a check in each box ☐ once you feel confident about your knowledge.

☐ Define performance, and terms pertaining to performance management

☐ Identify the importance of performance and how it is central to other HR functions

☐ Explain why performance is fundamentally controversial

☐ Define criterion development in terms of relevance, contamination, and deficiency

☐ Define Strategic Management and how it can be used to set performance guidelines

☐ Identify different types of organizational structure

☐ Define job analysis and its basic components

☐ Identify different methods for conducting job analysis

☐ Compare and contrast different theoretical models of performance dimensions

☐ Define extra-role performance and Organizational Citizenship Behaviors

☐ Identify the various purposes of performance evaluation

☐ Describe various types of errors that can be made in performance evaluation

☐ Explain different types of rating formats used in performance evaluation

☐ Explain the concept of After-Event Reviews to provide ongoing performance feedback

☐ Define and critique metrics of organizational performance

☐ Describe the progressive discipline approach to dealing with performance problems

☐ Explain some features that should be included in training performance raters

Chapter Overview

One of the fundamental goals of an organization is performance, which can be considered in terms of the individual, team, and/or organization. Employee performance has been defined as individual contributions toward organizational goals. A key component of organizational effectiveness is performance management, or the process of ensuring that employees can contribute to these goals. Performance management is critical to a variety of major HR functions, including recruitment, hiring, training, and compensating employees. Performance management also guides the work experience of individuals, helping them to sustain attention and energy toward the behaviors most likely to lead to desired outcomes for themselves as well as the organization.

One of the most difficult aspects of performance management is specifying the important dimensions of performance for employees, teams, and the organization. In fact, this process is very controversial and prone to various types of errors. Fortunately, there are many systematic ways to identify the right performance dimensions. This chapter will focus on strategic management, job analysis, and models of performance that transcend specific job titles. These approaches will be used to show how the correct performance dimensions can be identified.

From a Human Resources perspective, the "nuts and bolts" of performance management include the measurement and documentation of performance, or performance evaluation. This evaluation may consist of objective performance metrics and subjective evaluations made by supervisors, coworkers, clients, or customers. The remainder of the chapter covers ways to measure and evaluate performance, and the delivery of performance-related feedback.

The Importance of Performance and Its Management

There are many potential uses and applications of performance and its management. An abbreviated list of these is provided below.

- Communication. Employees need to know what is expected of them and how they should dedicate their energy at work.

- Feedback. Employees lose direction and motivation if performance feedback is not provided.

- Rewards. High-performing employees want tangible and intangible rewards and recognition for the good work they have done, or they will be motivated to seek employment elsewhere.

- Personnel decisions. In addition to compensating high-performing employees, it is wise to document reasoning behind hiring, promotions, layoffs, or disciplinary actions.

- Workforce planning. To adapt to the current and future needs of the organization, it is necessary to predict and manage performance needs for the future.

- Organizational accountability. The identification of performance provides a framework for identifying what went right and what did not.

Performance Is Controversial!

Despite being one of the most fundamental Human Resource topics, performance and its management are also among the most controversial. One of the essential controversies actually surrounded the definition of performance (e.g., Campbell, 1993). This author and his colleagues noted that performance is actually the <u>behavior</u> that is directed toward some goal, not the outcome of the behavior. This is a critical distinction because employees often have more control over their behaviors than an outcome, particularly in a turbulent economy. However, this important distinction is often overlooked because those with a vested interest in the organization are more concerned with outcomes, especially as they relate to profit.

Other controversies surrounding performance include choosing which performance factors to use, how performance should be measured, what the performance feedback is to be used for, and how frequently it should be evaluated. As indicated in the sidebar, giving performance feedback is one of the most dreaded tasks that managers face. Suzanne Lucas describes the conflicted opinions that may be experienced by those who know performance evaluation is valuable. Often the evaluation is equally dreaded by the employee receiving the feedback.

To add to the controversy, researchers and practitioners have disagreed on the fundamental dimensions of performance. At the heart of this controversy are the questions (for any given job): What exactly does it mean to be "successful" ... how do we know who is good at it? These questions are at the heart of an intriguing issue that has plagued Workplace Psychology, known as the Criterion Problem (e.g., Austin & Villanova, 1992). In order to address this problem, we must cover the issue of criteria and criterion development. These concepts overarch the entire topic of performance and its management. It is worthwhile for organizations to invest substantial time in the development of performance criteria.

Problems with the "Yardstick" of Criteria ...

BOB FOUND A DIFFERENT YARDSTICK FOR SUCCESS AND HE FELT SWELL.

Criteria and Its Development

Recall that Chapter 1 identified "Criterion Development" as one of the key training areas for Workplace Psychology. What, exactly, is a **criterion**? The formal definition for a criterion is an accepted standard, or "yardstick," for making a judgment about something. Performance is often referred to as the criterion with which individuals, groups, or organizations can be judged. As we shall see in Chapter 3, performance is the criterion that HR attempts to predict with hiring practices such as interviews or work samples. Similarly, investors are interested in business performance as the standard of the value of the organization. It is not surprising that many organizations have the same basic goals in terms of performance outcomes: to be profitable and successful over time, and to be respected in the community or industry. Other goals exist, to be sure, and a basic set of guiding principles is typically used to direct and assess organizational performance over time. These are also used to direct the basic functions of Human Resources Departments.

Although it seems straightforward to think about performance, at first glance, it is, in fact, one of the greatest areas of disagreement. The problems become evident when considering the requirements for the "accepted standards," particularly as they relate to performance. As it turns out, many dimensions of performance are subjective in nature and controversial because people cannot agree on them. Emphasizing some aspects of performance can have unintended consequences on other aspects, and real-world collection of performance data can be cumbersome or inaccurate. Grizzle (2002) has discussed the problematic side effects of quantifying work. These may include problems such as focusing on the wrong outcomes of performance or politicizing the work environment.

It is important for organizational leaders to think carefully about the development of performance management. Terms that are useful to describe the criterion problem include **criterion contamination**, **criterion deficiency**, and **criterion relevance**. Essentially, these terms describe accuracy versus error. The diagram below illustrates this point:

Imagine that the first circle (on the left) consists of what you have defined as performance. The second circle (on the right) is the entire realm of <u>true</u> performance. The overlap is the extent to which you have accuracy in your measurement and have acceptable criterion development. Everything else is measurement error.

Criterion contamination = things that are measured that are unrelated to true performance

Criterion deficiency = real aspects of performance that are not measured

Criterion relevance = the correct measurement of real performance; measurement will be useful to organization and employee

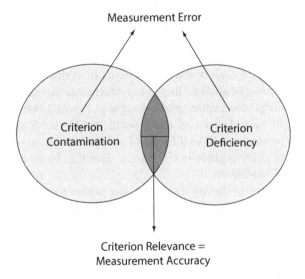

How can an organization maximize the accuracy—and minimize the error—in defining and evaluating performance? A very good starting point is to consider the purpose of the existence of the organization, and the direction it is striving toward. These issues are addressed in a process known as strategic management.

Strategic Management

Many topics in workplace psychology can be considered in terms of different units or levels. This is particularly true of performance (Griffin, Neal, & Parker, 2007). Whereas employee performance and performance management are typically the purview of Human Resources, overall organizational performance is typically the responsibilities of founders, executives, and/or shareholders. Not always, but in many cases, those in charge of organizational performance have some formal and informal training in business administration, and work closely with Human Resources to align company-wide objectives with day-to-day management of employees. It is fundamentally important that those in HR be fluent regarding organizational performance; therefore, a few of the most basic concepts will be presented here.

Guiding principles of strategic management include formal statements related to the organization's mission, vision, and values. A **mission statement** provides an overarching definition of the organization, who it serves, and how it is different from other organizations. A **vision statement** is typically a concise, future-oriented statement of where the organization is heading, and is typically intended to be inspirational in nature. A **values statement** highlights the higher-level ideals that the organization aspires to, and is used to provide expectations about the way that business will be conducted.

Any well-formulated treatment of performance within organizations should be built around its strategic management. In fact, all major Human Resources functions should be in alignment with strategic management. Essentially, this is a process that depicts the course of direction for a company, including a time line for outcomes and evaluations of whether or not these outcomes have occurred.

One of the best features of a strong strategic management process is the use of clearly established goals and measurements to evaluate progress relative to these goals. The use of goals to increase performance is one of the most well-supported findings in workplace psychology (e.g., Lewin, 1944; Locke & Latham, 1991), and will be addressed in more detail in Chapter 5 as a motivational technique. The acronym **SMART goals** has been used to describe the important features of goals to guide performance: Specific, Measurable, Achievable, Relevant, and Time-bound.

The goals identified during strategic management can (and should) be used to set performance metrics throughout the organization, from "big picture" outcomes such as profit margins and market share to team outcomes such as collaborative productivity down to the individual worker's output. Linking the entire performance management system with strategic management is one way to ensure good communication about business goals to employees, and also that the performance measures taken of teams and individuals do link clearly to organizational goals (for an excellent review, see Pun & Sydney, 2005). An example of how performance measures can be linked to unit objectives is provided at the end of this chapter (taken from Pritchard, Harrell, DiazGranados, & Guzman, 2008).

The flowchart depicts the major stages in the strategic management process. The first stage is planning, which sets basic parameters such as the scope, who

Mission statement = the basic purpose of the organization in terms of what it does and who it serves; the framework for guiding the strategy

Vision statement = a future-oriented, inspirational statement of what the organization is striving toward

Values statement = the guiding principles in terms of ideals, principles, and beliefs about business conduct

SMART goals = an acronym to summarize features of goal setting that enhance their usefulness; the goals should be specific, measureable, achievable, relevant, and time-bound.

shall be involved in strategic management, and the timeframe under consideration. During environmental scanning, a wealth of information is gathered to make the most accurate forecasts possible. This information includes internal and external scans to delineate where strengths can be built to maximize the probability of success. Examples of these information-gathering approaches include SWOT analysis, PEST analysis, and Porter's Five-Factor model. For an internal scan, the **SWOT analysis** provides an assessment of the organization's strengths, weaknesses, opportunities, and threats. In terms of the external scan, the **PEST analysis** provides information about the landscape in terms of the political, economic, social, and technological environments. Porter's Five-Factor model focuses a little bit more closely on the specifics of the industry. It includes the gathering of information relevant to reliance on suppliers, existing competition and the likelihood that new competition will appear, the diversity of the customer base, and the cost pricing of alternative products.

This information will help guide the specific movements that can be taken in the business environment. These movements are defined and implemented in the formulation and execution of the strategy. The last step in the sequence involves ongoing assessment of the effectiveness of the strategy per measurements defined during the strategy development.

The organization's strategic planning should be used to guide the process of performance communication, measurement, and evaluation. Specific, measurable objectives should be developed for work teams and individuals. A clear and ongoing process of performance management should be used to ensure that performance outcomes are happening in desired ways. The manner in which a strategic plan is best implemented is dependent upon organizational structure.

The Strategic Planning Process

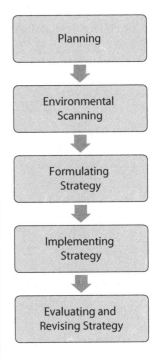

Organizational Structure

As we have seen, key performance objectives should be derived from the strategic management process. This should include performance related to the overall mission, vision, values, and financial objectives of the organization as a whole. One way in which strategic management is linked to team and individual performance is through the **organizational structure**, which sets the reporting relationships among people and jobs within the organization. These reporting relationships are often graphically represented in the **organizational chart**.

Organizational structure influences the communication patterns, reporting relationships, division of labor, delegation of authority, and sometimes the physical locations of employees. Decisions about how to set the structure for the organization are very important and should be set in terms of maximizing the **line of sight** of the organization's goals to the unit and employee. Research has identified some of the key features that create an alignment of organizational goals throughout its departments (Beehr, Glazer, Fischer, Linton, & Hansen, 2009). These include communication of goals, effectiveness of managers, and employee development practices (skill improvement, role clarity, participation,

Organizational structure = describes the formal reporting relationships among employees

Organizational chart = a graphic representation of the organizational structure

Line of sight = the extent to which something is clearly visible in the daily working world of employees

and empowerment). Of critical importance to performance management and communication is a structure that is designed to align strategic management goals throughout the organization. Some common options for organizational structure are described briefly below.

Functional Organizational Structure. This is the most common type of organizational structure, in part due to its intuitive appeal. Here, the structure is made in terms of the major departments in the organization. Many organizations have the following major departments: Operations, Productions, Marketing, Accounting, HR, and Technology. The assumption of this type of structure (which may or may not be correct) is that employees working within these departments have common goals that funnel to/from the aggregate. As mentioned above, this structure has intuitive appeal but the overarching organizational objectives can get lost if not carefully linked for employees.

There is a variety of other types of organizational structure that differently affect the flow of communication and performance management. A **geographic organizational structure** is similar to the functional structure, but rather than reporting based on departments, the reporting structure is based on geographic location. This can be the case when certain sales regions are in effect. Another intuitive type of organizational structure is based on the product line. Here, the reporting relationships are made in terms of service to a particular product only. This is called a **product-based structure**. In a **matrix-style organizational structure**, employees report to two managers. Although this type of structure can help with the exchange of information, it is important that communication does not create conflicting performance expectations.

Seamless Organizational Structure. The seamless organizational structure appears to a trend for the future. The idea behind the **seamless structure** is to raise the level of communication based on need, rather than formal channels. Due to the ease of contacting people in the organization, it is not as necessary to formalize a particular flow of information. Rather, networks of communication form as a function of project-based work. This structure can work well if the organization has a team-based appraisal and reward system in place, as well as a knowledge management system. The use of seamless structures will increase to the extent that organizations rely on autonomous work teams rather than formal management channels.

Functional Organizational Structure = a structure based on the fundamental purpose of the department

Geographic organizational structure = a structure based on physical location

Product-based structure = a structure based on the product line or service to be delivered

Seamless structure = a structure based on autonomous work groups or teams; uses technology to enhance communication and performance management across formal reporting relationships

Performance Metrics

Thus far, performance has been introduced as the most fundamentally important feature of any organization. It is basically its reason for being. To evaluate progress relative to goals, there is a wide variety of performance metrics at the organizational, team, and individual levels.

A good performance management system should be creative in the development of performance metrics. An example of performance metrics using overall organizational goals applied to specific job titles is provided at the end of the chapter (Pritchard et al., 2008). These authors have created a performance management system that is based on goal setting and communicating feedback. The name of their system is ProMES (Productivity Measurement and Enhancement System). Another approach to managing performance is the **balanced scorecard**. This process is driven by objectives and measurements to maximize accountability in four key areas: financial outcomes, customer data, internal business processes, and talent management.

Balanced scorecard = a performance management system that incorporates financial and nonfinancial metrics

Metrics of Financial Performance: Organizational

There are many metrics of organizational performance. For instance, many find it important to be aware of financial measures. These standard metrics are used to describe the fiscal picture of the organization. Basic accounting principles and reports can be used to present data related to this type of performance.

- **Balance Sheet**. The balance sheet displays a snapshot of the organization's monetary situation on any given day, typically the last day of an accounting period. The balance sheet summarizes the financial picture by presenting the assets as a function of liabilities (financial negatives) and equity (financial positives).

- **Accounts Receivable Ledger**. This statement shows, in a detailed fashion, the amount of money that is still owed to the organization, and by whom.

- **Market Cap**. For publicly traded companies, the market cap can be used as a metric of financial performance. It is the mathematical product of the dollar value per share and the total number of shares.

Market Cap = the monetary value of a company's publicly traded shares

Metrics of Performance: Department

Some performance metrics make sense to gather at the level of the department, or team. A considerable amount of research in workplace psychology has been invested in team performance (for comprehensive reviews, see Wildman, Bedwell, Salas, & Smith-Jentsch, 2011, or Cannon-Bowers & Bowers, 2011). These authors have documented some of the factors that affect team performance, as well as some common views of team performance. In general, these authors suggest that the effectiveness of teams should be measured in terms of: (a) an increase in the ability of the team to perform well in the future; (b) behavioral and attitudinal consequences for individual team members; and (c) team outputs. The list below contains some common categories of team outputs.

- **Productivity Measures**. Productivity measures include the sum total of what has been created in a given time period. It may include things such as reports generated, units built, or new product lines initiated.

- **Efficiency Measures**. Efficiency measures are those that demonstrate the amount that has been accomplished relative to an input variable. For example, human resources may tout their efficiency with measures such as cost per hire, or the ratio of the organizational workforce to that of the HR staff.

- **Break-Even Analysis**. The break-even analysis tracks and displays the achievement of outcomes that justify the financial and time investment of any activity. Another way to say this is that the activity has "paid for itself." A break-even analysis can be very important for demonstrating the value added of an endeavor such as employee training.

- **Employee Opinion Measures**. Survey data can be assessed to summarize important opinions about a team's performance. These data can be useful to report what the group is "doing right," as well as areas that are needed for improvement. This is addressed in further detail in Chapter 7 (Employee Relations).

These "big picture" features are important to performance management, but so are the specific details of employee day-to-day productivity that is defined in terms of each job. To raise the criterion relevance for what makes a particular employee good at his or her job, it is necessary to consider information from a job analysis.

Job Analysis

Job description = a detailed description of the responsibilities and activities performed on the job; often delineates essential and nonessential functions

A job analysis is a detailed description of the key elements of each job. It can be considered to be the building blocks of workplace psychology because through defining the job, we can ascertain key dimensions of performance, how to hire the right people, and what to train. The components of a job analysis include the job summary, job description, and job specification.

A **job summary** is a brief overview of the job and provides a synopsis for prospective employees. The **job description** contains a very detailed description of the day-to-day behaviors required for the job and the outcomes that can be expected from them. In contrast to describing the <u>activities</u>, the **job specification** provides a description of the <u>employee</u> in terms of knowledge, skills, or other attributes needed to be successful at the job.

Job specification = an explanation of specific knowledge, skills, education, or physical characteristics that an employee needs to have in order to do the job

Cost-cutting trends in organizations have changed the nature of the formal job analysis process. In today's workforce, employees are expected to work in teams and to quickly pick up new job assignments. Nevertheless, it is useful for organizations to have an ongoing job analysis process to help in performance management and knowledge management.

There are many different methods of conducting a job analysis. A "shortcut" approach is to use **benchmarking**. This relies on preexisting analyses that have been conducted in other organizations or are part of industry standards. These standards can then be adapted to fit within any particular organization. Another method of job analysis is to conduct on-site job observations of employees. This has the advantage of a realistic view of daily work, but can have a disadvantage in terms of whether the observations adequately represent the typical job requirements. Another method of job analysis is the employee interview and/or questionnaire. An advantage to this approach is that the questions are standardized and yield a large volume of information. A potential disadvantage is that employees may exaggerate certain components of their work in order to look impressive. Many different job analysis tools have been created, such as the Functional Job Analysis (FJA) and the Position Analysis Questionnaire (PAQ). These approaches consist of a detailed series of questions for a job analyst to pose to job incumbents or other Subject Matter Experts (SMEs).

In defining the most important aspects of performance for any given job title, raters are asked to evaluate the frequency, difficulty, and importance of a list of job actions. An example blank worksheet is provided on the next page for you to see how the data could be collected. The exact rating formats for making these judgments can be adapted to make sense within any organization; examples are provided in detail elsewhere (e.g., Morgeson & Dierdorff, 2011).

[see *Job Analysis: Task Rating* on the next page]

Strategic management and job analysis are extremely useful in the correct specification of performance. In building a performance management system, there is an additional resource for potential performance dimensions. This final source of information to develop performance criteria consists of features of performance that may occur across jobs. Various theorists have attempted to create taxonomies or systems that can describe these basic performance factors. A summary of these will be given below.

Models of Performance

Campbell's 8-factor Taxonomy. An early model of performance was the 8-factor taxonomy (Campbell et al., 1993). These authors believed that it was important to distinguish between the outcomes of performance, and performance as conceptualized as a behavior. They formulated a theory of job performance consisting of the following eight dimensions, which could describe essential features of any job: (a) job-specific task proficiency; (b) non–job-specific-task proficiency; (c) written and oral communication; (d) effort; (e) personal discipline; (f) teamwork performance; (g) leadership; and (h) administration.

Benchmarking = the process of comparing one's business practices with existing information or the best practices in an industry

Cambell's 8-factor Taxonomy = a theory of performance which consists of eight dimensions, and shifts focus from outcomes to behavior

Job Aid

Job Analysis: Task Rating

Use this or a similar form for SMEs to individually rank tasks from their job analysis results by frequency, difficulty, importance (or other factors, as necessary). Most of the definitions are blank so that you can define them as needed.

Please use the following scale to rate each task based on how often you do this task in your job (frequency), how difficult it might be for a person to learn this task (difficulty), and how important doing this task accurately is to your work (importance). Write the rating number in the appropriate columns for each task.

Frequency	Difficulty	Importance
0 = Never do it	0 = Anyone could figure it out	0 = No impact to the business if done incorrectly
1 =	1 =	1 =
2 =	2 =	2 =
3 =	3 =	3 =
4 =	4 =	4 =

Task	Frequency	Difficulty	Importance

The material appearing on this page is not covered by copyright and may be reproduced at will.

Organizational Citizenship Behaviors (OCBs). A key distinction made in this model of performance is that of in-role versus extra-role performance. **In-role performance** is that which is consistent with essential job responsibilities as identified in a job analysis. This is generally considered to be a function of skills, training, effort, and cognitive ability (Fletcher, 2001). **Extra-role performance** is that which, as the name implies, goes beyond the formal descriptions of the job to contribute to coworkers and/or the organization. Extra-role aspects of performance are considered more likely to be a function of personality and motivation (Fletcher, 2001).

Researchers who focused on extra-role performance identified the importance of "individual behavior that is discretionary, not directly or explicitly recognized by the formal reward system, and that in the aggregate promotes the effective functioning of the organization" (Organ, 1988, p. 4). These behaviors have also been referred to as contextual performance (Borman & Motowidlo, 1993). Although the specific dimensions have varied according to the researcher, some of the key concepts include behaviors such as those listed below.

It is important to note that there may be a blurring of in-role and extra-role behaviors in some situations (e.g., Vey & Campbell, 2004). For instance, in many service-oriented jobs, the dimensions of courtesy and conscientiousness may, in fact, be an essential job function. In any case, researchers have helped to shine a light on an aspect of what people consider to be a "good employee" in ways that may not be recognized during formal performance evaluations.

Counterproductive Work Behaviors (CWBs). In contrast to OCBs, **counterproductive work behaviors** consist of antisocial behaviors (Sackett, 2002). Examples of CWBs include theft, drug or alcohol use, destruction of property, misuse of time, poor attendance, and inappropriate verbal and physical actions (Gruys & Sackett, 2003). Clearly, organizations are concerned about these types of antisocial behaviors, and so they have received much attention in workplace psychology over the past decade. Later in the chapter, emphasis will be given on how to best handle CWBs in a performance management process known as progressive discipline.

Bartram's Great Eight Competencies. **Job competencies** are broad statements and basic characteristics that describe what it takes to be successful in an organization. **Competency modeling** is the process of defining the success factors for different jobs. Using a competency modeling approach to performance, Bartram identified eight dimensions (e.g., Bartram, 2005) that define the competencies across jobs. In addition, the Great Eight model specified the potential links between the competencies and their links to personality traits. These eight competencies are: (1) leading/deciding; (2) supporting/cooperating; (3) interacting/presenting; (4) analyzing/interpreting; (5) creating/conceptualizing; (6) organizing/executing; (7) adapting/coping; and (8) enterprising/ performing.

Applications. The previous sections have examined ways for identifying critical performance dimensions. This can be done by combining information from

Helping Behavior (e.g., altruism, courtesy)

Initiative (e.g., enthusiasm, conscientiousness)

Sportsmanship (e.g., not complaining)

Organizational Loyalty (e.g., maintaining commitment)

Organizational Compliance (e.g., following rules)

Civic Virtue (e.g., getting involved with governance)

Competency modeling =the use of job competencies to identify what is needed to succeed at a given job

strategic management, job analysis, and theory-based models of performance. Spending time on performance specifications will ensure that the criterion development is complete and relevant. This, in turn, will help employees understand what is expected of them and how they can contribute to the organization's goals. This is only part of the performance picture, however. It is also necessary to decide how to measure and deliver performance appraisal.

Performance Appraisal

There are many methods of appraising performance, and each is associated with different advantages and disadvantages. **Performance appraisal** is defined as a variety of activities through which employers conduct assessments of employees, with goals of measuring competence, providing feedback, and/or appropriately distributing rewards (Kline & Sulsky, 2009). Although there are many potential benefits of performance appraisal, there are also a large number of potential problems. As reflected in the sidebar blog 'How to Write Performance Appraisals', performance appraisals often create negative reactions, even if the need for them is recognized.

Some of the problems associated with performance appraisal have been described earlier under the Criterion Development section, and other reasons center on fundamental problems with measurement. Performance is a complex construct, and measures that attempt to assign a number can often miss the mark. Good appraisal measures are: reliable, representative, job related, accepted by employees, and fairly easy to gather and report. Unfortunately, this is not an easy task. To help meet these goals, it is useful to consider both objective and subjective forms of appraisal data.

Types of Appraisal Data

Objective Appraisal Data.

Objective performance data are based on observable, countable aspects of work or its output. Examples of objective data include sales volume, new contracts executed, work attendance rates, or rate of product defects. One of the major advantages to this approach is that it is very clearly business related, as the data speak to outcomes that are important to the organization. A related advantage is that these data direct employee attention and effort to desirable outcomes. As such, it also lends itself to goal-setting programs. Another advantage is that because it is directly observable (countable), it may be perceived as less prone to biases or interpersonal/political factors.

There are several disadvantages to this type of data, however. At a practical level, they may be cumbersome to collect. In terms of validity, there may be problems with construct validity, wherein the measure (such as sales volume) fundamentally taps into a factor other than performance (such as economic market conditions). If the objective data involve behavior (such as greeting customers), a problem with sampling may occur in which it is unclear when and how often data should be taken. Finally, many jobs have only a few (if any) objective performance indicators, leaving much of the performance domain unmeasured. Due to the potential problems with objective measures, it is often preferable to supplement the use of objective data with subjective data.

Subjective Appraisal Data.

In contrast to objective data, subjective data cannot be directly observed or counted. It relies on the judgments of people by other people. In the context of performance appraisal, those making the judgments are called **raters**. The rater is most frequently the direct supervisor. An expanded view of performance can be obtained by asking additional raters' opinions, such as those of coworkers, subordinates, or customers. This is often referred to as **360-degree feedback**, (also multisource feedback), a performance evaluation system that incorporates views from all sides. It should be noted that some research has reported some problems with this approach, such as a lack of honest and constructive feedback and appropriate follow-up on data provided (e.g., Overeem, Wollersheim, Driessen, Lombarts, van de Ven, Grol, & Arah, 2009; Morgeson, Mumford, & Campion, 2005).

Multi-rater Appraisal, or 360° Feedback

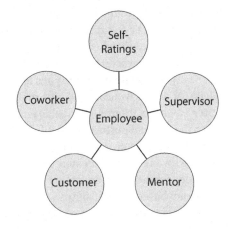

Subjective data have an advantage in that they can tap into useful performance constructs that cannot be directly measured, but are also prone to various types of biases and personal errors. In fact, there is an extensive documentation of these biases and errors in the field of social psychology known as social perception. Overall, these are characterized by the tendency to believe that we know more than we actually do, and by letting our personal likes and dislikes influence our judgments about performance. Collectively, these errors contribute to criterion contamination, in that ratings are influenced by factors unrelated to performance.

self-appraisal. Perhaps I should have said that there "may be" exaggeration, but the principle still stands: Don't take everything they write with blind faith.

3. Ask your employees' clients about their performance. What did you say? They don't have clients because you are in finance? Hogwash. Finance works with all different departments. Who do you meet with? Who do your employees meet with? Speak with them.

4. Look through your sent E-mails. You've forgotten a lot. Trust me. Look through them and see what happened.

5. Don't fall into the look-at-only-the-last-30-days trap. Now, I would tell you to work extra hard the 30 days before appraisals are due so your boss will think you are brilliant, but don't fall into that trap with your people. Try to look at the whole year.

6. If you set goals for the year, refer back to them and base your appraisal on that.

7. When it's all written, send a copy to your employees before you meet with them. Why? Because anything negative you have to say (and most likely even your star performers have a couple of areas for improvement) will go across much better if they've had time to think about it. If you just present it in a meeting, they are immediately on the defensive and feel like they've been blindsided. So, let them read it, ponder it, and then meet with them.

(source: http://money. usnews.com/money/blogs/outside-voices-careers/2008/09/18/ how-to-write-performance-appraisals)

Social perception is the process of evaluating another person in terms of their traits and motives. It may be something that is required, as in the case of performance appraisal; it may also be a process that happens subconsciously. If kept private it can be harmless, but if expressed verbally or through behaviors, it can be beneficial for the recipient of a positive evaluation, and harmful for the recipient of a negative evaluation. Let's take a look at the many forms that social perception biases and errors may take.

Distributional Errors. People may have implicit beliefs about variability in performance. Most variables, in fact, follow a normal distribution, or bell curve. This means that most people are "average," with a few exceptionally high and a few exceptionally low. It should be noted that this may or may not be the true distribution for a particular performance dimension, but it is true for many. Other examples of distributions include bimodal, positively skewed, or negatively skewed. Beliefs about distributions become a problem when they do not match reality (thereby creating data contamination). One of the more common distributional errors for performance appraisal is the negative skew, also known as **rating inflation**. This is extremely prevalent in education, commonly referred to as "the easy A." In the workplace, a rater may inflate ratings to avoid hurting someone's feelings, to avoid negative job consequences for the employee (particularly in today's economy), or because they do not have documented information to support a low rating. On the other hand, a rater may be a perfectionist or have other reasons to be "tough" on employees, and subsequently rate them lower than they actually deserve (creating a positive skew).

Stereotyping. **Stereotyping** occurs when a rater believes that all members of a certain group have the same characteristics. Stereotypes may be positive or negative, true or false. Many people hold **stereotypes** about performance based on age, gender, ethnicity, or attractiveness. In performance evaluation, this is a problem when the rater is wrong about a particular employee, using their stereotypical beliefs rather than actual performance information. Although it may be bad to inflate ratings based on stereotypes, it is particularly harmful to the employee if the ratings are lowered based on stereotyping. This situation results in employment **prejudice**. Prejudice is an action that unfairly discriminates against a member of a group based on that status alone.

Halo effect. The **halo effect** occurs when a rater has some positive performance information about an employee, such as punctuality, and generalizes it to all other performance dimensions. This is based on a false correlation, and results in an employee looking like an "angel" for overall performance.

Horns effect. This is the opposite of the halo effect. In this case, the rater has some negative performance information and it affects all other performance ratings. For instance, an employee may be habitually late to work but highly productive once there. A **horns effect** would occur if the rater could not look past the tardiness and rated the employee as low in productivity as well. The horns effect makes the employee look like a "devil" for overall performance.

Similar-to-me-effect. If the rater deems the employee as sharing a common characteristic or background, there might be an "in-grouping" effect. The rater

---

Social perception = the process of collecting information about another person and making judgments about him or her

Rating inflation = a rating error in which a rater makes evaluations that are higher than the true evaluation

Stereotyping = a type of social perception in which a rater believes that everyone in a group shares characteristics, regardless of whether or not this is the case

Halo effect = a rating error in which a rater allows a single favorable attribute to affect the perception of all other job dimensions

Horns effect = a rating error in which a rater allows a single negative attribute to affect the perception of all other job dimensions

may view this common trait so favorably that they exhibit rating inflation for that employee. A **similar-to-me-effect** always results in ratings that are higher than true performance.

Anchoring. A cognitive error that influences ratings is starting with an expectation of what that rating should be. For instance, if a rater receives a favorable rating, the employee is likely to receive one as well. More of a problem from the employee's perspective, however, is that the same effect occurs if the rater receives an unfavorable performance rating. (Latham, Budworth, Yanar, & Whyte, 2008).

Fundamental Attribution Error. Authors in the field of social perception have made a distinction in the sources that raters may attribute the behavior of another to (e.g., Kelley, 1965). One such source of attributions relates to internal causes, such as personality characteristics or other traits that a person carries. In contrast, external causes are those that are based upon the situation. The **fundamental attribution error** describes an error that people make, in which they believe that they understand the reasons behind another's behavior. In making this attribution, they overemphasize internal causes in addressing the "why" question. This means that people are fairly quick to make enduring judgments about other people on the basis of fairly limited behavioral information.

Rating Formats in Appraisals

Subjective appraisal data relies upon opinions, and requires a rating scale or other format for providing these opinions. Research has invested a great deal of effort into designing such formats (MacDonald & Sulsky, 2009). Some of the most common include the graphic rating scale, the behaviorally anchored rating scale, and the behavior observation scale. Other formats require the rater to compare employees' performance against each other, such as employee ranking or forced distribution. These are described briefly below.

The **graphic rating scale** is perhaps the simplest type of rating format. It provides a graphic display of performance scores that vary from low to high on either end of a performance dimension.

Arrives to work on time

Similar-to-me effect = a rater preference for other people who share characteristics with the rater

Fundamental attribution error = an error in social perception in which people overestimate the impact of personal traits (internal traits) in guiding another person's behavior

Graphic rating scale = a rating format that is anchored at either end of a performance dimension

More details can be provided to this basic form of rating scale. For instance, additional "anchors," or labels, can be added to the scale to ensure that all raters have common reference points. One such approach is known as the **Behaviorally Anchored Rating Scale (BARS)** approach. In this rating format, scale anchors are provided that display what a worker has done (or would be most likely to do) on a given performance dimension. Another anchored rating scale is the **Behavioral Observation Scale**, in which the labels are presented in terms of the frequency of observed behavior.

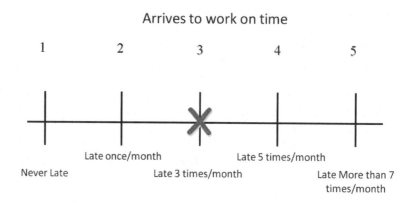

Other rating formats are based upon comparisons among employees' performance. In the **ranking method**, the appraiser makes a listing of employees in terms of highest to lowest performer. This approach can be problematic with large numbers of employees and can result in a competitive culture at work. In the **forced distribution method**, the rater is required to rate performance using a bell curve, with the majority of employees rated in the average range and a small number at the high end and the low end. A major problem with this approach is that it may or may not reflect the actual performance distribution. It also may create competition among employees.

One of the many criticisms of performance appraisal is that it often contains overall impressions, or references to performance incidents that happened months prior to the time of the actual performance review. This has a judgmental or punitive feel, and does not help to adjust performance as needed at the relevant time. To address these concerns, an alternative to periodic performance appraisals is the use of After-Event Reviews to manage performance.

Ongoing Feedback: After-Event Reviews

Performance appraisals that are conducted once or twice per year miss out on major goals of performance management in terms of feedback, recognition, and corrections of performance mistakes. An alternative approach is to implement a program of ongoing performance feedback that is delivered as closely as possible to a performance-related event. A system that can be used during training or performance appraisal is the **After-Event Review** (Busby, 1999; Ellis, Mendel, & Nir, 2006). According to these authors, AERs "intensify cognitive elaboration of experiential data, under the assumption that this process will ultimately promote the necessary behavioral changes" (Ellis & Davidi, p. 857). Essentially, this practice involves reviewing the performance event, and then encouraging a process of self-explanation, data verification, and feedback. This will lead to a deep level of processing for the employee about what went right and what went wrong in a given circumstance.

After-Event Review = providing immediate feedback about performance events on the job

Applications of ongoing performance management have also been referred to as Painless Performance Improvement. This approach focuses on how to intervene in situations where an employee has made a mistake at work. The supervisor's task is to address the incident as quickly as possible, simply stating what was observed and how it differs from performance expectations. Here too, the emphasis is on encouraging the employee to take responsibility for performance by providing immediate feedback.

Progressive Discipline

Overall, this chapter has focused on the benefits of using strategic management, job analysis, and models of performance to clearly define and measure important behaviors and outcomes at the individual, team, and organizational levels. Doing so will unify efforts toward important goals, as well as provide important communication throughout the organization. This view of performance management takes a proactive and positive view of the process of defining and measuring performance.

There are circumstances, however, where performance management takes on a more punitive approach. Consider the case of an employee who is consistently late or absent to work, or one who undermines team efforts by gossiping about other employees. In these cases, it is necessary for a manager to clearly communicate the performance-related problems, and steps that must be taken to address them. This process is known as **progressive discipline**.

Progressive discipline = a process of documenting performance-related problems and specific employee changes needed to address the problems

All steps of the progressive discipline process involve communication and documentation. The manager will start by having a serious, informal conversation with the employee, clearly specifying the nature of the problem and a time line for performance measures to change. If the evaluation time line does not yield the agreed-upon changes, the manager should prepare a written document for a second formal conversation. At this time, the employee may be asked to sign understanding of the conversation and necessary changes for continued evaluation. The next stage involves a written reprimand documenting any existing problems. Finally, the employee may be terminated if the problems continue.

It is important to note that the steps in this process only need to be carried out if the problems continue. Alternatively, the manager may decide that all the steps will not address the problem and an employment termination would be the best case of action. Due to the nature of at-will employment, it is not necessary to go through each of these steps. In fact, having a formal, published system of progressive discipline can be a mistake, in that employees will expect that process as a matter of policy. However, at the discretion of management and Human Resources, this process can provide a clear way to ensure that an employee termination was not due to a simple misunderstanding.

Rater Appraisal Training and some "How-to's"

A final point about performance management concerns the importance of providing training for those responsible for documenting and delivering performance feedback. It can be a mistake to assume that all managers are good at conducting performance appraisals. They should be trained at length in terms of the performance management system, how to collect information about employees' performance, and how to appropriately convey this information. The list below contains some additional features that should be emphasized during appraisal training.

- *Gather Documentation.* Researchers have demonstrated the importance of keeping documentation in order to be able to provide specific performance feedback (Cannon-Bowers & Bowers, 2011). This is particularly important for progressive discipline, as well as for performance management systems that do not provide ongoing feedback. The use of objective performance data is ideally suited to documentation and should be included as part of a performance management system.

- *Use Principles from Organizational Justice.* Performance appraisal can be an emotionally charged topic for employees. It is of utmost importance that people feel they have been treated fairly, particularly during performance feedback. Workplace psychologists have identified some of the forms that perceptions of justice can take (for an early review, see Greenberg, 1990; Greenberg, 2011). These include procedural justice (the fairness of the process), distributive justice (the fairness of how rewards are allocated), and interactional justice. Interactional justice refers to the perception of being treated with respect and dignity, and being allowed to voice one's opinions. An effective performance management system should be built upon these principles from the organizational justice literature.

- *Neutrality.* An important feature of providing performance feedback is to keep observations free of emotions, or assumptions about causation. As mentioned earlier, a common error of social perception is to presume that the causes of behavior are trait-related (internally caused) rather than caused by the environment. Research has shown that managers' assumptions about the extent to which behavior is internally caused led them to make mistakes in judging subsequent performance (e.g., Heslin & VandeWalle, 2008). To avoid these types of problems, it is important to stick to the information at hand.

- *Preparation.* Another essential feature to performance feedback is to be well prepared. The amount of information an appraiser gathers for the meeting will directly affect the usefulness of the appraisal. Some "how-to" checklists are provided on the following pages to help with the preparation and delivery of performance information.

Checklist: Preparing a Performance Review

Here are some suggestions for "getting it all together" before an annual performance review meeting.

1. Remind the employee of the performance review process:

☐ Identify potential dates for the meeting.

☐ Review with the employee how to prepare for the meeting (for instance, do you want him or her to do a self-appraisal first, to come prepared with a list of accomplishments?)

2. Determine sources for performance data: Compile a list of sources of data about the employee's performance (the performance plan; feedback from clients, internal customers, peers; accomplishment reports).

3. Review and analyze the data:

☐ Analyze the data gathered from a variety of sources.

☐ Avoid personal biases.

☐ Assess performance against each performance goal.

☐ Support each observation with examples and specific details.

4. Determine rating: Calculate overall rating for the entire year (or portion of year, if appropriate).

5. Prepare to summarize at the end of the meeting:

☐ What are the strengths?

☐ What are the areas for improvement?

☐ What are the implications for professional or career development activities for the next year?

6. Communicate to the next-level manager:

☐ Share written review.

☐ Share rationale for rating.

☐ Solicit views from next-level manager and ask to support your decision.

7. Confirm the performance review data.

The material appearing on this page is not covered by copyright and may be reproduced at will. **15**

Job Aid

Checklist: Conducting a Performance Review

Here are the steps to follow when conducting a successful performance review.

1. Open the meeting:

☐ Establish rapport.

☐ Explain the purpose of the review.

2. Create dialogue:

☐ Encourage the person to talk.

☐ Listen; don't interrupt.

3. Review the goals and standards: All feedback should refer to these goals and standards.

4. Keep feedback objective: Feedback should focus on behaviors, actions, and performance, not personality.

5. Discuss accomplishments:

☐ Solicit person's view first.

☐ Supplement person's view with your view.

6. Discuss areas for improvement:

☐ Solicit person's view first.

☐ Supplement person's self-feedback with your view.

7. Discuss performance rating.

8. Discuss future performance cycle in light of strengths and areas for improvement.

9. Develop a plan for training or professional development for the next year.

10. Summarize meeting.

11. Agree on follow-up or progress checks, as appropriate.

16

The material appearing on this page is not covered by copyright and may be reproduced at will.

Putting it All Together

Considering the material in this chapter, here are a few "take-home" ideas for making sure you have a good performance management system:

- Recognize that the main goal is to establish major performance objectives at the organizational, team, and individual levels—don't get bogged down in performance management details!

- Use a current and relevant Strategic Management system to derive objectives that match the organization's mission, vision, and values.

- Be sure that the formal organizational structure matches a natural flow of performance objectives. Communication is an essential component of performance management.

- Use current and relevant Job Analyses to fine-tune performance management for each job title. Highlight and recognize the important features of each job function.

- Consider theoretical models of performance to see if your system is missing anything. Specifically, address both in-role and extra-role performance dimensions.

- For performance appraisals, use a combination of objective and subjective measurements. Be sure all measures are job related and easy to collect/compile. Don't allow office politics or personal biases to sneak into the ratings.

- Consider the feasibility of 360-degree feedback for subjective measurements to get a more complete picture.

- Performance management requires an ongoing conversation between supervisor and employees. Use After-Event Reviews as a model to guide discussions.

- Periodic formal performance reviews should recognize accomplishments and identify progressive areas for development in the future.

- Significant negative performance should be handled under a separate performance management system. Use the Progressive Discipline Approach to document incidents as they occur and communicate clearly what the employee needs to change.

- Provide training to everyone who will be conducting performance appraisal—don't assume that people already know how to give feedback in a constructive manner.

Spotlight On Research

Emotional Intelligence and Contextual Performance

Introduction

Devonish, D., & Greenidge, D. (2010). The effect of organizational justice on contextual performance, counter-productive work behaviors, and task performance: Investigating the moderating role of ability-based emotional intelligence. International Journal of Selection and Assessment, 18(1), 75–86.

Organizational Justice = perceptions of fairness within an organizational setting. One component is procedural justice, or perceived fairness about the process used to make decisions.

Contextual Performance = voluntary, positive job behaviors that go beyond task requirements and contribute to organizational functioning.

Emotional Intelligence = the set of abilities related to perception and management of emotions to facilitate positive outcomes.

Research Question:

Does the relationship between organizational justice and contextual performance depend on the level of emotional intelligence?

Method

450 participants were recruited at their work site and asked to complete a packet of surveys. Response rate was 46.8%.

Anonymity and confidentiality were preserved with the use of confidential research codes rather than employees' names.

A variety of survey measures were taken on validated scales. Contextual performance (Coleman & Borman, 2000).

Procedural justice (Moorman, 1991).

Emotional intelligence (Wong & Law, 2002).

Participants were thanked and debriefed.

Results

Participant Summary

▢ 9 organizations in Barbados(N=211)

▢ 54.5% women; 45.5% men

▢ Average age = 36 years

Results

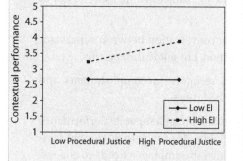

There was a main effect of emotional intelligence, such that those with higher emotional intelligence had higher contextual performance.

There was an interaction (see graph). Those with high EI responded more favorably to high procedural justice in terms of their contextual performance.

Discussion: Directions for Future Research

Studies should identify other moderators of the justice-performance relationship.

In terms of application, organizations should foster both procedural justice and development of emotional intelligence.

Examples: Linking Objectives to Performance Indicators

Examples of objectives and Indicators

Organizational Consultants

Setting: This unit worked with clients doing individual assessments of various types ranging from one-day assessment to multiple-day assessment centers.

Objective 1. Profitability
  Indicator 1. Cost Recovery. Average amount invoiced per assessment divided by cost for that assessment.
  Indicator 2. Billable Time. Percent monthly billable time on days when any assessment function is done.
  Indicator 3. Billing Cycle Time. Average number of days between billing trigger and invoice submission.
Objective 2. Quality of Service
  Indicator 4. Validity of Selection Assessments. Percentage of hits: people assessed predicted to be high performers who turn out to be high performers and those predicted to be marginal who are marginal. Index is based on a 6-month follow-up.
  Indicator 5. Cycle Time. Percentage of assessment reports going out that went out on time.
  Indicator 6. High Quality Experience of Participant. Percentage of participants giving "satisfied" and "very satisfied" ratings at the time of assessment.
  Indicator 7. Customer Satisfaction. Percentage of "satisfied" and "very satisfied" to customer satisfaction measure.
  Indicator 8. Consultant Qualifications. Percentage of licensable consultants who are licensed within 2 years of joining the firm.
  Indicator 9. Ethics/Judgment Training. Percentage of staff with a minimum of 4 hours ethics/judgment training in the last 12 months.
Objective 3. Business Growth
  Indicator 10. Assessment Revenue. Average revenues for the last 3 months from the assessment function.
Objective 4. Personnel Development and Satisfaction
  Indicator 13. Personnel Skill Development. Number of actual tasks the person had been trained on divided by the number of possible tasks that person could be trained on.
  Indicator 14. Personnel Satisfaction. Average number of "OK" and "good" days per person per month based on data entered when each person entered his or her weekly time card.

Photocopier Repair Personnel

Setting: Technicians go out on service calls to repair customers' photocopiers.

Objective 1. Quality: Repair and maintain photocopiers as effectively as possible.
  Indicator 1. Mean copies made between service calls
  Indicator 2. Percentage repeat calls
  Indicator 3. Percentage of preventive maintenance procedures correctly followed
Objective 2. Cost: Repair and maintain photocopiers as efficiently as possible.
  Indicator 4. Parts cost per service call
  Indicator 5. Labor time per service call
  Indicator 6. Percentage of repeat service calls caused by a lack of spare parts
Objective 3. Administration: Keep accurate records of repair and maintenance
  Indicator 7. Percentage of required repair history information filled in correctly
  Indicator 8. Percentage of parts warranty claims correctly submitted.
Objective 4. Attendance: Spend the available work time on work-related activities.
  Indicator 9. Percentage of labor contract hours actually spent on the job.
Objective 5. Ambassadorship: Behave as correctly as possible on the job.
  Indicator 10. Percentage of important social behaviors shown on the job as measured by customers' ratings.

SOURCE: Pritchard, R. D., Harrell, M. M., DiazGranados, D., & Guzman, M. J. (2008). The productivity measurement and enhancement system: A meta-analysis. *Journal of Applied Psychology, 93*(3), 540–567.

Chapter Exercises

Science: Replication and Extension

<u>Instructions:</u> Consider the Spotlight on Research summarized in this chapter. Address each of the following items by using two or three complete sentences on a separate sheet of paper.

1.   What do you think were the strengths of this research?

2.   What were the weaknesses?

PROPOSAL: If you conducted a follow-up study, what you would include in terms of:

3.   A sample of participants (whom would you study?)

4.   Variables you would include and hypotheses you would make (what would you test, specifically?)

Sequencing: Identify the Correct Order

<u>Instructions:</u> Consider the stages presented below. Label each one with a number (next to the stage), and describe why each is important on a separate sheet of paper.

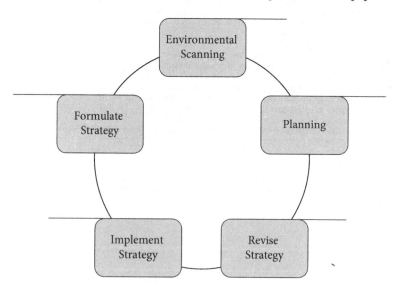

Short Essay Questions

Instructions: Please address the following essay questions briefly, writing in complete sentences on a separate sheet of paper.

1. Briefly describe any three purposes of performance management.

2. Define three terms that relate to whether or not performance criteria have been adequately specified.

3. What is Strategic Management, and how does it relate to performance management?

4. Define Job analysis, and explain how it is related to performance management.

5. Compare and contrast any three errors of social perception.

6. Describe the sequence of steps used in progressive discipline and its overall purpose.

Topics: Relate to Your Own Life

Instructions: Choose one or more of the topics below to write about a related experience from your own life.

- The criterion problem. Describe a situation from your life in which people did not agree about what was "good" performance. Feel free to choose your experience from different life domains such as performance as a student, a parent, a sports team player, or employee.

- Your experiences with performance appraisal. Was your review accurate? Why or why not? Did it clarify performance standards and/or motivate you to do well? Discuss the overall system in terms of its strengths and weaknesses.

- Extra-role performance. Do you believe that extra-role performance such as OCBs should be a part of the formal appraisal system? Why or why not? Explain your own experiences with in-role versus extra-role performance.

Index

References and Recommended Readings

Austin, J. T., & Villanova, P. (1992). The criterion problem: 1917–1992. *Journal of Applied Psychology, 77*(6), 836–874.

Bartram, D. (2005). The Great Eight Competencies: A Criterion-Centric Approach to Validation. *Journal of Applied Psychology, 90*(6), 1185–1203.

Beehr, T. A., Glazer, S., Fischer, R., Linton, L. L., & Hansen, C. P. (2009). Antecedents for achievement of alignment in organizations. *Journal of Occupational and Organizational Psychology, 82*(1), 1–20.

Borman, W. C., & Motowidlo, S. J. (1993). Expanding the criterion domain to include elements of contextual performance. *Personnel Selection in Organizations*, 71–98.

Buchner, T. (2007). Performance management theory: A look from the performer's perspective with implications for HRD. *Human Resource Development International, 10*(1), 59–73.

Campbell, J. P., McCloy, R. A., Oppler, S. H., & Sager, C. E. 1993. A theory of performance. In N. Schmitt, W. C. Borman, and associates (Eds.), *Personnel selection in organizations:* 35–69. San Francisco: Jossey-Bass.

Cannon-Bowers, J. A., & Bowers, C. (2011). Team development and functioning. In S. Zedeck (Ed.) *APA handbook of industrial and organizational psychology, vol. 1: Building and developing the organization* (pp. 597–650). Washington, DC: American Psychological Association

Catano, V. M., Darr, W., & Campbell, C. A. (2007). Performance appraisal of behavior-based competencies: A reliable and valid procedure. *Personnel Psychology, 60*(1), 201–230.

Devonish, D., & Greenidge, D. (2010). The effect of organizational justice on contextual performance, counterproductive work behaviors, and task performance: Investigating the moderating role of ability-based emotional intelligence. *International Journal of Selection and Assessment, 18*(1), 75–86.

Ellis, S., Mendel, R., & Nir, M. (2006). Learning from successful and failed experience: The moderating role of kind of after-event review. *Journal of Applied Psychology, 91*(3), 669–680.

Ellis, S., Ganzach, Y., Castle, E., & Sekely, G. (2010). The effect of filmed versus personal after-event reviews on task performance: The mediating and moderating role of self-efficacy. *Journal of Applied Psychology, 95*(1), 122–131.

Fletcher, C. (2001). Performance appraisal and management: The developing research agenda. *Journal of Occupational and Organizational Psychology, 74*(4), 473–487.

Fletcher, C., & Perry, E. (2001). Performance appraisal and feedback: A consideration of national culture and a review of contemporary and future trends. In N. Anderson, D. Ones, H. Sinangil, & C. Viswesvaran (Eds.), International handbook of industrial, work and organizational psychology. Beverly Hills, CA: Sage.

Fodchuk, K. (2007). Work environments that negate counterproductive behaviors and foster organizational citizenship: Research-based recommendations for managers. *Psychologist-Manager Journal, 10*(1), 27–46.

Griffin, M. A., Neal, A., & Parker, S. K. (2007). A new model of work role performance: Positive behavior in uncertain and interdependent contexts. *Academy of Management Journal, 50*(2), 327–347.

Greenberg, J. (1990). Organizational justice: Yesterday, today, tomorrow. *Journal of Management, 16,* 399–432.

Greenberg, J. (2011). Organizational justice: The dynamics of fairness in the workplace. In S. Zedeck (Ed.), *APA handbook of industrial and organizational psychology, vol. 3: Maintaining, Expanding, and Contracting the Organization* (pp. 271–328). Washington, DC: American Psychological Association.

Grizzle, G. A. (2002). Performance measurement and dysfunction: The dark side of quantifying work. *Public Performance and Management Review, 25,* 363–369.

Gruys, M. L., & Sackett, P. R. (2003). Investigating the dimensionality of counterproductive work behavior. *International Journal of Selection and Assessment, 11*(1), 30–42.

Hagood, W. O., & Friedman, L. (2002). Using the balanced scorecard to measure the performance of your HR information system. *Public Personnel Management, 31*(4), 543–557.

Kacmar, K. M., Collins, B. J., Harris, K. J., & Judge, T. A. (2009). Core self-evaluations and job performance: The role of the perceived work environment. *Journal of Applied Psychology, 94,* 1572–1580.

Kline, T., & Sulsky, L. (2009). Measurement and assessment issues in performance appraisal. *Canadian Psychology/Psychologie canadienne, 50*(3), 161–171.

Latham, G. P., Budworth, M., Yanar, B., & Whyte, G. (2008). The influence of a manager's own performance appraisal on the evaluation of others. *International Journal of Selection and Assessment, 16*(3), 220–228.

Lievens, F., Sanchez, J. I., Bartram, D., & Brown, A. (2010). Lack of consensus among competency ratings of the same occupation: Noise or sub-

stance? *Journal of Applied Psychology, 95*(3), 562–571.

MacDonald, H., & Sulsky, L. (2009). Rating formats and rater training redux: A context-specific approach for enhancing the effectiveness of performance management. *Canadian Journal of Behavioral Science, 41,* 227-240.

Morgeson, F., & Dierdorff, E.C. (2011). Work analysis: from technique to theory. In S. Zedeck (Ed.), *APA handbook of industrial and organizational psychology, vol. 2: Selecting and Developing Members for the Organization* (pp. 3–42). Washington, DC: American Psychological Association.

Morgeson, F. P., Mumford, T. V., & Campion, M. A. (2005). Coming Full Circle: Using Research and Practice to Address 27 Questions About 360-Degree Feedback Programs. *Consulting Psychology Journal: Practice and Research, 57*(3), 196–209.

Organ, D. W. (1997). Organisational citizenship behavior: It's construct clean-up time. *Human Performance, 10,* 85–97.

Overeem, K., Wollersheim, H., Driessen, E., Lombarts, K., van de Ven, G., Grol, R., & Arah, O. (2009). Doctors' perceptions of why 360-degree feedback does (not) work: A qualitative study. *Medical Education, 43*(9), 874–882.

Pritchard, R. D., Harrell, M. M., DiazGranados, D., & Guzman, M. J. (2008). The productivity measurement and enhancement system: A meta-analysis. *Journal of Applied Psychology, 93*(3), 540–567.

Podsakoff, P. M., MacKenzie, S. B., Paine, J., & Bachrach, D. G. (2000). Organizational citizenship behaviors: A critical review of the theoretical and empirical literature and suggestions for future research. *Journal of Management, 26*(3), 51--563.

Pun, K., & Sydney, A. (2005). A performance measurement paradigm for integrating strategy formulation: A review of systems and frameworks.

International Journal of Management Reviews, 7(1), 49–71.

Sackett, P. R. (2002). The structure of counterproductive work behaviors: Dimensionality and relationships with facets of job performance. *International Journal of Selection and Assessment, 10*(1-2), 5–11.

Sackett, P. R., Berry, C. M., Wiemann, S. A., & Laczo, R. M. (2006). Citizenship and Counterproductive Behavior: Clarifying Relations between the Two Domains. *Human Performance, 19*(4), 441–464.

Vey, M. A., & Campbell, J. P. (2004). In-Role or Extra-Role Organizational Citizenship Behavior: Which Are We Measuring? *Human Performance, 17*(1), 119–135.

Wildman, J. L., Bedwell, W. L., Salas, E., & Smith-Jentsch, K. A. (2011). Performance measurement at work: A multilevel perspective. In S. Zedeck (Ed.), *APA handbook of industrial and organizational psychology, vol. 1: Building and developing the organization* (pp. 303–341). Washington, DC: American Psychological Association.

Workforce Planning
Hiring And Legal Issues

3 Chapter Outline

Learning Objectives

The list of objectives below is your guide for organizing the content of this chapter. After you have read the chapter, you can test your proficiency by ensuring that you can address each of the objectives. Place a check in each box □ once you feel confident about your knowledge.

- ☐ Define terms related to workforce planning
- ☐ Explain the importance of performance management for recruitment and hiring
- ☐ Describe various recruitment strategies
- ☐ Discuss affirmative action programs during recruitment
- ☐ Identify the components of a multistage model of hiring
- ☐ Discuss how to screen job applicants
- ☐ Identify legal issues related to giving and seeking reference check information
- ☐ Discuss the appropriate use of interviews and different types of interviews
- ☐ Explain the concept of work samples and their use in hiring
- ☐ Define traits that may be assessed during the selection process
- ☐ Explain the benefits of using a Realistic Job Preview
- ☐ Discuss the use of sensitive information during hiring: drug and medical testing
- ☐ Identify paperwork that must be completed after hiring
- ☐ Discuss activities that should be included in new employee orientation
- ☐ Discuss the use of Succession Planning
- ☐ Describe the Civil Rights Act as it applies to hiring, and Title VII of that act
- ☐ Identify protected classes that are covered by employment law
- ☐ Define validity during hiring: face validity, content, concurrent, and predictive

Chapter Overview

The goal of workforce planning is to use information from performance management (Chapter 2) to help find ideal employees for the organization. This can be a difficult task, but it can be made more effective and manageable by utilizing an organized process of recruitment, hiring, and succession planning for the workforce based on performance needs.

The performance management system provides the specific details of what a person needs to do for valued on-the-job performance. These details should be used during recruitment to locate and encourage talented applicants to apply for jobs. Recruitment is also the place to implement affirmative action programs, particularly if the workforce is underrepresented in terms of the demographic makeup of the local labor market. Advertising the position to the greatest number of qualified people will raise the potential for making good hires.

From this applicant pool, the organization implements its hiring system for selecting the people with the best fit for the positions, a process also known as personnel selection. The purpose of this system is to selectively funnel a large number of candidates down to the best ones. Techniques that may be part of this system include screening tools such as application forms or résumés. From that point, applicants who seem to be a good fit may be selected for interviews or work samples. If necessary, additional practices such as drug testing or credit checking may be included. Integrating performance management with hiring should also include the long-range process of succession planning. This leads to smooth transitions of employees to higher-level positions that need to be filled, and the accomplishment of strategic planning objectives.

Access to employment is considered a civil rights issue. Unfair employment discrimination, whether intentional or not, is not permissible. However, an organization is allowed to have the hiring system of its preference, as long as it can be shown to be clearly job related. Workplace psychology has many data-based techniques to demonstrate the fairness and job-relatedness of a hiring system.

"You seem to have ALL the qualities we're looking for, Mr. Burke. You're not real, but we'll just have to work around that."

Linking Hiring to Performance Management

The purpose of a hiring system is to find fully qualified job candidates. In a perfect world, workforce planning would find the ideal employees exactly as they are needed. Having a workforce of ideal candidates would maximize the performance of the organization (all other things held constant). As indicated in the cartoon, it is not realistic to find a flawless job candidate. However, information from workplace psychology can be used to recruit and identify the best possible job candidates.

Recall that performance management combines essential information from strategic management and job analyses to define the work that needs to be done. This information should guide the process of workforce planning. The following section provides a brief overview of some of the ways these concepts should be integrated.

Strategic Management ⇨ Mission, Vision, and Values ⇨ Job Competencies. Job competencies are overarching abilities that can be demonstrated in different ways. Remember that part of the strategic planning process includes the specification of the overall purpose and ideals of the organization. For example, a mission or vision statement might suggest job competencies related to "teamwork skills" or "innovation." This information should be included in the hiring system. For this example, applicants who cannot provide evidence of ability related to innovation and teamwork would not be the best job candidates.

Strategic Management ⇨ Organizational Culture ⇨ Job Turnover. An organizational mission and vision that are consistent with a meaningful organizational culture will support employees who match that culture. This process has been studied as part of the Attraction-Selection-Attrition framework (e.g., Schneider, 1987; Billsberry, 2007). Essentially, this model indicates that attrition is partly a function of a lack of person/organization fit. People whose needs and values do not match the organization will leave, if and when they can. Others with better fit will be integrated into the organization.

Strategic Management ⇨ Performance Goals ⇨ Workforce Planning. Strategic management directs the organization by specifying future goals, as well as how to evaluate goal progress. This roadmap provides the crucial information that needs to be the cornerstone of the long-range hiring plan known as succession planning. Clearly, any major changes such as organizational restructuring or a merger will have direct implications for short- and long-term hiring goals.

Establishing Hiring Criteria

Job Analysis ⇨ Job Specification ⇨ Initial Screening. As already described in Chapter 2, job analysis is the process of documenting a detailed description of each job title. This includes any necessary characteristics someone must have to be successful at work. These characteristics are listed in the job specification. One of the clearest links between performance management and hiring is to use the job specification to screen out applicants who cannot demonstrate these characteristics. They will not be able to do the job well and therefore should not be hired.

Job Analysis ⇨ Job Description ⇨ Interview and Performance Tests. Another major segment of the job analysis consists of the job description, which describes the actual work activities for a given job title. This information should be used to derive questions for the interview, and any other work samples or tests that are used during hiring. Workplace psychologists have expertise in using job requirements to derive high-quality selection instruments. The quality of these instruments is measured in terms of various forms of reliability and validity; these are described in greater detail at the end of the chapter.

The previous section has outlined some of the many ways that performance management is a necessary precursor to hiring the right people to reach the organization's goals. The remainder of the chapter examines some of the theory, research, and legal issues related to good hiring practices.

Recruitment

A good recruitment plan is proactive in nature, allowing time to find the right people to hire. A recruitment plan incorporates information from changes in strategic direction, staffing requirements, and turnover data. The key to recruitment is to cast as broad a net as possible to reach qualified **applicants**. This includes recruiting applicants from internal sources (within the company) as well as external sources. There are advantages and disadvantages to each strategy, reviewed below.

Internal Recruitment

Typically, employees appreciate the opportunity to be considered for new positions, particularly if it means a promotion or development opportunities. Therefore, attempting to fill positions from current employees should be part of the ongoing performance management system. To facilitate internal recruitment, a database known as a **skill inventory system** should be maintained. This database contains documentation of employees' KSAOs (knowledge, skills, abilities, and other characteristics). A **job bidding** system allows employees to express interest in a position, even if there are no job openings at the time. By contrast, a **job posting** system announces position openings to current employees.

The main advantage to internal recruitment is that the organization already has a track record of performance for these applicants. Another potential advantage is meeting employees' expectations for promotion opportunities upon establishing this record. However, this potential advantage can become a disadvantage if it results in unhealthy competition or resentment among coworkers vying for the same position. To guard against this possibility, organizations should employ the findings from organizational justice research introduced in Chapter 2. This research (e.g., Smith, Organ, & Near, 1983; Greenberg, 2011) demonstrates that internal applicants should understand the selection policies (procedural justice) as well as a clear communication process that shows respect for the employee (interactional justice).

External Recruitment

There are situations in which the employer may desire or require new skills, or a fresh perspective from someone who has not been part of the organization. If this is the case, it is important to identify the recruitment sources that will yield the highest number of qualified applicants. There is a large number of potential sources for external recruitment, including:

• Job fairs

• Career centers

• Employee referrals

- Employment agencies
- College placement centers
- Internet job sites

The job requirements should be carefully considered in evaluating which recruitment sources to use. For instance, posting job announcements in online or print publications has the advantage of reaching a large number of people, and so it is a desirable strategy for an entry-level position. If specialized skills are required, they should be clearly stated in the job announcement. This will make it easy to screen out applicants who do not have the requisite skills. In addition, it suggests a targeted recruitment strategy, such as educational or certification institutes, or trade associations. Professional journals and websites are another avenue of external recruitment that will likely yield a qualified applicant pool.

Affirmative Action Programs (AAPs)

A topic that is relevant to external recruitment is **affirmative action**. The Department of Labor requires affirmative action programs from all employers who have 50 or more employees and who receive federal contracts in excess of $50,000. These programs must be established within 120 days from the contract's date of origin. Such contractual obligations are monitored by the Office of Federal Contract Compliance Programs (OFCCP).

A common misconception about affirmative action is that it is based on setting quotas for minorities during hiring. An additional misconception regarding affirmative action programs is that they may force out good employees who do not have a minority status. Affirmative action programs were never intended to result in the hiring of people who were not qualified for a job, and any such implementation is not helpful to the organization or its employees. In fact, these incorrect perceptions have been associated with negative reactions to the programs (e.g., Unzueta, Gutiérrez, & Ghavami, 2010; Heilman, Block, & Lucas, 1992; Heilman, McCullough, & Gilbert, 1996). As one might expect, stronger prejudices against minority groups relate to more negative reactions to AAPs (e.g., James, Brief, Dietz, & Cohen, 2001).

It is more appropriate to think about affirmative action programs as maintaining an awareness of the existing representation of protected groups throughout the organization, and encouraging diversity by actively recruiting from a variety of sources. In fact, survey results (SHRM, 2010) indicate that the most frequently used diversity practice used by organizations was in the area of recruitment (79%).

- Promotes improvement in quality of web sites and other e-publications as required.

Qualifications:

- Extensive knowledge of web applications and technologies, such as HTML, CSS, and Javascript. Ruby on Rails is a plus.

- Software knowledge including: Camtasia, Director, Fireworks, Photoshop, Soundforge, Dreamweaver, Freehand, ImageReady, Shockwave, and Macromedia Flash.

- Must have the ability to collaborate with internal and external groups.

- 4-5 years of experience in web interface design or web-based graphic design, B.A. or B.S. in graphic design, art, or related field or equivalent academic or work experience.

- Extensive written and oral communication skills.

- Audio/Video demonstration technologies experience is preferred.

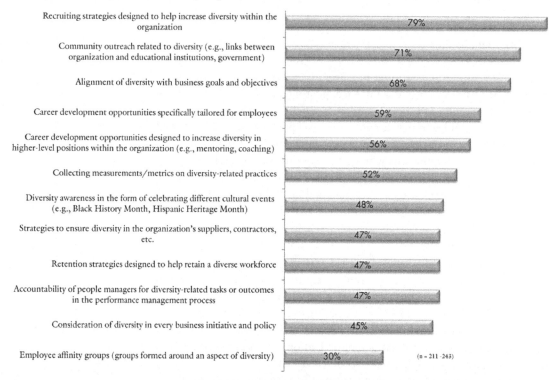

(Source: http://www.shrm.org/Research/SurveyFindings/Documents/10-DiversityFlier_FINAL_spotlight.pdf)

A reliance on a single source of recruitment (such as employee referrals) may limit the demographic diversity of applicants. The information gathered in an affirmative action program will help identify whether or not an organization needs to expand its recruitment efforts to match the local labor market in terms of demographic representation.

There are several components in an affirmative action program. As part of reporting requirements, organizations must file Form EEO-1 with the Equal Employment Opportunities Commission and the Office of Federal Contract Compliance Programs. This form reports the frequencies of male and female employees by ethnicity and position category. The information that must be recorded is included in the chart below.

Section D—EMPLOYMENT DATA

Employment at this establishment—Report all permanent full-time and part-time employees including apprentices and on-the-job trainees unless specifically excluded as set forth in the instructions. Enter the appropriate figures on all lines and in all columns. Blank spaces will be considered as zeros.

JOB CATEGORIES		OVERALL TOTALS (SUM OF COL. B THRU K)	MALE					FEMALE				
			WHITE (NOT OF HISPANIC ORIGIN)	BLACK (NOT OF HISPANIC ORIGIN)	HISPANIC	ASIAN OR PACIFIC ISLANDER	AMERICAN INDIAN OR ALASKAN NATIVE	WHITE (NOT OF HISPANIC ORIGIN)	BLACK (NOT OF HISPANIC ORIGIN)	HISPANIC	ASIAN OR PACIFIC ISLANDER	AMERICAN INDIAN OR ALASKAN NATIVE
		A	B	C	D	E	F	G	H	I	J	K
Officials and Managers	1											
Professionals	2											
Technicians	3											
Sales Workers	4											
Office and Clerical	5											
Craft Workers (Skilled)	6											
Operatives (Semi-Skilled)	7											
Laborers (Unskilled)	8											
Service Workers	9											
TOTAL	10											
Total employment reported in previous EEO-1 report	11											

NOTE: Omit questions 1 and 2 on the Consolidated Report.
1. Date(s) of payroll period used: 2. Does this establishment employ apprentices?
   1 ☐ Yes   2 ☐ No

(Source: http://www.eeo1.com/EEO1Form.pdf)

An activity that may be included as part of an affirmative action program is to conduct a workforce analysis, which is essentially an organizational chart that displays the breakdown of the workforce in terms of gender, race, and wages. This chart helps to identify any areas of potential underrepresentation of demographic groups per job title, or wage disparities by gender or race. Another proactive approach to diversity management is to conduct a SWOT analysis (described in Chapter 2). An example of this analysis is included below.

Diversity SWOT Analysis

In terms of diversity, analyze the organization's, or team's, strengths, weaknesses, opportunities, and threats (SWOTs). Based on the answers to the SWOT analysis, divide answers into areas to work on and establish goals, objectives, and action plans to complete. Fill out the blank diversity plan provided.

Strengths

What are our strengths in providing a culture that supports diversity? (Or, what strengths in valuing diversity does this team display?)

Weaknesses

What weaknesses do we have in providing a culture that supports diversity?

Opportunities

What external opportunities exist that we can take advantage of to increase our ability to support diversity?

Threats

What external threats do we foresee that could hinder our success in creating a culture that encourages and supports diversity?

Diversity Plan

Goal:

Objective:

Action Plan (resources and due dates):

Measurement:

Savings or Efficiencies:

It should be noted that several cases of **"reverse discrimination"** have been filed. One of the most famous cases was *California Board of Regents v. Bakke* (1978), which dealt with college admissions. The Supreme Court ruled that quotas cannot be established, but that race could be a factor in deciding among qualified applicants. This idea was upheld several decades later in *Gratz v. Bollinger* (2003), where it was ruled that areas of underrepresentation could be addressed in furthering the university's mission of advancing diversity. Allegations of reverse discrimination are not limited to university settings. Overall, the courts have been consistent in ruling that selection quotas are not allowed, but that using minority status to address underrepresentation is acceptable. Even if an organization is not legally required to maintain an affirmative action program, it is useful to keep track of the diversity of job candidates located through different recruitment approaches. A high-quality recruitment strategy will yield a large number of qualified, diverse applicants to consider when hiring for a position.

Selection Techniques: Hiring

Organizations need an effective system of hiring. The more critical and complex the positions, the more attention to detail the system requires. The following section describes some of the considerations for organizations to implement a thorough selection system.

Applicant Tracking

It is important to anticipate how many job applicants there will be during the hiring process. For a highly specialized or rare skill, it may be possible to consider each set of application materials in their entirety. However, when recruiting for jobs that will yield a large number of applicants, it will be necessary to create an applicant tracking and communication system. This system will involve decisions about time lines and types of communication with applicants, accessibility of files, and delegation of responsibility over the process.

A Multistage Model of Hiring

Selection processes should advance from the most simple and inexpensive to the most complex and costly. The first stage of selection involves screening for basic essential qualifications. This can be done via a resume or application forms, with basic reference checks to advance candidates to the next step. The next stage is more substantive in nature, involving interviews and/or work samples. Some organizations also invest in contingent selection practices such as credit checks, drug testing, or medical testing.

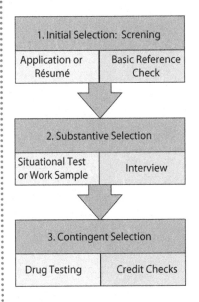

1. Initial Selection: Screening Applicants

It is important to screen applicants on the basis of whether or not the applicant has the necessary job specifications and competencies. The initial selection stage can be used to screen out applicants who do not have the requisite background, knowledge, skills, or abilities required to do the job. Using these selection techniques will help hone in on the applicants who most closely fit the needs of the position. Two fairly straightforward ways to accomplish this goal are the application and the employee résumé, both of which may be collected online. An advantage to using the job specification for screening is that you can quickly scan applications and résumés for the information you are looking for. Applicants who pass initial screening for job specifications can proceed on to the next stage of the selection process: background and reference checks.

Background and Reference Checks. A large number of applicants provide dishonest information on their résumés and/or applications. There have been many widely publicized instances of résumé fraud, including the chief executives of Yahoo, RadioShack, and Bausch & Lomb. A study conducted by the Society of Human Resource Management in 2003 reported 41 percent of job applicants lied about their education, and 23 percent fabricated professional licensure. Therefore, it is worthwhile for employers to take the time to substantiate the information provided on these sources. If the information is a matter of public record such as professional licensure, it is fairly easy to verify.

Other information, however, can only be obtained by asking for it. An employer may ask the candidate for professional references, or may contact a former employer listed on the application. Sometimes the information provided is limited, because the reference source may be concerned about accusations of **defamation** if it can be shown that any information given verbally is false. Similarly, the source may be charged with **libel** if the information given in a written format is false. Therefore, when requesting or providing information, it is important to stick to information that is factual and clearly job related. Another idea is to obtain written consent from the job applicant that you have their permission to provide job-related information. At a minimum, you will be able to ascertain whether applicants have been truthful about factual information contained on their applications. If the applicant has performed well, often the reference will reflect this.

Conducting a **reference check** allows the organization to screen out applicants who do not have the qualifications they have claimed. This enables more attention to be given to substantive selection techniques. A few such techniques are described below, including the employment interview, work samples, and trait assessments.

2. Substantive Selection

Applicants who have successfully passed the screening stage of the selection process may be considered in more substantial selection techniques. Often these techniques are conducted on-site, and involve a meeting with hiring managers, members of the department, and those in Human Resources.

Interviews

The interview is the most prevalent substantive selection method used in the United States (Huffcutt & Culbertson, 2011). The best way to create interview questions is in concert with the job analysis, so all questions are specific and job related. In this way, the candidate can be asked directly if they are capable of satisfying the job requirements. This will also avoid the risk of asking questions that violate employment law (such as the ADA, 1990).

There is a long history of research on the employment interview, dating back almost one hundred years ago (Scott, Bingham, & Whipple, 1916). Periodic reviews of the employment interview have been conducted every few decades (Wagner, 1949; Ulrich & Trumbo, 1965), which highlight the issues of the day. Overall, research has shown that interviews do have validity in terms of correlations with job performance. There are some features of interviews that have been shown to heighten validity.

One such feature is the use of the **structured interview** (versus the unstructured interview). The essence of the structured interview is to develop a standardized list of job-related questions for each job applicant. This does not

Defamation = verbal communication of information that provides a negative image of a person and is false

Libel = written communication of information that provides a negative image of a person and is false

Reference check = the process of confirming the accuracy of information provided on a résumé or job application

Structured interview = the use of standardized questions for each job candidate

mean that a hiring manager must follow a script. Obviously, there should be flexibility to establish rapport and ask relevant follow-up questions. Some practitioners are hesitant to use a structured approach and prefer to rely on intuition (Highhouse, 2008). However, including the same, job-related questions for each candidate ensures consistency and minimizes the possibility that the interviewers' personal biases will affect their judgments.

Another type of standardized interview format is the **behavior description interview** (Janz, 1982). The emphasis of this type of interview is to ask for specific instances of job-related behaviors. This interview feature improves validity by emphasizing the behaviors that the applicant can apply to the hiring organization. A **situational interview** (Latham, Saari, Pursell, & Campion, 1980) can be tailored to create hypothetical situations of interest to the organization. Again, the key here is to find specific details of how the applicant approaches and responds to situations. For instance, an applicant may be given specific details about a given working environment, such as interacting with an irate customer who has a particular complaint, and asked how they would respond. The notion of raising standardization by including details of the situation is further developed by using work samples or simulations.

Behavior description interview = the inclusion of questions that ask for specific behavioral examples of past performance instances

Situational interview = the inclusion of questions that ask about what job candidates would do in hypothetical situations

Work Samples and Simulations

A component that may be added to substantive selection tactics is a work simulation. Again, hiring managers and those in HR should be creative in applying a **work sample** that clearly relates to the ability to do the job. Some examples of this type of substantive selection technique include:

Work sample = a method of substantive selection in which the applicant is asked to perform samples of job-related tasks

- Lecture. A 15–20 minute lecture is often called a lecturette. This can be used as a selection technique for those who will be teaching or giving presentations.

- Problem-Solving Tests. Engineers and software programmers may be asked to solve some standard problems to ensure that they have technical competence and can explain their reasoning.

- Sales Pitches. Candidates who will be working in sales may be asked to provide a demonstration of how they would engage potential customers or clients.

- Lab Tests. Those who will be working in a science lab (e.g., chemists, forensic scientists), may be asked to work with lab samples and conduct quantitative analyses.

- Administrative Tasks. An applicant for a secretarial position may be asked to type a letter, which can be coded for speed and accuracy.

Work samples provide a simulation of the work environment and allow the job candidate to demonstrate specific job-related behaviors. These samples allow the organization to make assessments of the candidate's professional competency and presentation skills. They have advantages in that they show clear positive correlations with job performance (Roth, Bobko, & McFarland, 2005). In addition, they are less prone to racial differences in test scores than some other assessments, as described below (Roth, Bobko, McFarland, & Buster, 2008). If possible, the work sample can be a valuable part of the substantive hiring process.

Trait Assessments

There are other options for substantive selection techniques, including various types of **trait assessments**. Research has generally supported correlations with job performance for these measures. However, they can lead to negative reactions from applicants because the items on the assessments do not always clearly relate to job requirements. In fact, a review of applicant reactions across countries shows clear patterns of preferences for interviews and work samples over other substantive techniques (Anderson, Salgado, & Hülsheger, 2010). Thus, organizations may choose to use these techniques only if it is deemed necessary to supplement the other components of the hiring system.

- *Cognitive Ability Tests.* These questionnaire-style tests are often used to measure reasoning and intellect. Well-known tests include the Watson-Glaser Critical Thinking Test and the Wonderlic Personnel Test. Although cognitive ability tests do correlate with job performance across a variety of job titles, they are not perceived favorably and can be prone to racial biases (Anderson et al., 2010; Roth et al., 2008).

- *Personality Tests.* These questionnaire-style tests are often used to measure aspects of personal beliefs and views of the world. Well-known tests include the NEO-PI, the Hogan Personality Inventory, and the Guilford-Zimmerman Temperament Survey.

- *Integrity Tests.* The idea behind a trait-based **integrity test** is to predict a job applicant's likelihood of stealing from the organization. These tests present a series of statements to which applicants rate their level of agreement such as, "It's okay to skim a little money off the top from time to time." They also incorporate "fake good" items such as, "It is wrong to take a pencil home from work." Although these items have been shown to correlate moderately with job performance and counterproductive work behaviors (Van Iddekinge, Roth, Raymark, & Odle-Dusseau, 2012), they are among the least favorably perceived by job applicants (Anderson et al., 2010). Organizations concerned about employee theft may be more inclined to assess integrity via background checks or contingent selection techniques, described below.

Realistic Job Preview

The **realistic job preview** (RJP) is not a selection technique, but it is useful to include as part of a candidate's on-site visit. The realistic job preview consists of describing a typical working day, allowing observations of the work site, and meetings with current job incumbents. The RJP also allows an opportunity for applicants to ask questions about the job, the work unit, or the organization that they might not otherwise have thought about. The organization can use the RJP to clarify the job requirements, as well as to promote positive features of the job.

Research on the realistic job preview indicates that it is associated with lower job turnover and higher ratings of job satisfaction, although the strength of the association is moderate (Phillips, 1998). In addition, the usefulness of the RJP depends somewhat on the availability of alternative positions and the applicant's level of choice in declining a job that doesn't match expectations (Breaugh, 2008). Nevertheless, since the RJP is quick and inexpensive, it is worthwhile to include during an on-site meeting.

3. Contingent Selection

This final selection stage is generally the most expensive and time consuming, so it is wise to limit its use to candidates one would like to hire. As always, information gathered during this stage must be clearly related to the requirements of the job. Some information that may be of interest to the organization may be considered personally sensitive to the job applicant. In these cases, it is important to be aware of existing legislation and the correct handling of personal information. Drug testing and credit checks are two such types of sensitive information that may be used during contingent selection and will be considered here.

Drug Testing

There are conflicting views on the topic of testing for the use of illegal drugs. Some believe that use of any substance that is against the law should be subject to testing in employment. Others think that personal consumption of substances away from the worksite is a lifestyle choice, and therefore is irrelevant if it does not affect job performance. Research tends to support moderate correlations between the use of drugs and various health and work problems, and this extends to the use of alcohol (as described in the Spotlight in Research, Chapter 6; Liu, Wang, Zhan, & Shi, 2009).

A reasonable compromise regarding this controversy has been taken by many organizations. It is assumed that drug testing is not necessary unless otherwise indicated through erratic behavior, observations of drug use at work, or workplace accidents. If events such as these occur, it is more easily accepted that drug testing is reasonable. However, the government has initiated a more proactive stance on illegal drugs for organizations that receive federal funding.

Drug-Free Workplace Act of 1988. This legislation requires that all organizations that receive federal contracts of $100,000 or more will ensure a workplace free of illegal drugs. Basically, this means that they will publish and maintain drug awareness programs, and notify the federal government if an employee is found to be using illegal drugs. Although it does not mandate regular testing for drugs, the organization may choose to do so as part of its antidrug program.

Credit Checks: Fair Credit Reporting Act (1970)

Many employers are interested in considering a candidate's financial history, particularly for jobs that require financial responsibility or access to money. In fact, a survey study found that almost half of all employers use credit check

The most heavily researched personality inventory is the NEO-PI, also known as the "Big Five." The personality dimensions of the **Big Five** are:

- Emotional stability = not neurotic, anxious

- Extraversion = people oriented, outgoing

- Openness to experience = cultured, inquisitive

- Conscientiousness = dependable, detail oriented

- Agreeableness = easygoing, calm

Of these traits, conscientiousness has been shown to correlate most strongly with job performance across a variety of job titles (Barrick & Mount, 1991; O'Neill & Allen, 2011).

information (SHRM, 2010). This step is most likely to be taken for jobs in investment, accounting, and senior management positions that control financial resources.

The Fair Credit Reporting Act (1970). This legislation was enacted in part to govern the use of financial history information. Unlike most employment legislation, this act applies to all employers regardless of scope or size. This act requires the employer to inform the candidate of their intent to check information from a credit report, and to obtain written consent to do so. It also requires the employer to inform the employee if an adverse action is to be made on the basis of this information, and allows the employee to challenge the accuracy of the information. Finally, the act protects the privacy of this information and specifies proper disposal of it. The following example provides a form that covers all aspects of background checks.

Authorization for Background Investigation

Full Legal Name _____

If applicable, other names used during the last 5 years:

_____

Current Address: _____

Current Phone: _____

Current Email: _____

Social Security Number: _____

Date of Birth: _____

Gender: M / F

Position Applying for: _____

Residence History (last 5 years):

City and State	Dates Resided

As a candidate for the above-referenced position, I understand that [insert company name] may conduct a background investigation, including education and employment verification and credit and criminal record investigation, for employment purposes. If I am refused employment due to the results of the background investigation, I understand that I may request an explanatory meeting with [insert name]. Such a request must be made within 5 working days of my notice. Failure to provide complete and accurate information will be case for disqualification/termination of employment.

Signature: _____   Date: _____

_____

This section of the chapter has provided an overview of how to develop a good system of finding qualified job applicants. Research (SHRM, 2012) has investigated the influence of selection information on hiring decisions. These data suggest that the most important factors are: good organizational fit, specific work experience and skills, good presentation during the interview, and favorable background checks.

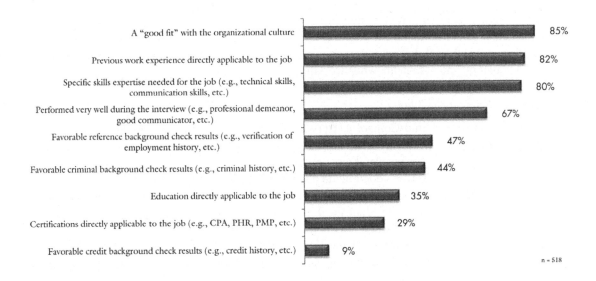

(Source: http://www.shrm.org/Research/SurveyFindings/Articles/Documents/CCFlier_FINAL)

Post-Selection

Having found the best candidate, there are several things that must be done to get the new employee "into the system." For instance, employment laws have been enacted to use the workplace as a way to track parents who owe child support and the immigration status of workers. In addition to these administrative details, it is important to help new employees with their transition into the organization. The following section will explore some of the steps an organization should take following hiring.

Details and Paperwork

Offer of Employment

The offer letter stipulates a formal invitation for employment at the organization. A written, signed employment letter reduces the possibilities of disagreements about the employment conditions. The written letter should include the date, job title, starting salary or hourly rate, and note that the offer is subject to the results of any contingent hiring practices (e.g., drug testing, medical or background checks). It is important to avoid phrases that may be, or may imply, a long-term employment contract. In fact, some would suggest that the letter should explicitly state that it is not a contract of employment, and iterate that the relationship is "at will." This means that either party can terminate the working relationship at any time. The offer letter should be signed by a company official as well as the new employee.

New Hire Reporting Form

Organizations are required to report the names and addresses of all new hires within 20 days, so that the information can be added to the National Directory of New Hires. The purpose of this database is to track parents who are delinquent on child support payments, and also to ensure that people do not collect unemployment benefits while working.

Verifying Employment Eligibility

The Immigration Reform and Control Act (1986) was enacted for the purposes of verifying employment eligibility to work in the United States. An applicant does not need to be a U.S. citizen to legally gain employment. However, he or she does need to provide certain documentation to be considered eligible for hire. These documents must verify both identity and employment authorization. Examples of documents that accomplish both include: U.S. passport, employment authorization card with photo, or Permanent Resident Card. If these are not available, the prospective employee may use one document to establish identity (e.g., driver's license, school ID card, voter registration) and another to establish eligibility (e.g., social security number, birth certificate, Native American tribal document, or employment authorization issued by the Department of Homeland Security). Verification of employment eligibility is confirmed on Form I9, *Employment Eligibility Verification*. The employer is required to store these forms and be prepared to submit them to the U.S. Bureau of Citizenship and Immigration Services, if requested.

Tax Withholding

All new employees must complete Form W-4, the *Employee's Withholding Allowance Certificate*. This form documents the number of dependents (withholding allowances) and marital filing status of employees. These factors relate to the rate of income tax that is deducted from each paycheck. Employees may change this form as their life circumstances change to adjust their income tax withholding rate.

New Employee Orientation and Related Activities

Once the employee has accepted the job and arrives to work, it is important to provide a thorough employee orientation. The orientation is often referred to as **onboarding**, which provides a good visual analogy of pulling someone who might be adrift at sea onto the ship (of the organization). These activities have several purposes. First, the new employee should be made welcome to the organization. As mentioned in Chapter 1, the nature of the exchange relationship indicates that spending time during this phase will raise commitment to the organization. Another major endeavor during this time is to provide **organizational socialization**, which helps the new employee adapt to the new environment (Bauer & Erdogan, 2011). Part of this process involves an introduction to the **organizational culture**. Many organizations require a formal new employee training session to accomplish these goals. Additional methods for socializing new employees include providing an employee handbook and mentoring programs.

A recent poll (SHRM, 2011) found that over 80 percent of respondents reported that their organizations conduct onboarding activities. Data from this survey also suggest that the provision of communication, training, and resources are the most useful during new employee socialization.

In your opinion as an HR professional, how important are the following activities for the successful adjustment of newcomers and for facilitating their performance, engagement and retention?

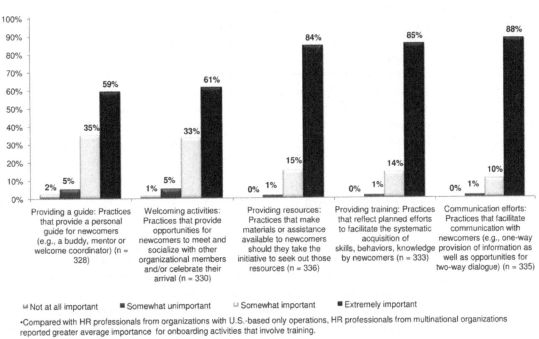

◻ Not at all important   ■ Somewhat unimportant   ◻ Somewhat important   ■ Extremely important

•Compared with HR professionals from organizations with U.S.-based only operations, HR professionals from multinational organizations reported greater average importance for onboarding activities that involve training.

Note: Percentages may not total 100% due to rounding.

(source: http://www.shrm.org/Research/SurveyFindings/Articles/Pages/OnboardingPractices.aspx slide 14)

The Employee Handbook

There are numerous purposes for the **employee handbook**. It provides a description of the organization's history, purpose, vision, and mission, as well as an organizational chart representing the organizational structure. It welcomes the new employee and highlights the benefits of employment at the organization, such as employee discounts, education or training opportunities, and paid holidays.

The handbook must also address rules and the consequences for violation of those rules. It should specify exactly what is expected of the new employee in terms of attendance, punctuality, dress code, theft, consumption of substances, and technology use at the workplace. The handbook may include a list of resources and contact information for questions that arise. Many organizations ask employees to sign a form indicating that they have received and read the employee handbook.

Mentoring Programs

Mentoring programs pair a higher-level, veteran employee (the mentor) and a less experienced employee (the protégé). The **mentoring** dynamic is classically represented in the apprenticeship form of training, where a one-on-one relationship exists to guide the protégé toward professional competence. Informal mentoring programs exist in virtually every organization.

The key to these programs is that the senior employee takes an interest in the career development of the junior employee. In this manner, they can help the newer employee navigate the steps necessary for professional success. This includes providing job-related advice, explaining the proverbial "ropes" of the organization, networking with valuable contacts, and making political affiliations. One of the downsides to informal mentoring is that they can form on the basis of the similar-to-me bias (described in Chapter 2), and therefore can be less available to those who do not share demographic similarity to the mentor.

Some organizations have attempted to get around this problem by formalizing their mentoring programs. In this case, protégés are assigned to a mentor, who is asked to help them. This has the advantage of ensuring that everyone has equal access to the program. However, a potential downside is that the dynamic of the relationship may not generate the level of interest required for the protégé to succeed.

Succession Planning

Another element of workforce planning concerns keeping an awareness of the current workforce in terms of talent management and replacing people who will be leaving the organization. It is important to be proactive in these endeavors to avoid rushed decision making. The integration of long-term strategic planning and performance management is needed for succession planning. However, survey data (SHRM, 2011) revealed that only 23 percent of organizations have a formal succession planning program. Those that do are more likely to be large (greater than 2,500 employees) and more likely to have complex structures (Naveen, 2006).

Succession planning refers to a wide variety of activities aimed at long-term workforce planning. It is the process of assessing both planned and unplanned turnover, particularly in key positions in the organization. It is generally recognized that there are four components of a formal succession plan (Capella, 2011):

1. Identifying the job titles that will be covered in the planning process.

2. Forecast upcoming turnover within those jobs.

3. Identification of candidates within the organization who can fill those jobs.

4. Leadership development, special job assignments, and other training to prepare those candidates.

Related activities include identifying and managing talent within the organization, mentoring, and providing for growth opportunities and skill development. A **skills inventory** is typically a database that contains a listing of employees and specialized skills, certification, and training each has achieved. This inventory should be directly tied to Training and Development activities (Chapter 4), wherein successfully completed training programs are logged into the database. Another tool that can be used during succession planning is a **replacement chart**. This chart contains four categories into which employees may be placed: replace, ready for promotion, develop for future promotion, or satisfactory in current position.

Long-range approaches to workforce planning can be speculative in nature. Inquiring when a person intends to retire or otherwise leave the organization may be considered to be personally intrusive, and that person might not have a particular date in mind. In addition, those who have been identified for development may not succeed in their preparations, or may leave the organization before the promotion occurs.

Skill inventory system = an information management system (often a database) for documenting specialized skills or training

Replacement chart = a succession planning tool to identify performance potential of employees

The chapter thus far has presented some guidelines and creative ideas for workforce planning. The coverage of this topic will now turn to legal and professional issues that should be integrated into the process of recruiting and hiring employees.

Legal Issues in Workforce Planning

There are a multitude of potential legal issues involved in workforce planning, particularly the hiring of employees. Attending to these issues benefits both the organizations and the employees. Hiring guidelines should follow a "common sense" logic based on fairness, and be crafted to prevent potential legal problems. Keeping detailed documentation is an important element of any hiring system. All hiring managers should be fully trained regarding these legal and professional issues.

Negligent Hiring

One of the most straightforward reasons to be diligent during hiring is to avoid allegations of negligent hiring. **Negligent hiring** occurs when an organization does not adequately vet its employees, particularly in situations that place other people at risk. Specifically, an organization's liability hinges on whether: (1) They should have known the person was unfit; (2) there is a foreseeable risk; and (3) injury to a person was caused by this employment. Some clear-cut cases of negligent hiring are presented below.

Negligent hiring = failing to ensure the safety of customers, clients, or employees through inadequate hiring practices

Negligent Hiring Cases: Employer Found Guilty

Following are examples of *negligent hiring cases* in which the employer was found guilty:

- A furniture company was found liable for $2.5 million for negligent hiring and retention of a deliveryman who savagely attacked a woman customer in her home. (Tallahassee Furniture Co., Inc. v. Harrison)

- A nursing home was found liable for $235,000 for the negligent hiring of an unlicensed nurse with numerous prior criminal convictions who assaulted an 80-year-old visitor. (Deerings West Nursing Center v. Scott)

- An employee with a criminal record sexually abused a child; his employer was found liable for $1.75 million for negligent hiring and retention. (Doe v. MCLO)

- A vacuum cleaner manufacturer was found liable for $45,000 because one of its distributors hired a door-to-door salesperson with a criminal record who raped a female customer in her home. The manufacturer should have required its distributors to conduct prehiring screening of door-to-door salespersons to prevent hiring of persons with criminal histories. (McLean v. Kirby Co.)

(Source: http://www.iso.com/Research-and-Analyses/ISO-Review/Negligent-Hiring-Employer-Risk.html)

This simply means that an organization needs to follow through on hiring practices. In particular, care should be taken in verifying identity through checking Social Security numbers or with the Department of Motor Vehicles. Other useful procedures include background checks, reference checks, and verifying the validity of information on an application blank or résumé. Additional checks such as credit history and drug use may be used, particularly if the employee will have access to sensitive materials on the job, or access to people's residences.

Equal Employment Opportunity

A careful system of workforce planning takes into account Equal Employment Opportunity (EEO). This philosophy is built upon the idea that people have fair access to achieving the portion of the American Dream that relates to employment. This means that workplaces in the United States are welcome places for people who are qualified for the work, regardless of religion, ethnicity, gender, or national origin.

Awareness of legislation and case law related to equal employment opportunity will help reduce the probability of legal battles. Equal employment opportunity law applies to most private employers, state and local government agencies, union organizations, educational institutions, and employment agencies. Thus, it affects a tremendous number of organizations and has resulted in a large number of litigation cases.

In deciding whether or not an organization is liable for violation of **Equal Employment Opportunity**, the courts place a great deal of weight in reaching a decision on the employer's "posture" relative to diversity and fairness. This posture is a function of many things, including the organization's communication of pro-diversity policies, implementation of an affirmative action plan, and maintenance of documentation. The remainder of this chapter will address some of the laws related to EEO.

Employment Law

There is a host of legal issues related to recruitment and hiring. Central to this discussion is the notion of a **protected class**. This term indicates membership in a group that has historically encountered unfair discrimination. Equal employment opportunity law is in place to correct historical imbalances for these groups. This body of law is so detailed, that full coverage would require separate dedicated texts. To highlight some of this material, a very brief summary of legislation surrounding protected classes follows.

Protected Classes: Gender, Religion, Race, Color, National Origin

Title VII of the Civil Rights Act of 1964. The first federal legislation to specifically address illegal discrimination in employment was Title VII of the Civil Rights Act of 1964. The other titles of this act address other potential arenas of unfair discrimination. Title VII specifically listed as protected classes: sex (now referred to as gender), religion, race, color, and national origin for most private employers with more than 25 employees. This Civil Rights Act also established a government agency called the **Equal Employment Opportunity Commission** to oversee its enforcement. In addition to responding to claims of EEO violations, the EEOC collects annual reports about the demographic makeup of the workforce from all employers of more than 100 employees (and those with 50 employees receiving federal contracts).

Early Legal Cases Involving Title VII. Title VII gave specific legal ground to people who had been unfairly discriminated against at work because of membership in a protected class. For instance, in the case of *Rosenfeld v. Pacific Railway* (1968), stereotypes that women were unable to lift 30 pounds were used as grounds to deny promotion to Lily Rosenfeld. This employment decision was made despite the employee having an otherwise excellent performance record and the capability of lifting 30 pounds. Title VII made it illegal to rely on such stereotypes in eliminating people from consideration for jobs.

A quick recap of the EEOC 2010 stats:

• 36,258 charges of retaliation discrimination (up 7.8%)

• 35,890 charges of race discrimination (up 6.9%)

• 29,029 charges of sex discrimination (up 3.6%)

• 25,165 charges of Americans with Disabilities Act violations (up 17.3%)

• 23,264 charges of Age Discrimination in Employment Act violations (up 2.1%)

• 11,304 charges of national origin discrimination (up 1.5%)

• 3,790 charges of religious discrimination (up 11.9%)

• 1,044 charges of Equal Pay Act violations (up 10.8%)

• 201 charges of Genetic Information Nondiscrimination Act violations (first year recorded)

(Source:http://www. fosterthomas.com/blog/ bid/36337/2010-EEOC-Results-Show-Increase-in-Employment-Practices-Liability-Claims)

Another major case related to Title VII was *Griggs v. Duke Power* (1971). In this case, the Supreme Court held that Title VII proscribes not only overt discrimination, but also practices that are fair in form but discriminatory in operation. If one demographic group is systematically eliminated from consideration, the employer must then be able to show that their hiring procedures are job related and consistent with business necessity.

Another significant decision was made by the Supreme Court in *Albemarle Paper Co. v. Moody* (1975). Although the employer tried to present evidence in court that their hiring practices were related to job performance, the quality of the evidence was poor. More specifically, ratings of job performance were only provided in the form of subjective supervisor ratings, and only for senior level employees. Thus, this information did not relate clearly to the entry-level applicants or their performance. This was an important decision because the Supreme Court made it clear that evidence must be of legitimate quality. In essence, this meant that organizations needed to take equal employment opportunity seriously.

Executive Order 11246 (1965). An executive order is a presidential proclamation that can be signed directly into law. These have been used to legislate equal employment opportunity that affects organizations receiving federal grants. The year following the Civil Rights Act of 1964, such an executive order was signed into effect by President Lyndon Johnson, prohibiting employment discrimination by organizations with 50 or more employees receiving federal contracts of $50,000 or more. This order also required the implementation of affirmative action programs. The purpose of these programs is to include a nondiscriminatory policy, document the inclusion of protected classes in the organization, compare these to the available workforce, identify discrepancies, and to set goals to remedy these discrepancies.

Equal Pay Act (1963). The Equal Pay Act prohibits wage discrimination for men and women performing substantially equal work for the same organization. Compensable factors in determining the similarity of the work include: effort, skill, responsibility level, and working conditions. Although this was a progressive attempt to limit pay discrimination based on gender, in practice it is very difficult to measure the concept of "substantially equal work" (see Chapter 5 for a discussion of job evaluation). Also, due to many employment practices of pay secrecy, it is difficult for an employee to know when unfair pay practices are in place. Thus, as indicated in the graph, women typically earn 70 to 85 percent of the salary of men, depending upon the industry. The construction industry is the closest to reaching "equal pay." There are many arguments about why women typically earn less. These include lower career commitment among women, choice of lower-paying career paths, and time taken away from the workplace due to family needs (particularly those involving children). Whatever the reason, data across most professions indicate that there is still a substantial gender pay gap.

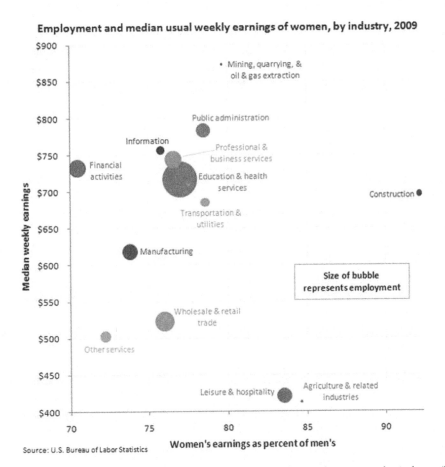

Employment and median usual weekly earnings of women, by industry, 2009

Source: U.S. Bureau of Labor Statistics

(Source: http://economix.blogs.nytimes.com/2011/02/17/the-gender-pay-gap-by-industry/)

Lilly Ledbetter Fair Pay Act (2009). The Supreme Court had ruled in 2007 that there was a 180-day statute of limitations on claims of pay discrimination, and the clock started on the first unfair paycheck distributed. The Lilly Ledbetter Act (so named after the Supreme Court case *Ledbetter v. Goodyear Tire and Rubber Co.*) changed this statute of limitations so that the 180-day clock started with <u>each</u> discriminatory paycheck. This legislation makes it easier for employees to identify and protest unfair pay.

Protected Class: Age (over 40)

The Age Discrimination in Employment Act (1967). This legislation applies to private organizations with greater than 20 employees, and most government agencies. It was initiated by a concern that older workers would be discriminated against so that companies could continually operate with cheaper (younger) labor. The ADEA made it illegal to discriminate against job applicants or current employees on the basis of age for anyone aged 40 years or older. The act does not protect people who are younger than 40, even if they are "older" compared to other workers (see *General Dynamics Land Systems v. Cline*, 2004).

There are various exceptions to protections for older workers, such as those for executives who are older than 65 years, have been in their positions for longer than two years, and are eligible to receive at least $44,000/year in retirement benefits. Other exceptions include situations for which it is recognized that an advanced age may limit the capacity to perform a job, such as firefighter or law enforcement officer. Other legislation related to protecting older workers in terms of their compensation and benefits is described in Chapter 6. This has recently become an important topic due to the rapid changes in benefits packages and health care options.

Protected Class: Veterans

It is important that veterans be able to find gainful employment. A recent professional survey by the Society of Human Resources Management (2012) indicated that most organizations had hired U.S. veterans, but that only 13 percent of respondents reported being "very aware" of effective recruitment resources. Issues of high unemployment among military servicepersons has received media and political attention.

Vietnam Era Veterans Readjustment Assistance Act (1974). This act was initiated by a concern that war veterans would be discriminated against. It applies to employers who have federal contracts of $25,000 or more. Such employers are to provide affirmative action and actively recruit vets who served 180 or more active duty days between 1964 and 1975, or any disabled veterans during this time period.

Uniformed Services Employment/Reemployment Rights Act (1994). This legislation was based upon a concern that military personnel would lose pension and promotion rights due to required active duty service. This act requires employers to grant leave for five years, and to reinstate the employee upon his or her return. In addition, the employee is allowed to keep all health care benefits, and to accrue all pension and seniority benefits as if employment had not been interrupted.

Protected Class: Disability

The Rehabilitation Act (1973). This act was initiated by a concern that prejudices against physical challenges (such as impaired mobility) would limit employment opportunities for disabled people who are capable of successful job performance. This act prohibited employment discrimination for federal employees, federal contractors, or any organization receiving federal funding.

Americans with Disabilities Act (1990). This legislation greatly expanded coverage for qualified persons with disabilities who require a reasonable accommodation to perform the job. It applies to all organizations with more than 15 employees. It also requires that organizations be accessible to people with disabilities. However, according to the ADA, employers are not required to make accommodations that would result in undue financial hardship.

The handling of reasonable accommodations is actually based on common sense, although in practice it can be mishandled by either the employer or the employee. For a job applicant, the employer's appropriate handling is to present the requirements of the job and ask the employee if he or she can meet those requirements. If the prospective employee cannot, but could with a feasible accommodation, the appropriate response would be to explain the nature of this request.

It is the responsibility of a current employee who develops a disability that interferes with the job to request a meeting with a manager to discuss possible accommodations. The interactive process involves employees explaining the nature of their disabilities and making suggestions for accommodations to allow them to do the job.

Facts About the Americans with Disabilities Act

Title I of the Americans with Disabilities Act of 1990 prohibits private employers, state and local governments, employment agencies and labor unions from discriminating against qualified individuals with disabilities in job application procedures, hiring, firing, advancement, compensation, job training, and other terms, conditions, and privileges of employment. The ADA covers employers with 15 or more employees, including state and local governments. It also applies to employment agencies and to labor organizations. The ADA's nondiscrimination standards also apply to federal sector employees under section 501 of the Rehabilitation Act, as amended, and its implementing rules.

An individual with a disability is a person who:

- Has a physical or mental impairment that substantially limits one or more major life activities;
- Has a record of such an impairment; or
- Is regarded as having such an impairment.

A qualified employee or applicant with a disability is an individual who, with or without reasonable accommodation, can perform the essential functions of the job in question. Reasonable accommodation may include, but is not limited to:

- Making existing facilities used by employees readily accessible to and usable by persons with disabilities.
- Job restructuring, modifying work schedules, reassignment to a vacant position;
- Acquiring or modifying equipment or devices, adjusting or modifying examinations, training materials, or policies, and providing qualified readers or interpreters.

An employer is required to make a reasonable accommodation to the known disability of a qualified applicant or employee if it would not impose an "undue hardship" on the operation of the employer's business. Reasonable accommodations are adjustments or modifications provided by an employer to enable people with disabilities to enjoy equal employment opportunities. Accommodations vary depending upon the needs of the individual applicant or employee. Not all people with disabilities (or even all people with the same disability) will require the same accommodation. For example:

- A deaf applicant may need a sign language interpreter during the job interview.
- An employee with diabetes may need regularly scheduled breaks during the workday to eat properly and monitor blood sugar and insulin levels.
- A blind employee may need someone to read information posted on a bulletin board.
- An employee with cancer may need leave to have radiation or chemotherapy treatments.

An employer does not have to provide a reasonable accommodation if it imposes an "undue hardship." Undue hardship is defined as an action requiring significant difficulty or expense when considered in light of factors such as an employer's size, financial resources, and the nature and structure of its operation.

An employer is not required to lower quality or production standards to make an accommodation; nor is an employer obligated to provide personal use items such as glasses or hearing aids.

An employer generally does not have to provide a reasonable accommodation unless an individual with a disability has asked for one. If an employer believes that a medical condition is causing a performance or conduct problem, it may ask the employee how to solve the problem and if the employee needs a reasonable accommodation. Once a reasonable accommodation is requested, the employer and the individual should discuss the individual's needs and identify the appropriate reasonable accommodation. Where more than one accommodation would work, the employer may choose the one that is less costly or that is easier to provide.

Title I of the ADA also covers:

- Medical Examinations and Inquiries
  Employers may not ask job applicants about the existence, nature, or severity of a disability. Applicants may be asked about their ability to perform specific job functions. A job offer may be conditioned on the results of a medical examination, but only if the examination is required for all entering employees in similar jobs. Medical examinations of employees must be job related and consistent with the employer's business needs.

  Medical records are confidential. The basic rule is that with limited exceptions, employers must keep confidential any medical information they learn about an applicant or employee. Information can be confidential even if it contains no medical diagnosis or treatment course and even if it is not generated by a health care professional. For example, an employee's request for a reasonable accommodation would be considered medical information subject to the ADA's confidentiality requirements.

- Drug and Alcohol Abuse
  Employees and applicants currently engaging in the illegal use of drugs are not covered by the ADA when an employer acts on the basis of such use. Tests for illegal drugs are not subject to the ADA's restrictions on medical examinations. Employers may hold illegal drug users and alcoholics to the same performance standards as other employees.

It is also unlawful to retaliate against an individual for opposing employment practices that discriminate based on disability or for filing a discrimination charge, testifying, or participating in any way in an investigation, proceeding, or litigation under the ADA.

Federal Tax Incentives to Encourage the Employment of People with Disabilities and to Promote the Accessibility of Public Accommodations

The Internal Revenue Code includes several provisions aimed at making businesses more accessible to people with disabilities. The following provides general – non-legal – information about three of the most significant tax incentives. (Employers should check with their accountants or tax advisors to determine eligibility for these incentives or visit the Internal Revenue Service's website, www.irs.gov, for more information. Similar state and local tax incentives may be available.)

- Small Business Tax Credit (Internal Revenue Code Section 44: Disabled Access Credit)
  Small businesses with either $1,000,000 or less in revenue or 30 or fewer full-time employees may take a tax credit of up to $5,000 annually for the cost of providing reasonable accommodations such as sign language interpreters, readers, materials in alternative format (such as Braille or large print), the purchase of adaptive equipment, the modification of existing equipment, or the removal of architectural barriers.
- Work Opportunity Tax Credit (Internal Revenue Code Section 51)
  Employers who hire certain targeted low-income groups, including individuals referred from vocational rehabilitation agencies and individuals receiving Supplemental Security Income (SSI) may be eligible for an annual tax credit of up to $2,400 for each qualifying employee who works at least 400 hours during the tax year. Additionally, a maximum credit of $1,200 may be available for each qualifying summer youth employee.
- Architectural/Transportation Tax Deduction (Internal Revenue Code Section 190 Barrier Removal):
  This annual deduction of up to $15,000 is available to businesses of any size for the costs of removing barriers for people with disabilities, including the following: providing accessible parking spaces, ramps, and curb cuts; providing wheelchair-accessible telephones, water fountains, and restrooms; making walkways at least 48 inches wide; and making entrances accessible.

(Source: http://www.eeoc.gov/facts/fs-ada.html)

Protected Class: Genetic/Family History of Medical Problems

Genetic Information Nondiscrimination Act (2008). Indirectly, this act stemmed from a concern over the ballooning costs of health care. With the increasing identification of genetic markers for health disorders, it was thought that some people might be discriminated against due to the presence of these markers or a family history of such a disorder. GINA mandates privacy of all health-related information, and makes it illegal to use genetic information for employment decisions. Some examples relevant to GINA are provided in the sidebar.

As the review above indicates, it is important to have an awareness of the notion of protected classes and the legislation related to them. Blatant discrimination against people in these groups is referred to as **adverse treatment**, and can be used to bring about an employment lawsuit if there is any documentation or corroboration of this treatment. However, simply claiming that one's organization does not unfairly discriminate against protected classes is not good enough (although it is a good starting place).

HR departments need to be prepared to show that the system of hiring people is clearly related to the jobs they will be doing. A forward-thinking organization therefore is prepared to address the validity of their hiring processes. These issues have been clearly addressed in the Uniform Guidelines for Employee Selection, described below.

Uniform Guidelines for Employee Selection (1978)

Confusion about the basic principles that should be used to hire people led to the development of selection guidelines. The agencies involved with writing and approving the guidelines were the Equal Employment Opportunity Commission, the Department of Labor, the Civil Service Commission, and the Department of Justice. The guidelines were developed for any situation that could be considered as employee "selection," including hiring, promotion, job retention, or specialized training designations if they relate to promotion decisions. It is good to note that (in addition to avoiding legal problems), these guidelines are based in common sense ideals that should appeal to both hiring managers and job applicants.

A key term is **adverse impact**. Adverse impact occurs when any source of information used during selection results in membership of a protected class being eliminated from consideration to a greater extent than others. What is the difference between groups that needs to be evident to suggest adverse impact? The guidelines and the courts have adopted the "4/5th rule" as **prima facie** evidence of adverse impact. The **4/5th rule** means that the selection rate of candidates of a protected group must be at least 80 percent that of the selection rate of a comparison group (the group with the highest percentage of candidates remaining). If it is below 80 percent, there is an indication that the process may be unfairly discriminatory.

However, this is not the end of the process, as far as the guidelines are concerned. Any selection procedure that creates adverse impact may still be lawful if it can be demonstrated that it is job related, and that there are no other comparable methods that do not create adverse impact. How can job-relatedness be established? There are several methods of doing this.

Recall from Chapter 1 that validity is an important concept in establishing the truth or appropriateness of any measurement. Validity studies can be used to demonstrate the job-relatedness of a selection source. Numerical and professional data are necessary to demonstrate validity, and the courts will require this information. **Criterion-related validity** relies on the demonstrated correlation between scores on the selection source and measures of job performance (such as those described in Chapter 2). This can be established by using information from the applicants who are subsequently hired. This is known as **predictive criterion-related validity**. Criterion-related validity can also be established by using selection source and performance data from job incumbents. This is known as **concurrent criterion-related validity**. Criterion-related validity is the best method for establishing the job-relatedness of a selection source because it is direct data to this effect.

Sometimes it is not possible to establish criterion-related validity due to small sample sizes or other practical problems with collecting data. There are other approaches that may be used to establish validity. For instance, **construct validity** exists when a selection source can be shown to be correlated with other, previously validated measures that have conceptual similarity. Finally, the **face validity** of a selection test refers to the extent to which there is a clearly apparent link between hiring and job requirements. It is important that applicants perceive this type of validity during hiring.

The Uniform Guidelines describe how employers can ensure that selection procedures are clearly related to job requirements. It is fairly straightforward to maintain a fair and legal selection system by implementing these recommendations and using common sense. As mentioned throughout the chapter, merging the concepts from Chapter 2 (Performance Management) and Chapter 3 (Workforce Planning) will result in a workforce that can achieve its organizational goals

Criterion-related validity = the extent to which scores on the selection test correlate with job performance

Predictive criterion-related validity = the extent to which job applicants' scores on the selection test at one time correlate with their job performance at another time

Concurrent criterion-related validity = the extent to which job incumbents' scores on the selection test correlate with their job performance

Putting it All Together

Considering the material in this chapter, here are a few "take-home" ideas for making sure you have a good hiring system:

- Start with your performance management system! What will a person taking this job need to be able to do for the organization?

- Both the strategic planning and job analyses are critical tools to be used in developing a hiring system.

- Recruitment of qualified applicants may occur from within the organization or external sources. It is important to cast as wide a recruitment net as possible to be sure to get high-quality applicants.

- Affirmative action programs are part of a valid workforce planning effort that maintains awareness of the diversity of one's organization relative to the local labor market.

- Hiring systems should consist of a multistage approach, starting with screening applicants based on the job specifications.

- More substantive stages of hiring systems include interviews and work samples. These should be structured and geared toward job-related behaviors.

- If the position requires it, contingent selection tactics such as drug testing, medical testing, or financial background may be used.

- Employee orientation activities and an employee handbook will help to socialize the new employees to the organization.

- Equal Employment Opportunity is a principle that advocates fairness in the employment arena and also tries to ensure that unfair discrimination does not occur.

- A "protected class" is a group that is protected by employment law. The reasoning is that members of certain groups traditionally have been unfairly discriminated against and require legal protections.

- Protected classes include gender, religion, race, color, national origin, age, veteran status, disability, and genetic markers.

- The Uniform Guidelines for Employee Selection have been developed to clarify what organizations need to do to ensure their hiring systems are valid and do not unfairly discriminate against applicants.

- There are many types of validation evidence that may be used to support the use of a given selection test.

Spotlight On Research

Emotions and Interviewing

Introduction

Interview = a very popular method for gathering information about job applicants. It often creates anxiety for job seekers.

Research has suggested that people use impression management tactics such as emotional suppression. Emotional suppression is thought to be a stressor and to increase cognitive load.

Women have been shown to be more expressive of emotions in a wide variety of circumstances.

Research Question:

Are there gender differences in emotional suppression during interviews, and does suppression relate to anxiety perceived by oneself and others?

Method

Participants were recruited through a research website and offered 15 euros for participation.

All participants were told that they would be interviewed and would be video recorded for an external evaluation.

Task: Participants took part in a series of tests and an interview. The interview was prerecorded and participants had one minute to address ten questions, such as:
  "What qualifies you for this position?" and "What are your weaknesses?"

Measures (a subset of all the measures taken)
  Subjective emotional state (Wallbott & Scherer, 1991). Items such as anxiety, depression were rated on a 10-point scale.
  Emotional suppression (4-point scale). *"During the job interview, did you try to suppress or hide your feelings (e.g., insecurity, anxiety)?"*
  Rater's evaluation of emotional state (Wallbott & Scherer, 1991). Items such as anxiety, depression were rated by trained evaluators of the videos using a 10-point scale.

Results

Both men and women reported some degree of anxiety.

There was a complex interaction. Women who suppressed emotions reported significantly higher anxiety, although this was not found by those making an external rating (see graph).

Discussion: Directions for Future Research

Studies should assess personality characteristics related to interview strategies.

Future research can explore whether women have a greater tendency to withdraw from career opportunities that require emotional suppression.

Sieverding, M. (2009) "Be cool!" Emotional costs of hiding feelings in a job interview. International Journal of Selection and Assessment, 17(4), 391–401.

Participant Summary

☐ *Undergraduate Students (N=74)*

☐ *37 women; 37 men*

☐ *Average age = 26.4 years*

Results

	Self-rating	External rating
Men (Suppressors)	2.0	1.9
Women (Suppressors)	4.2	2.0
Men (Nonsuppressors)	2.1	1.7
Women (Nonsuppressors)	2.2	3.1

Chapter Exercises

Science: Replication and Extension

<u>Instructions:</u> Consider the Spotlight on Research summarized in this chapter. Address each of the following items by using two or three complete sentences on a separate sheet of paper.

1. What do you think were the strengths of this research?

2. What were the weaknesses?

PROPOSAL: If you conducted a follow-up study, what you would include in terms of:

3. A sample of participants (whom would you study?)

4. Variables you would include and hypotheses you would make (what would you test, specifically?)

Sequencing: Identify the Correct Order

<u>Instructions:</u> Consider the stages presented below. Label each one with a number (next to the stage), and describe why each is important on a separate sheet of paper.

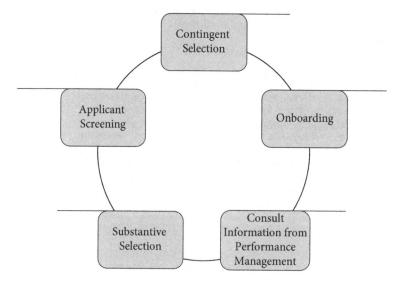

Short Essay Questions

<u>Instructions</u>: Please address the following essay questions briefly, writing in complete sentences on a separate sheet of paper.

1. Specifically, describe any two ways that performance management principles relate to employee hiring.

2. List and briefly describe any four groups of employees who are part of a "protected class."

3. What is the basic purpose of validity in hiring tests? Briefly define any three types of validity as it relates to hiring.

4. Describe the purpose of an affirmative action program. What information is contained in EEO-1?

5. Explain any three characteristics of interviews that enhance predictive validity.

6. Describe any three onboarding practices that can be used to help new hires adjust to the organization.

Topics: Relate to Your Own Life

<u>Instructions</u>: Choose one of the topics below to write about a related experience from your own life. Use the space at the bottom of the page to document your experiences and opinions.

• Internal versus External Recruitment. Discuss your experiences with the pros and cons of filling positions from within the organization, as compared with filling positions with newcomers to the organization.

• Affirmative action programs. What exposure have you had to affirmative action? Was it positive, negative, both, or neither?

• Interviews. Consider features of an interview that can be used to raise its validity. To what extent were these included (or not included) in the last interview you took part in? Explain.

Index

References and Recommended Readings

American Educational Research Association, American Psychological Association, & National Council on Measurement in Education (1999). *Standards for educational and psychological testing.* Washington, DC: American Psychological Association.

Anderson, N., Salgado, J. F., & Hülsheger, U. R. (2010). Applicant reactions in selection: Comprehensive meta-analysis into reaction generalization versus situational specificity. *International Journal of Selection and Assessment, 18*(3), 291–304.

Arthur, W., & Day, E. A. (2011). Assessment Centers. In S. Zedeck, S. Zedeck (Eds.), *APA handbook of Industrial and Organizational psychology, vol. 2: Selecting and developing members for the organization* (pp. 205–235). Washington, DC: American Psychological Association.

Barrick, M. R., & Mount, M. K. (1991). The Big Five personality dimensions and job performance: A meta-analysis. *Personnel Psychology, 44*(1), 1–26.

Billsberry, J. (2007). Attracting for values: An empirical study of ASA's attraction proposition. *Journal of Managerial Psychology, 22*(2), 132–149.

Breaugh, J. A. (2008). Employee recruitment: Current knowledge and important areas for future research. *Human Resource Management Review, 18*(3), 103–118.

Capella, P. (2011). Succession Planning. In S. Zedeck, S. Zedeck (Eds.), *APA handbook of Industrial and Organizational psychology, vol. 2: Selecting and developing members for the organization* (pp. 673–690). Washington, DC: American Psychological Association.

Conway, J. M., Jako, R. A., & Goodman, D. F. (1995). A meta-analysis of inter-rater and internal consistency reliability of selection interviews. *Journal of Applied Psychology, 80*(5), 565–579.

Griggs v. Duke Power Co., 401 U.S. 424 (1971).

Equal Employment Opportunity Commission (1978). *Uniform guidelines on employee selection procedures.* Washington, DC.

Heilman, M. E., Block, C. J., & Lucas, J. A. (1992). Presumed incompetent? Stigmatization and affirmative action efforts. *Journal of Applied Psychology, 77*(4), 536–544.

Heilman, M. E., McCullough, W. F., & Gilbert, D. (1996). The other side of affirmative action: Reactions of nonbeneficiaries to sex-based preferential selection. *Journal of Applied Psychology, 81*(4), 346–357.

Highhouse, S. (2008). Stubborn reliance on intuition and subjectivity in employee selection. *Industrial and Organizational Psychology: Perspectives on Science and Practice, 1*(3), 333–342.

Huffcutt, A. I., & Culbertson, S. S. (2011). Interviews. In S. Zedeck, S. Zedeck (Eds.), *APA handbook of Industrial and Organizational psychology, vol. 2: Selecting and developing members for the organization* (pp. 185–203). Washington, DC: American Psychological Association.

James, E., Brief, A. P., Dietz, J., & Cohen, R. R. (2001). Prejudice matters: Understanding the reactions of Whites to affirmative action programs targeted to benefit Blacks. *Journal of Applied Psychology, 86*(6), 1120–1128.

Janz, T. (1982). Initial comparison of patterned behavior description interviews versus unstructured interviews. *Journal of Applied Psychology, 67*, 577–580.

Latham, G. P., Saari, L. M., Pursell, E. D., & Campion, M. A. (1980). The situational interview. *Journal of Applied Psychology, 65*, 422–427.

Moody et al. v. Albemarle Paper Company, 474 F .2d 134 (1973).

Newman, D. A., Hanges, P. J., & Outtz, J. L. (2007). Racial groups and test fairness, considering history and construct validity. *American Psychologist, 62*(9), 1082–1083.

O'Neill, T. A., & Allen, N. J. (2011). Personality and the prediction of team performance. *European Journal of Personality, 25*(1), 31–42.

Outtz, J. L. (2011). The unique origins of advancements in selection and personnel psychology. In S. Zedeck (Ed.) *APA handbook of industrial and organizational psychology, vol. 2: Selecting and developing members for the organization* (pp. 445–465). Washington, DC: American Psychological Association.

Phillips, J. M. (1998). Effects of realistic job previews on multiple organizational outcomes: A meta-analysis. *Academy of Management Journal, 41*(6), 673–690.

Ployhart, R. E., & MacKenzie, W. I. (2011). Situational judgment tests: A critical review and agenda for the future. In S. Zedeck, S. Zedeck (Eds.), *APA handbook of Industrial and Organizational psychology, vol. 2: Selecting and developing members for the organization* (pp. 237–252). Washington, DC: American Psychological Association.

Roth, P. L., Bobko, P., & McFarland, L. A. (2005). A meta-analysis of work sample test validity: Updating and integrating some classic literature. *Personnel Psychology, 58*(4), 1009-1037.

Roth, P., Bobko, P., McFarland, L., & Buster, M. (2008). Work sample tests in personnel selection: A meta-analysis of Black-White differences in overall and exercise scores. *Personnel Psychology, 61*(3), 637–662.

Schneider, B. (1987). The people make the place. *Personnel Psychology, 40*(3), 437–453.

Scott, W. D., Bingham, W. V., & Whipple, G. M. (1916). Scientific selection of salesmen. *Salesmanship, 4*, 106–108.

Seijts, G. H., & Kyei-Poku, I. (2010). The role of situational interviews in fostering positive reactions to selection decisions. *Applied Psychology: An International Review, 59*(3), 431–453.

Sieverding, M. (2009). "Be cool!": Emotional costs of hiding feelings in a job interview. *International Journal of Selection and Assessment, 17*(4), 391–401.

Society for Industrial and Organizational Psychology, Inc. (2003). *Principles for the validation and use of personnel selection procedures* (4th Edition). College Park: Maryland.

Title VII of the Civil Rights Act, as amended, 42 U.S.C. 2000e (1964).

Unzueta, M. M., Gutiérrez, A. S., & Ghavami, N. (2010). How believing in affirmative action quotas affects White women's self-image. *Journal of Experimental Social Psychology, 46*(1), 120–126.

Van Iddekinge, C. H., Roth, P. L., Raymark, P. H., & Odle-Dusseau, H. N. (2012). The criterion-related validity of integrity tests: An updated meta-analysis. *Journal of Applied Psychology, 97*(3), 499–530.

Training and Employee Development

4 Chapter Outline

Learning Objectives

The list of objectives below is your guide for organizing the content of this chapter. After you have read the chapter, you can test your proficiency by ensuring that you can address each of the objectives. Place a check in each box ☐ once you feel confident about your knowledge.

☐ Define training and other employee development terms

☐ Explain why training is important to employees and organizations

☐ Explain the input-process-outcome elements of the training process

☐ Define training needs assessment and its components

☐ Define a learning objective and how it should be written

☐ Contrast various training methods in terms of advantages and disadvantages

☐ Discuss how to arrange the learning environment for training implementation

☐ Define and explain each of the criteria for training evaluation

☐ Define the "transfer problem" and ways to address it

☐ Identify the components of a return-on-investment analysis

☐ Identify theoretical learning principles that should be part of training

☐ Define employee development and identify its purposes

☐ Explain the use of coaching in employee development

☐ Explain job assignments as an employee development tactic

☐ Identify assessment tools that can be used in employee development

☐ Define the continuous learning organization and why it is beneficial

Chapter Overview

Within the context of organizations, training is defined as a planned effort to raise job-related knowledge, skills, and abilities. The goals are to improve both employee and organizational functioning. It is useful to think about training activities in terms of stages in an input-process-outcome model. This model helps to ensure a systematic and thorough training program.

Input activities that occur prior to training are known as a needs assessment, which essentially brings a strategic planning approach to the training endeavor. Process activities involve implementation of the training program and incorporation of principles from learning theories. This stage should include both theoretical and practical best practices for training delivery. The outcome stage involves evaluation of the training program. This includes measures of: reactions to training, knowledge gained, behaviors applied to the job, and improvements to the organization. All of these stages create and support the training learning objectives, which specify what the trainees should know, and be able to do, upon successful completion of the training program.

Whereas training often deals with current job demands, employee development is typically based on planning for the future. Development activities are geared toward preparing high-potential employees for advancement in the organization. One approach to employee development involves interpersonal relationships such as coaching or mentoring. Another is the use of planned job assignments such as job rotation or job enrichment. Other activities such as performance appraisal, assessment centers, or personality indicators can provide useful feedback for development. Each of these developmental activities can help to ensure that employees are ready for future assignments.

This chapter concludes with a discussion of a continuous learning organization. An organization with a continuous learning culture places a high value on training, learning, and the sharing of knowledge.

Why Is Training Important?

Organizations in the United States spend millions of dollars annually on training employees as a way to improve job performance and increase profits (e.g., Velada, Caetano, Michel, Lyons, & Kavanagh, 2007; Noe, 2010). Research has shown a positive relationship between the use of training and job-related skills, learning outcomes, and performance (Arthur, Bennett, Edens, & Bell, 2003), organizational productivity (Zwick, 2006), and team effectiveness (Aguinis & Kraiger, 2009).

Training has direct effects on learning. In addition, it demonstrates an investment in employees and thus is a symbol of value. This, in turn, affects the social exchange relationship (described in Chapter 1). Finally, training can reduce liability associated with negligent employee behavior or safety violations.

Training and development can help organizations address fundamental questions and issues such as:

- What are the critical objectives of training?
- How should the content of training be delivered?
- Have trainees gained necessary knowledge in training?
- Are trainees confident that they can do their jobs?
- Do learned skills transfer back to the job site?
- Does the organization value the currency of skills?
- What is the benefit of training relative to its cost?

A systematic approach to training and development of employees will raise their preparation to perform well and to innovate, and these outcomes will be reflected in the bottom-line outcomes for the organization. This chapter will address practical applications of training and well-known psychological theories of learning.

A Training Input-Process-Outcome Model: An Overview

Many topics in workplace psychology can be considered in terms of input variables, the change process, and outcome measures. A systematic approach to training should include attention to activities prior to, during, and following training.

Pre-training activities are often addressed during the training **needs assessment**. Other important activities during this time include preparing employees for change (e.g., demonstrating that the potential benefits will outweigh the potential costs). Information obtained during the needs assessment will address whether or not training is necessary to meet organizational objectives. It will inform the development of a training design, which specifies the details of subsequent training activities.

The training implementation should carefully follow the training design, paying careful attention to basic learning principles. This phase also involves a host of practical activities, such as how to set up the training environment, how to deliver the training content, and the provision of training materials.

The final component of the training program is the outcome evaluation. This requires assessing whether training is being applied back to the job site and benefiting the organization as intended. Each of these stages will be described in greater detail in the following pages.

A model that is popular in applied training programs is represented by the acronym ADDIE. The ADDIE model includes the following components of training: **A**nalysis, **D**esign, **D**evelopment, **I**mplementation, and **E**valuation. Thorough models of employee training include a significant investment to

Stages of a Training Program

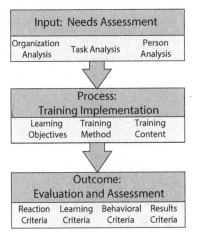

Needs assessment = a formal planning method to determine organizational objectives and whether these can be met with training

activities before, during, and after training to ensure the effectiveness of the program.

Input: Needs Assessment

Needs assessment is defined as the process of determining the organization's objectives, and whether these can be met by training (Arthur et al., 2003). Essentially, the training needs assessment involves collecting a lot of information from a variety of sources prior to committing to training. The needs assessment is typically considered in terms of three phases of analysis: organization, task, and person.

Organization analysis = the use of business plans to identify the potential need and benefit of a training effort; includes organizational goals, resources, and environment

Organization analysis. During the organizational analysis, the training is aligned with strategic planning so that it furthers the organizational mission. Specifically, one of the purposes of a performance management system is to reveal any performance discrepancies between business objectives and the results achieved. One of the aims of the organizational analysis is to ascertain whether these performance discrepancies can be addressed with training and development, or whether they require a different approach. If a different approach is identified (for instance, the existing equipment is too slow), there is no need to pursue training until better equipment has been purchased.

However, if training needs have been identified, it is important to clearly specify the appropriate long- and short-term goals for the training. This phase also requires a realistic assessment of the requisite budget and timeframe for the training. In addition, specific targets can be identified for the measurable outcomes of training.

If training is supported during the organizational analysis, specific learning objectives can be developed to address the performance discrepancies. The job skills most frequently identified as lacking within the workforce include "people skills" such as supervision leadership, and communication (Davenport, 2005).

Task Analysis. With the results of the organization analysis in hand, it is necessary to examine the actual job requirements. Some of these data can be obtained from current job descriptions. Other sources of information include interviews with job incumbents or observations of the work site. A final report of a task analysis will include the jobs that were analyzed, the tasks performed at the job, and the Knowledge, Skills, Abilities, and Other characteristics (KSAOs) necessary to excel at each task. This will give the information needed to refine the learning objectives.

Task analysis = the examination of job requirements to address training needs

Person Analysis. As the name indicates, this analysis is considered at the level of the employee. As such, it can be the most controversial phase of the needs assessment because Equal Employment Opportunity Law (discussed in Chapter 3) also applies to the opportunity to participate in training and development activities. For this reason, most organizations choose to develop training

Person analysis = consideration of individual-level performance and training needs

around a particular job skill or department rather than at the level of individuals. However, it can be useful for organizations to link the person analysis to employee development as part of the performance management system. With the increased use of computer-based training modules, it is easier to manage training at the individual level.

The person analysis includes a consideration of employees in terms of their training needs. A potential source of information for this analysis is a performance appraisal that highlights training deficits; another is a career development plan that specifies training requirements for promotion. Another consideration regarding the person analysis is to invest pre-training effort to raising trainees' readiness, as well as their understanding of the benefits of the training. This process of managing worker perception is a fundamental feature of any change endeavor. A basic model for implementing change was introduced by Lewin (1952), and is summarized in the sidebar graph.

Process: Training Implementation

The process of training should be focused on maximizing the trainees' learning. There are many practical ideas such as providing learning objectives, discussion questions, and handouts. There are also many theory-driven concepts that have been shown to raise learning in a wide variety of workplace and educational settings.

Learning Objectives

The **learning objectives** are perhaps the most important feature that links the three phases of the Input-Process-Outcome model. The things that are identified as important for trainees to know and do during the needs assessment phase should be emphasized during training implementation. These objectives are also used to evaluate training effectiveness in the outcome stage.

It is important to provide clearly written learning objectives to trainees. Each objective should specify the performance (in terms of knowledge or skill) that is expected upon successful completion of training. The learning objectives are extremely helpful for trainees because they provide a clear framework and set of expectations.

Choice of Training Method(s)

Ideally, the training content should be presented to trainees using a variety of different methods. This multi-method approach (also referred to as a blended approach) will help to balance out the strengths and weaknesses of each. In addition, the variety will help to maintain the interest of the training group.

A common distinction between methods is whether they are conducted on site (at the work place) or off site (e.g., a training facility or classroom). As discussed in Chapter 1 on the topic of research methods, being on site enhances

Perceived Skill Gap

Skill Gap	Percent
Managerial and supervisory skills	55
Communication and interpersonal skills	51
Leadership and executive-leva skills	45
Process and project management skills	27
Technical IT, and systems skills	23
Customer service skills	20
Professional or industry-specific skills	19
Sales skills	17
Basic skills	11

Source: Davenport (2005).

Unfreezing	• Assessing Belief Systems • Explaining why Change is Beneficial
Change	• Implementing Training • Providing a Suppportive Environment
Refreezing	• Establishing Ongoing Culture • Checking that Old Habits have not Returned

Learning objectives = the specification of what trainees need to know and/or be able to do at the conclusion of the training

realism but detracts from the control over learning. By contrast, being off site allows for a focused approach to training, but requires additional attention to the application of knowledge and skills to the job. The following section provides a brief description of some of the many methods for delivering training content, with a summary of the potential advantages and disadvantages of each.

On-the-Job Training

One of the most popular training methods, particularly for new employees, is on-the-job training (OJT). This typically involves a current, experienced employee showing the newcomer how the job is done. A mistake that is often made by organizations is to have an informal program that does not dedicate attention to the steps needed for success (see graph). The lack of structure in OJT can result in confused newcomers, and unwilling "trainers" who have neither the time nor motivation to fit training into their regular job responsibilities.

Effective OJT requires that learning objectives are clearly specified and supported by the trainer. The important stages of this process are presented in the sidebar. To optimize learning, trainees must attend to the training material and store it in long-term memory. Trainees should then perform the tasks, at first with feedback from the trainer, and then on their own. On the job, the workplace environment should include features that motivate employees and reinforce the skills that were learned in training.

Trainees must attend to the training material and store it in long-term memory. Trainees should then perform the tasks, at first with feedback from the trainer, and then on their own. On the job, the workplace environment should motivate employees to reinforce skills learned in training.

There are several strengths and weaknesses to this training method. These include:

Advantages:

- training is clearly related to actual job conditions

- easy for the trainer to modify content as needed

Disadvantages:

- can be overwhelming for trainees and trainers

- can detract from either job performance or training

Apprenticeship

Another training method that would be considered "on site" is that of the apprenticeship. This is a special type of training for those who are trying to earn their license in an applied trade. These trades typically require that the trainee complete an experience component of hundreds of hours, under the supervision of someone who has a current license.

Advantages:

- training is clearly related to actual job conditions
- easy for the trainer to modify content as needed
- the trainee can earn money and required experience

Disadvantages:

- trainees may not be prepared for the work
- quality of training depends on the work relationship

Lecture

The lecture method consists of the trainer delivering content through the spoken word. On its own, it is usually considered to be a passive method, in that the trainer presents the material and the trainee listens and takes notes. Of course, a good trainer will bring more active methods to the presentation such as question/answer and group discussion. The lecture is a good tactic when there are a large number of people who need to learn basic, factual information that does not require hands-on practice.

Advantages:

- can reach a large number of people at once
- fairly inexpensive, compared to other methods
- content can be easily modified by the trainer

Disadvantages:

- trainees can become easily distracted
- limited practice/feedback opportunities

Computer-Based Training (CBT)

Another popular method for delivering training content is computer-based training, which can be made readily available on a website. This too, is a good method for presenting factual information that does not require the use of specialized job-related equipment. Another major bonus of computer-based training is that it can include self-tests to ensure mastery of material before the trainee proceeds to additional training content.

Advantages:

- can be accessed by trainees at their convenience
- can include self-test modules to ensure mastery

Stages Required for Effective On-the-Job Training

1. Attention = the trainee perceives the intended training principles

2. Retention = the trainee saves learned principles into long-term memory

3. Production = the trainee is able to produce job-related behaviors under supervision

4. Motivation = the job environment supports the trainee using learned skills on the job

Disadvantages:

- can be expensive to develop

- not easy to quickly modify content as needed

A related term is "e-learning," which is acquisition of material delivered with CBT, or "m-learning," which includes mobile devices. Other potential benefits of e-learning are given in the chart. It is important to recognize that not all trainees will be engaged with online delivery of training material, and there is also a risk for distractions (such as social networking sites).

Attributes and Benefits of E-learing

Attribute	Benefit
Shorter learning time, often much shorter	• Less time away from productive work • Lower training costs
Adapts to learner needs (i.e., learning mastery is fixed but individual learning times may vary)	• Minimized time away from productive work (people return to work as quickly as individually able) • No waiting for those needing extra time • Extra attention for those needing more help
Actively involves learners; frequent activity	• In-depth learning experiences for each learner, not just for selected learners or those volunteering
Ensures learning	• No sliding by. Each learner must achieve and demonstrate competency.
Generates positive learner attitudes (When done well, learners often rate e-learning activities preferable over alternatives.)	• More enthusiastic participation • More receptivity • Greater likelihood learning will be applied to on-the-job performance
Provides consistent quality	• E-learning doesn't have bad hair days, headaches, or late nights out.
Allows instant, worldwide updates	• Through networked services, corrections, improvements, and new information can be made available to all learners instantly.
Is available 24/7/365	• Learning can start any day employees are hired or immediately upon assignment to new responsibilities. • Learning can be worked in and around higher priority activities. • Learner-managed schedules allow learners to work late into the night, in short sessions distributed throughout the day, or in long blocks of time. Whatever is best.
Is patient and treats all learners objectively and fairly	• Same options and same performance criteria for all learners • Blind to racial, cultural, gender differences • Offers no more or less learning support to any individual

Simulation

The simulation method is typically used when the training requires specialized equipment. For instance, you are probably familiar with the concept of flight and driving simulators. In these situations, it is desirable to practice "emergency" or crisis training in a controlled environment. Another use for simulations is to combine them with on-the-job training when equipment is required. In retail, trainees can practice taking orders using equipment as real orders are being placed with another employee. Other simulations involve the use of games or software that recreates a job-related skill (see example from Miller Brewing).

Minigames: Miller Brewing Company

Miller Brewing Company is testing a game called *Tips on Tap* for bartenders. The core gameplay is around the activities of being a great bartender, including serving up the perfect draught beer, carding customers, and serving them quickly for the goal of getting great tips.

Tips on Tap includes embedded minigames, including *Score Your Pour*, which teaches people how to pour beer using proper angle and height to achieve the perfect "head."

Score Your Pour provides a continuous practice environment for participants to precisely move the glass using the mouse, which measures distance and angle of the glass to the tap to create the proper head. Points are subtracted if participants hit the tap (bacteria buildup), or spill the beer (waste).

After each play, the participant gets feedback, tips, and motivational thoughts.

This level of kinesthetic knowledge is impossible using traditional linear methods of instruction, but it is also quite expensive, less convenient, and even often less instructional using real product. Jon Aleckson of Web Courseworks, the lead for the project, noted, "In the end, the minigame, *Score Your Pour*, is a reusable, updatable learning object that Miller Brewing Company can use in live classroom training, webinars, and as a part of a larger immersive learning simulation."

Advantages:

- can train how to handle emergency situations
- provides practice in a "real world" simulation

Disadvantages:

- can be expensive to develop
- difficult to quickly modify content of training

Role Playing

Role playing is similar to the simulation method, but here the focus is typically on interpersonal skills rather than the use of equipment. It involves "people skills" such as conflict management, delivery of sensitive information, or persuasion tactics during sales. It requires that trainees alternate taking on certain roles in which they simulate a real-world experience. Role playing requires careful supervision to accomplish the learning objectives, as well as the active cooperation of the trainees.

Advantages:

- addresses interpersonal skills better than other methods
- provides practice in a "real-world" simulation
- easy to quickly modify the content of training

Disadvantages:

- can seem contrived to participants
- only relevant for certain types of job skills

Training Content

The content of the training should be directly influenced by the learning objectives and the training method. Content should be created to present, enforce, test, and reward acquisition of the learning objectives. If the objective is to demonstrate a certain skill, the training method must include modeling of the skill, practice, and feedback sessions. If the objective is to gain knowledge, the method must repeatedly address the information and ensure that trainees understand and remember this information. The content of the training should be trimmed to the minimum possible length to fully address the learning objectives.

As stated above, the driving force of the training content is the learning objectives that have been developed through the phases of the needs assessment. Some common training programs include those directed toward diversity, customer service, or safety (covered in Chapter 6). Some specific content examples will be briefly reviewed below.

Training Content Example 1: Diversity

Diversity training is prevalent in U.S. organizations, and workplace trends of increased diversity will increase the need for diversity training. A survey study (SHRM, 2010) indicated that almost two thirds of all employees received mandatory diversity training (see graph).

Employee Level and Diversity Training

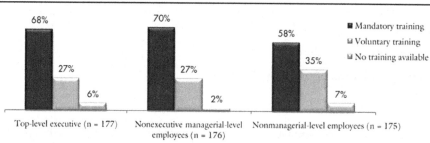

Note: Percentages may not total 100% due to rounding.

(Source: http://www.shrm.org/Research/SurveyFindings/Documents/10-DiversityFlier_FINAL_spotlight.pdf)

Diversity training may take several different forms (see Pendry, Driscoll, & Field, 2007). It may be simply to inform trainees about organizational policies regarding diversity. Another approach to diversity training is to enlighten participants about historical and ongoing diversity issues (e.g., prejudice, discrimination). Yet another approach is to build a cohesive social identity by asking participants to find commonality with each other (termed "conversity").

Training Content Example 2: Customer Service

The manner in which employees interact with clients and customers is of major concern to organizations. In a retail environment, this typically consists of:

- Greeting the customer
- Establishing rapport: using positive nonverbal behaviors, appropriate use of humor, and making connections
- Checking on the customer's needs
- Meeting and exceeding those needs
- Inquiring about additional services

For training, programs can be developed to clearly specify appropriate behaviors. Role playing can be employed to be sure that trainees can demonstrate customer service in a variety of situations. Trainees may also be challenged to expand their customer service view using exercises such as that provided on the next page.

[see *Governing Forces in Customer Service* on the next page]

In the chapter review thus far, performance management and the needs assessment are used to develop the learning objectives and training content. Integration of these tools can be used to shift the performance of the workforce toward desired outcomes (see Performance Distribution graph). Ideally, training should incorporate different methods of delivery to support these objectives. There are a number of other practical considerations that should be addressed in setting up the training environment, described in the following section.

Instructions: There are several key governing forces that affect customer service: mastery, positive attitude, healthy procedures, and shared vision and teamwork. Review the descriptions of those forces below and then answer the questions about how those forces are evident in your organization. Write down ideas about how you might improve in these areas.

Mastery: *Job Skills*

1. A desire to know and understand your job, why you do it, and how your role is important to others
2. Adequate training when you enter the company and ongoing training to update your job and technical skills
3. Knowledge and understanding of expectations
4. Desire to learn and practice new skills
5. Willingness to mentor others
6. Cross-training.

Mastery: *Communication Skills*

1. Continuously refining and practicing skills necessary to communicate effectively (including listening, empathizing, solving problems, flexibility, presenting a positive image, resolving conflicts, expressing appreciation, providing feedback, and offering support)
2. Practicing skills with internal customers and external customers.

Positive Attitude

1. Acting as an enthusiastic representative of your organization with commitment and genuine respect for others
2. Understanding that if you are positive, customers will be more positive
3. Acting with positive intent, courtesy, and goodwill
4. Being able to change your mindset to produce positive results
5. Knowing that attitude is all up to you—a good attitude is contagious!

Healthy Procedures

1. Having well-defined procedures to follow, with enough flexibility for you to work in the best interests of the organization and the customer
2. Knowing where to go for exceptions
3. Being able to get help with explanations
4. Understanding what decisions you can make and when you need approval
5. Using your empowerment to foster organizational goals and customer loyalty.

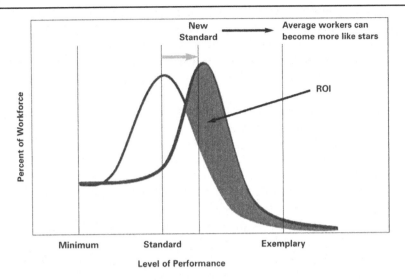

Other Practical Considerations

The trainer should carefully prepare the training environment to make sure that it is conducive to learning. Here are some of the administrative and learning features that should be addressed.

Training Design. Care should be taken in developing the training design. Prior to training, the design identifies how the training will take place, including: budget, timeframe, location, training method, and content. As with any study design (see Chapter 1), the training design should be scrutinized for potential pitfalls. All features of the design should be pilot tested for clarity and validity prior to implementation.

Environment. There are a number of common-sense considerations about the learning environment. Clearly, it is not acceptable to have external noises or other distractions, such as a heavily traveled area or building construction. It is important to maintain a comfortable temperature, which depends upon the level of physical exertion required for training activities. During pilot testing, the trainer should check that the environment is appropriate and that all equipment is functional.

Breaks. An important consideration is the use of breaks in training. Computer-based training allows for individual differences in the need for breaks, as trainees can proceed at their own paces (provided they master the material). Other methods that require trainees to sit and listen or practice with material should include a ten-minute break for approximately each two hours of training. If feasible, it is a good idea to provide some light snacks, water, and coffee for trainees.

Seating Arrangements. Computer-based learning requires that trainees have access to the Internet, but otherwise there is flexibility in terms of the timing and location of training. In a face-to-face environment, it is important to first consider the size of the training group and the complexity of the information to be presented. For instance, straightforward facts that need to be given to a large group of people can be given with an auditorium seating arrangement. If small group discussions are part of the training, the arrangement is better suited to a seating configuration around circular tables.

Handouts/Reference Materials. The learning objectives should be supported by the use of materials. To the extent that these objectives are complex or detailed, it is even more important to provide such references. Also, materials should be provided for important supplemental resources or people to contact for additional information.

Outcome: Training Evaluation

There are both summative and formative types of training evaluations. **Formative evaluation** is collected throughout the training with a specific goal to identify potential improvements to the training. **Summative evaluation**, however, is taken with a view to evaluating the training at its conclusion in terms of the learning and behavioral changes in the trainees.

An enduring model of training evaluation was developed by Donald Kirkpatrick. This framework describes the criteria to measure the effectiveness of training (Kirkpatrick, 1977; Kirkpatrick & Kirkpatrick, 2006). These include: reaction criteria, learning criteria, behavioral criteria, and results criteria. A good training program evaluation should include all of these outcomes. A summary of each is provided in the chart, and each will be described in further detail in the text below.

1. Reaction Criteria: Trainee Opinions

This level of training evaluation is just as it sounds: the reactions of the trainees to various aspects of the training. This type of training evaluation is the most frequently included because it is the easiest to assess. It simply requires distribution of a questionnaire to trainees at the conclusion of training. It is straightforward to summarize data that reflect perceptions of the training, and this is important because it relates to face validity and trainee motivation.

However, there are some limits to the usefulness of **reaction criteria**. Recall the discussion of criterion contamination and criterion deficiency (Chapter 2). For instance, many trainees appreciate and will respond favorably to a training environment that it is entertaining or easy. However, this may be unrelated to the amount the trainees learn or what they can do. Thus, it is necessary to evaluate the effectiveness of training in additional ways.

Formative evaluation = a type of training assessment that is conducted to improve the training

Summative evaluation = a type of training assessment that is conducted to determine the effectiveness of training

Reaction criteria = a type of training evaluation that is based on trainees' opinions and beliefs, typically measured with a survey

Sample Evaluation Statements That Reflect Assessment and Design

Training Design Statements

- The training objectives were clearly communicated and met my satisfaction.
- The pace of the training was appropriate for the topics covered.
- The level of difficulty of the content was appropriate for me.

Statements About the Instructor

- The instructor performed well overall.
- The instructor is knowledgeable about the subject matter.
- The instructor practiced effective time management.
- The instructor answered my questions adequately.

Statements About the Exercises

- I found the exercises valuable in helping my understanding of the concepts discussed and how to apply them.
- There was an adequate amount of time to practice the new skills.
- The exercises were helpful in learning the concepts covered.

Relevance Statements

- I will apply what I learned in my work.
- I will apply what I learned in my personal life.
- I will recommend this training to others in my department or organization.

Statements About the Logistics

- The seating arrangement was appropriate for the content and duration of the training.
- Visual media and lighting were conducive to participation and learning.
- Breaks, beverages, and snacks were ample for the session as it was scheduled.
- The length of the session was appropriate for the topic presented.
- I was able to see and hear the entire presentation.

Criteria of Training Effectiveness

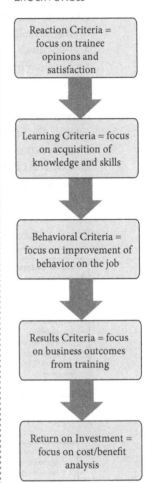

Reaction Criteria = focus on trainee opinions and satisfaction

Learning Criteria = focus on acquisition of knowledge and skills

Behavioral Criteria = focus on improvement of behavior on the job

Results Criteria = focus on business outcomes from training

Return on Investment = focus on cost/benefit analysis

2. Learning Criteria: Knowledge Tests

The next level of training evaluation concerns the extent to which the trainees learned the training material. This evaluation often occurs in the form of tests. It is an integral component of computer-based training. With other training methods, it may occur in the form of a written or verbal test. For instance, learning evaluations occur frequently in educational settings as examinations. Exam questions can take many forms: multiple choice, true-false, problem solving, matching terms, applications, interviews, or essays.

A tricky aspect of assessing **learning criteria** concerns <u>when</u> the assessment should take place. If it occurs during training, it can disrupt the flow of instruction or set a judgmental tone. Another problem with measuring learning at the training site is that it does not address whether long-term learning has taken place. However, attempting to track down employees once they have left the training site can create an administrative hassle. If practical, the training evaluation should assess learning both immediately following training and a few months hence to ascertain whether long-term changes have occurred.

3. Behavioral Criteria: Training Transfer

Training transfer refers to the extent to which material learned during training is subsequently applied to the job. In other words, behavioral criteria emphasize whether training actually affected job behaviors. Because this level of evaluation is considerably more complex, it is less likely to be included than

Learning criteria = a type of training evaluation that is based on trainees' knowledge, typically measured with a test

Training transfer = the extent to which behaviors learned during training are subsequently used at the job site

either reaction or learning criteria. This creates a problem in ascertaining whether training has been effective in changing on-the-job behaviors.

When behavior level data has been collected, researchers have identified a 'transfer problem' (Baldwin & Ford, 1988). The problem is that many training efforts are unsuccessful because they do not actually change job behaviors. Wexley and Latham (2002) investigated the transfer problem, and documented that initial behavioral transfer declined over time. They cited data that behavioral transfer fell from 40 percent immediately following training to 25 percent after six months, and 15 percent after one year.

This research makes it clear that learned behavior might not maintain over time unless it is built into an ongoing performance management system. For this reason, researchers have been very interested in the variables that relate to training transfer. A model of variables that help enforce transfer of training is provided in the figure. Note that there are learner characteristics, organizational variables, and aspects of the training design that can improve transfer of training. Organizations should address these concepts to avoid the transfer problem, and ensure that training behaviors are used on the job.

Training Transfer Process Model

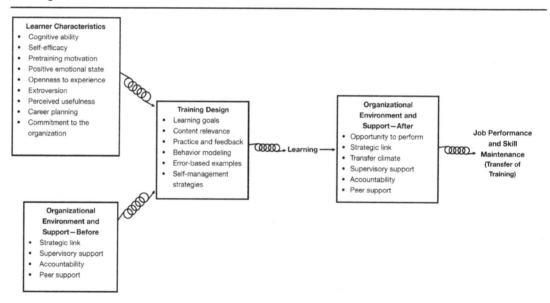

4. Results Criteria: Bottom-Line Outcomes

Results criteria refer to organizational outcomes such as profit, productivity, customer service, or product quality. These criteria are often not included in training evaluations because the direct link to training can be difficult to establish. Recall from Chapter 1 the difficulties involved when many variables affect an outcome, such as profit. Training is but one of many factors (such as economic conditions) that influence profit.

To avoid this problem, it is important to choose the results criteria that closely match the concepts covered during training. For instance, customer satisfaction data should be paired with customer service training, whereas employee accident rates should be linked with safety training. Including this type of data allows for a full evaluation of the training and can also be used during the cost/benefit analysis, described below.

5. Return on Investment (ROI): Cost/Benefit

This final level of training evaluation concerns whether the direct and indirect costs of training have been outweighed by the benefits in terms of improvements to job behaviors and organizational outcomes. The Return on Investment (ROI) provides an estimate of the dollar return from each dollar invested in training programs. It is one of the most persuasive means for demonstrating the direct value of the training. This will protect training from being cut from operational budgets.

The chapter thus far has defined the features required to have an effective training program, and the evaluation measures that should be taken to ensure that training goals have been met. The extent to which organizations include each of the evaluations are represented in the chart. These data demonstrate the declining attention to evaluation over the five stages. This is most likely due to difficulties in data collection, as described above.

The following section expands the discussion of training and development to include learning theories. Each theory focuses on a different aspect of learning, and the conditions under which it occurs. Training specialists should be familiar with these theories and how to apply them creatively.

What percentage* of your learning programs is evaluated at each level of the kirkpatrick/phillips five-level evaluation model?

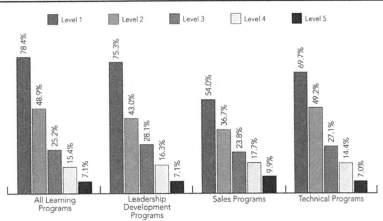

* Percentages are based on the group of respondents that use these Kirkpatrick/Phillips levels to any extent

Theoretical Perspectives on Learning

Psychology has a rich history of learning theories that can enhance the effectiveness of training. A brief review of these ideas follows, with a highlight on applications that can be integrated into training programs.

Adult Learning Theory

This perspective is based on the ways that adult learners are different from children in terms of their requirements for training (e.g., Knowles, 1975; Kaufman, 2003). In this regard, the study of learning has differentiated between **pedagogy** (relating to child education) and **andragogy** (relating to adult education). For instance, adults arrive at training with existing mental models based on their working experiences. Adult Learning Theory is based on the following learning principles:

- Drawing on experiences. The adult learner has a wealth of experience to incorporate with the learning material.

- Self-concept. The self-concept of the adult learner is to take responsibility as the person in charge of learning.

- Orientation to learn. The adult learner has an approach to new material that is based on its functionality.

- Readiness to learn. An adult will prefer training that is perceived as relevant to current needs.

- Motivation. An adult's motivation to learn is based on their own needs and goals rather than the expectations of others.

Applications. There are many ideas from Adult Learning Theory that can be applied to any training environment. It is important to keep in mind that adults have many needs in terms of what they want to get out of training. Thus, the trainer must keep the training interesting and job relevant. Trainees should be challenged to come up with unique ways to apply the knowledge to their work sites and to identify real-world examples of the training material. To further employ principles of andragogy, trainers should develop hands-on practice opportunities for trainees. This will help them engage with the material and realize the potential usefulness of it. Trainers should develop group discussion exercises to encourage knowledge sharing among trainees (particularly coworkers). See the table for additional applications of Adult Learning Theory.

Pedagogy = the study of how learning best occurs for children

Andragogy = the study of how learning best occurs for adults

LEARNING PRINCIPLE	IMPLICATION FOR TRAINING DESIGN
The adult is a partner with the facilitator in the learning process.	Participants should actively influence the learning approach.
Adults are capable of taking responsibility for their own learning.	Incorporate self-directed learning activities in the session design.
Adult learners gain through two-way communication.	Avoid overuse of lectures and "talking-to." Emphasize discussion.
Adults learn through reflection on their and others' experience.	Use interactive methods such as case studies, role-playing, and so forth.
Adults learn what they perceive to be useful in their life situations.	Make the content and materials closely fit the assessed needs.
Adults' attention spans are a function of their interest in the experience.	Allow plenty of time to "process" the learning activities.
Adults are most receptive to instruction that is clearly related to problems they face daily.	Promote inquiry into problems and affirm the experience of participants.
Adult learning culminates in action plans.	Include applications planning in each learning activity.
Adults do not typically see themselves as learners.	Give participants a rationale for becoming involved and provide opportunities for success.
Adults learn better in a climate that is informal and personal.	Promote getting acquainted and interpersonal linkages.
Adult learners apply learning that they have been influential in planning.	Diagnose and prioritize learning needs and preferences during the session as well as before.
Adults learn when they feel supported in experimenting with new ideas and skills.	Use learning groups as "home bases" for participants.
Adults are likely to have somewhat fixed points of view that make them closed to new ways of thinking and behaving.	Include interpersonal feedback exercises and opportunities to experiment.
Adults learn to react to the differential status of members of the group.	Use subgroups to provide safety and readiness to engage in open interchange.
Adults are internally motivated to develop increased effectiveness.	Make all learner assessment self-directed.
Adults filter learning through their value systems.	Provide activities that focus on cognitive, affective, and behavioral change.

Cognitive Psychology Perspectives

Cognitive psychology is the branch of psychology that emphasizes mental processes. This approach examines the acquisition of knowledge in terms of perception, information processing, and memory. When applied to training, it often highlights the importance of basic human capacities and limitations. One such approach is Information Processing Theory. The graph highlights the flow of information, with each link representing a potential problem for learning. The training material must first be attended to through basic sensory receptors. Once registered, the information goes into short-term memory. To the extent that the material is rehearsed and processed deeply, it will go into long-term memory. A response can be generated and will be strengthened to the extent that it is reinforced by the environment.

The Flow of Information in Training ...

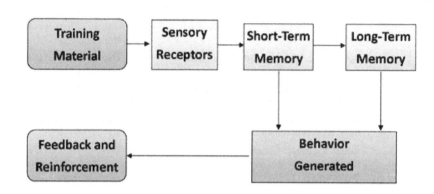

Declarative stage = a stage of learning and performance in which resources are dedicated to facts and rules

Procedural stage = a stage of learning and performance in which resources are dedicated to task processes.

Automatic stage, or automaticity = a stage of learning and performance related to task expertise

Research in the cognitive psychology tradition has found that people can attend to and process information at different rates, depending on their level of skill acquisition (see Anderson, 1985). A novice typically operates at the **declarative stage** of learning. During this stage, the trainee's resources are fully occupied with recitation of the details of the task. As skill progresses, in the **procedural stage**, the trainee's resources are no longer absorbed in attending to task details, and can focus on other aspects of performance execution. Finally, in the **automatic stage** associated with mastery of the skill, the person does not have to devote their cognitive processes to the task. Their performance seems to flow naturally and creatively.

Applications. Cognitive psychology perspectives emphasize that there are a limited number of things that people can notice at any given time, so it is important for the trainer to direct attention where it should be. The use and repetition of learning objectives is an excellent tool to maintain focus. Once attended to, information must be processed in a way that encourages the transition from short-term to long-term memory. Rehearsal is a concept that means the trainee should be given time to repeat the material. Chunking is another concept from cognitive psychology that can be used to enhance memory. It refers to grouping training material into meaningful "chunks" that help provide a learning framework. Another term from cognitive psychology is overlearning, which means that the link between long-term learning and behavior has become automatic (consistent).

Stages of learning suggest that people who have mastered the task (that is, achieved automaticity) may not be good trainers if they can no longer explain the task in terms of the declarative knowledge that is required by a novice. It is important to train the trainer to be able to relate to their audiences. Similar to Adult Learning Theory, asking trainees to apply training material will encourage processing the material in long-term memory. The final section of the model demonstrates that a response will be strengthened to the extent that it is supported by the environment. This idea will be covered further in the review of behavioral reinforcement.

Behaviorism and Organizational Behavior Modification

The **behavioral psychology** tradition (e.g., Skinner, 1953) has many implications for learning. The essence of this tradition is that people learn by associating consequences with behaviors. The most basic tenet of this theory is that a behavior linked to desirable outcomes is more likely to be repeated. Conversely, a behavior that is associated with undesirable consequences is less likely to be repeated. The immediate and frequent delivery of consequences following behaviors will strengthen learning (Thorndike, 1965).

Organizational Behavior Modification (OBM) is the application of the behaviorist tradition in psychology to organizations. It can be used as a system of performance management and can be used to increase learning during training. Research has documented the positive effects of OBM on performance (see Stajkovic & Luthans, 1997; Wilder, Austin, & Casella, 2009). OBM is based on a methodical process:

- defining desirable organizational behavior

- developing a system to measure the targeted behavior

- examining antecedents and consequences

- taking a baseline of the occurrence of those behaviors

- developing an intervention: altering the environment to reinforce desired behavior

- measuring the targeted behavior to observe results

Applications. Behaviorist principles contain many useful ideas for training and transfer of behaviors. First, the trainer needs to determine the appropriate reward for training behaviors. What constitutes the desirability of the consequence is a function of what the trainee considers to be rewarding, and this can vary from person to person. Appropriate rewards should be linked to desirable behaviors to strengthen the probability of these behaviors being repeated. In a training context this might be something like the use of verbal praise or recognition of accomplishment. Another potential reward is mastery of a task that has been linked to improved job performance. A simple example of positive rewards would be thanking trainees for responding to an open-ended question. Another example would be linking consequences to training attendance and completion. Reinforcement should be identified and emphasized by the trainer.

Behavioral psychology = a branch of psychology that emphasizes observable behaviors as a function of the environment

OBM is based on a methodical process:

- defining desirable organizational behavior

- developing a system to measure the targeted behavior

- examining antecedents and consequences

- taking a baseline of the occurrence of those behaviors

- developing an intervention: altering the environment to reinforce desired behavior

- measuring the targeted behavior to observe results

The fundamental premise of Social Learning Theory is that people learn by watching and imitating others (Bandura, 1977), also known as **modeling**. The classic research study demonstrated the modeling of behavior among children, who imitated an adult model they observed playing with toys. This research program showed that people will copy very specific behaviors.

Modeling = learning through watching and imitating the behavior of someone else

Social Learning Theory has many implications for training (e.g., Hoover, 2008). Some of these have already been discussed in the section describing On-the-Job training. These include the consideration that must be given to: attention, retention, production, and motivation. Social Learning Theory highlights that the likelihood of imitating behaviors is strengthened to the extent that the model experiences desirable outcomes, and that the model is a person with whom the viewer identifies. Part of the learning that occurs is vicarious, meaning that the trainee makes associations about consequences of behavior by watching what happens to the model. This implies that the trainer should model successful performance during demonstrations.

Self-efficacy = belief in one's own ability

Another part of the theory addresses the role of **self-efficacy**, or the belief in one's own ability to be successful at an endeavor. Research has supported a positive association between self-efficacy and training performance (Schwoerer, May, Hollensbe, & Mencl, 2005). An important role of the trainer (see Noe, 2010) is to raise the self-efficacy of trainees, as addressed in the applications section below.

Applications. Applications of Social Learning Theory are most relevant to on-the-job training. The trainer can carefully model the correct behaviors and emphasize the positive consequences associated with them. The trainer can also address self-efficacy by inquiring about the trainees' belief in their ability to do the task. They can raise self-efficacy by expressing belief in the trainee, and how they can improve over time. They can directly employ modeling tactics by showing the correct job behaviors and asking the trainee to attempt them. Specific corrective feedback and encouragement can be delivered as appropriate.

Employee Development

Employee development = discretionary activities to help specific employees prepare for future advancement in the organization

In addition to formal training programs, there are other ways to ensure that the workforce has the necessary knowledge, skills, and abilities to do their jobs. This can be accomplished using tactics for **employee development**. This refers to the methods that are available to help employees improve their skill sets in desired directions. Research (Pierce & Maurer, 2009) has shown that employee development opportunities are linked to organizational citizenship behaviors (introduced in Chapter 2). It is thought that providing development opportunities strengthens the workplace exchange relationship.

Employee development differs from training in several ways. Whereas training is often conducted to deal with current job demands, employee development is typically geared toward preparing the employee for future job needs or promotions. Another contrast is that training for job skills is often mandatory, but employee development is often optional. Therefore, the employee must take a greater level of responsibility toward ensuring that their career goals are being met by continuing their professional development.

The development planning process requires investment on the parts of both the organization and the employee. Recall that part of the performance management process involves performance feedback to employees. This feedback discussion should involve the identification of specific development goals if:

- The employee has a clear commitment to advancing

- The manager recognizes the potential for advancement. If this is the case, the manager should invest time and energy into developmental activities for the employee (see table).

Offering developmental opportunities for employees: role of the manager.

Key Aspects of the Manager's Role in Developing Employees	Associated Tasks
Administer and manage developmental opportunities	• Budget and provide funds for training activities • Facilitate staff coverage in order for employees to attend developmental programs • Inform employees of upcoming classes that you think would help them specifically • Track learning and completion of required training • Monitor and manage cross-training initiatives in your work group
Establish accountability	• Establish learning contracts before sending individuals to any developmental program • Give those who have just returned from training an on-the-job assignment that utilizes their new skills • Have participants who return from a session present a synopsis at a staff meeting about what useful information they learned, or have them give one-on-one training to colleagues
Lead by example	• Invest in your own continuous development • Accept that mistakes can happen • Embrace change and sharpen your skills at managing through change • Share and live our City values • Attend Citywide training yourself
Provide encouragement	• Nurture and encourage the potential in your employees • Provide feedback—positive and constructive—constantly • Promote initiative
Coach and mentor	• Assign work projects and provide opportunities to try out new skills • Help establish developmental goals and monitor progress toward goals • Delegate tasks • Encourage autonomy • Help connect employees with more seasoned employees and subject matter experts

These goals should involve both long-term career goals and the short-term developmental and performance activities necessary to achieve these goals. The following section provides a brief discussion of some of the many avenues of employee development.

Interpersonal Relationships

Mentoring has already been described in Chapter 3 (workforce planning) as a strategy to ensure that new employees are successfully integrated into the organization. Another form of employee development that is built upon an interpersonal relationship is **coaching**. Coaching refers to a peer, manager, or counselor who works with employees to set developmental goals and then to provide feedback and encouragement to meet those goals. Research (e.g., Gregory, Levy, & Jeffers, 2008) has identified that an effective coach has expertise in: establishing trust, gathering data, utilizing feedback, and providing motivation to clients.

Many people pursue life coaches as counselors in their private lives, and this approach may also be provided by organizations as part of an employee assistance program (described in greater detail in Chapter 6). Coaching may be based on goal setting, exploring and changing cognitions, or appreciative coaching (Orem, Binkert, & Clancy, 2007). Appreciative coaching is based upon a person's unique strengths and related opportunities, rather than focusing on deficiencies. The role of coaching within organizations has changed over the past decade in terms of how organizations invest in the future of employees (see table).

Coaching Trends

Coaching Then (a Decade or So Ago)	Coaching Now
Considered a punishment for "bad" managers and those who were "rough around the edges"	Considered a perk for employeess with potential; is a retention tool for high-performing managers
Provided by internal HR professionals and trainers or by hired external coaches	Essential leadership attribute
Stand-alone activity	Part of organizational initiatives, such as succession planning; is used in concert with mentoring and organizational networking
Directive, focused on specific skills or goals	Either directive or nondirective, emphasizing the learning process and ongoing growth and development
Less known and understood; membership in the International Coach Federation (ICF) was just under 4,000 in 1999	Growing and more accepted profession; ICF membership increased to more than 14,000 in 2008

Job Assignments

One of the best methods for enhancing the skills of employees is to give them challenging work assignments. This may include new projects, new clients, and fundamentally new job responsibilities. It can be similar to on-the-job training, in that the organization and the employee both benefit from the experience, provided that there is an experienced employee to oversee the work. Two concepts from the job design literature capture whether new job assignments increase the number of tasks that are done, or the responsibility associated with the tasks. **Job enlargement** describes the addition of tasks, whereas **job enrichment** describes increasing the responsibility level of the tasks. For example, job enlargement for a chef would mean an increase in the number of dishes to prepare. Job enrichment for a chef would mean making public appearances at culinary events to promote the restaurant.

Job enlargement = a job design strategy of increasing the number of tasks at the same level of responsibility

A formal program of managing job assignments is known as **job rotation**, or **cross training**. This program has the potential advantage of helping team members understand each other's workload while being trained to take on additional responsibilities. It often is provided for employees who work in the same department or physical location. For instance, restaurant employees may be trained to work in hosting, food service, busing tables, or simple food preparation. The use of cross training has many benefits beyond employee development. Because it helps coworkers understand each other's positions, it can build team cohesion. From a management perspective, it is extremely useful to increase staffing flexibility as needed. Finally, it can function to increase customer satisfaction by increasing the number of employees who can attend to their needs.

Job enrichment = a job design strategy of increasing the responsibility level associated with tasks

Job rotation = training and assigning employees to a variety of different jobs within the organization

Assessment Tools

Workplace psychology has developed a large number of assessment tools that can assist in employee development. We have already covered performance appraisal, and this can provide an excellent source for feedback. For instance, a simple feedback tool can be developed by using the multi-rater approach to the Great Eight Competencies (see Chapter 2). Using performance appraisals in this manner can guide development and avoid the attending problems when multi-rater feedback is used for compensation or promotion.

There is also a host of individual difference measures (e.g., "personality styles") that can be used to provide specific feedback for employee development. For example, the NEO-PI (Costa & McCrae, 1992) introduced in Chapter 3 can be used to provide developmental information about personality characteristics and their implications for work. One of the most commonly used is the Myers Briggs Type Indicator (MBTI). The MBTI (Myers & McCaulley, 1985) has been used for development of communication, team building, leadership, and understanding of different work styles. Through the use of a questionnaire, this development tool categorizes people's responses on four dimensions.

- Introversion/Extroversion

- Sensing/Intuition

- Thinking/Feeling

- Judging/Perceiving

The MBTI receives mixed reviews in terms of research. It has moderate test-retest reliability, face validity, and positive reactions from those who use it (e.g., Furnham & Stringfield, 1993). It also is useful as a development tool to teach that people have different styles that may affect work dynamics. As such, it can provide a cohesion-building tool for work teams. There is a certification process that is available to trainers who want to use the MBTI for employee development.

Formal Education

The performance management system may indicate that certain employees need additional education to enable them to be promoted. In other words, they may not currently have a necessary job specification, but could achieve it with additional education. A typical example is an employee who would like to be promoted to manager earning an executive Master's in Business Administration (MBA). In fact, there is a wide variety of professional degrees and certification programs available through local colleges, universities, or online programs.

Corporate universities = formal education that is specific to the requirements and culture of the trainees' organization

A trend followed by several large organizations is the creation of **corporate universities**. For instance, Caterpillar Inc. has developed a series of colleges (business processes, customers and markets, technical training, general studies, leadership, technology, and Six Sigma) that emphasize their business model. Other organizations using a corporate university include Deloitte Consulting, Whirlpool Corporation, Farmers Insurance Group, and Sprint Nextel Corporation. These corporate programs have the advantage of being built around the existing organizational culture, but a potential disadvantage of not bringing in new approaches to solving problems.

Assessment Centers

Assessment centers can be used for either employee development or a selection method for higher-level managerial positions (Arthur & Day, 2011). Assessment centers include a variety of work exercises and simulations that tap into cognitive ability, planning skills, problem solving, leadership, and communication. These exercises may include an in-basket simulation, role play, and a leaderless group discussion. The participants go through the entire battery of exercises, often over the course of a day or two. During this time, their behaviors are observed and recorded by trained assessors, creating an elaborate picture of the candidate's performance. Essentially, the **assessment center** provides a wide range of work and communication simulations, and can be used for identifying strong managerial candidates or for developmental feedback.

Assessment center = a series of job-related activities and simulations that can be used for employee development or personnel selection

The chapter thus far has presented the theory and practice of employee Training and Development. This information can be used to ensure that employees are well prepared for current and future job demands. A cross-cultural survey conducted by SHRM (2011) studied the practices deemed most effective in the United States, India, and the United Kingdom. The data (see figure) indicate that the most effective practices are organization specific. These include in-house development programs, coaching, on-the-job training, and job rotation. These findings were most pronounced in the United Kingdom. The final section of this chapter will focus on developing an organizational culture that supports Training and Development.

Which three learning and development practices do you believe are most effective? (%)

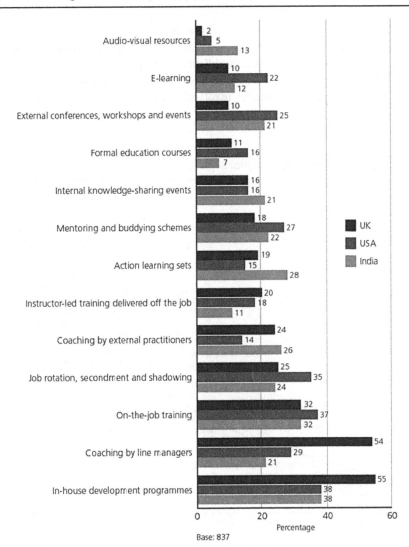

Base: 837

(Source: http://www.shrm.org/Research/SurveyFindings/Articles/Documents/CIPDandSHRMstudy.pdf)

Organizational Development Application: The Continuous Learning Organization

Organizational development (OD) is a process of implementing change that affects the entire organization. Organizational Development includes methods of directing the organizational culture in desired ways. There are many OD applications in workplace psychology. Some popular applications over the years have included Management by Objectives, Six Sigma, and Total Quality Management. In fact, any implementation of change that affects the entire organization can be thought of as Organizational Development.

An OD application that is relevant to Training and Development is the creation of a **continuous learning organization**. This application places a high value on continuous learning and innovation. Thus, it is a basic employment expectation that employees maintain currency in their skills. It should also be an accepted standard that both the employees and the organization share responsibility for managing skill development to meet the needs established in the performance management system. For instance, Caterpillar Inc. has created a set of activities to establish a culture of continuous learning. The graph illustrates the many procedures involved in the journey towards an organizational culture of continuous learning.

The Journey: building a continual organization.

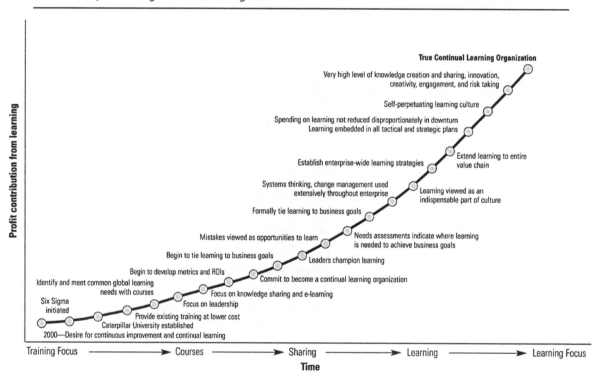

A culture of continuous learning creates an expectation of professional expertise, innovation, and sharing of knowledge. There are five descriptive components of an effective learning organization (popularized by Peter Senge, 1990). In this early conceptualization, the learning organization is based upon a:

- Mental model of the organization = ingrained assumptions about the work environment
- Vision for the future = sharing the organization's mission, vision, and strategy
- Pursuit of personal mastery = continually improving one's proficiency
- Team-based sharing of information = the use of knowledge management to pool resources
- Capacity to think at the organizational systems level = a skill that allows for advanced problem solving

Research has measured aspects of the learning organization by using a 55-item questionnaire called the Dimensions of Learning Organization Questionnaire (DLOQ; Watkins & Marsick, 1999). Correlational studies have shown that aspects of a learning organization are associated with positive employee outcomes such as job satisfaction and job commitment (Jeong, Lee, Kim, Lee, & Kim, 2007) as well as financial indicators such as earnings per share and net income per employee (Davis & Daley, 2008).

A trend toward continuous learning is also evident in professions that require licensure (introduced in Chapter 1). This applies to virtually all licensed professions, including fields as diverse as dentistry, carpentry, counseling, and Human Resources. To demonstrate professional currency, these careers require continuing education activities, and some also require periodic passage of a certification examination. In the future, employees of most professions will be expected to engage in continuous learning across the career lifespan.

Putting it All Together

Considering the material in this chapter, here are a few "take-home" ideas for making sure you have a good understanding of Training and Employee Development:

- Training is a planned process aimed at increasing employees' skills in ways that further organizational goals.

- Prior to training, a training needs assessment should be conducted. The needs assessment identifies whether training is needed, and if so, who needs training and what needs to be trained.

- It is important to have full organizational support and employee awareness of the benefits of training.

- The training design is a blueprint of how the training will take place, including: budget, timeframe, location, training method, and content.

- Learning objectives should specify exactly what the trainees should gain from the training in terms of knowledge and skills. These objectives guide training content, delivery, and training evaluation.

- Trainers should invest time to ensure that the learning environment is comfortable and free of distractions.

- An evaluation of the effectiveness of training is important. Full evaluations include trainee reactions, learning, job behaviors, and organizational outcomes. A cost-benefit analysis may be included.

- Theories of learning provide additional tools for creating an effective learning environment.

- Employee development activities are those geared toward preparing individuals for future job opportunities.

- Developmental activities include coaching, job assignments, formal education, and assessments with feedback.

- A continuous learning organization describes an organizational culture that places a high value on the currency of skills and the expectation that learning is an ongoing job responsibility.

Spotlight On Research

Goal Orientation and Training

Introduction

Training transfer = the extent to which material learned during training is actually used back on the job.

Goal orientations = how people approach achievement situations.

Research Questions

Do goal orientation and individualism/collectivism relate to learning and intentions for training transfer?

Method

Participants took part in an engineering training course and took a 25-item knowledge test, developed by Subject Matter Experts. They took the test both before and after training and answered survey measures (using a 1–5 rating scale):

1. Individualism/collectivism (Hofstede, 1980).

   e.g., *"My personal identity, independent of others, is important to me."*

2. Goal orientation (VandeWalle, 2001).

   e.g., *"The opportunity to learn new things is very important to me."*

3. Transfer intentions (developed by the authors)

   e.g., *"I will apply the techniques I learned in training as soon as I return to my job."*

4. Motivation to learn (Noe & Schmitt, 1986)

   e.g., *"I would like to improve my skills."*

Results

Results showed a link between goal orientations, individualism/collectivism, and training outcomes (motivation and transfer).

Low performance goal orientation was related to higher training outcomes, as was collectivism.

Collectivism interacted with goal orientation to affect motivation to learn (see graph).

Discussion: Directions for Future Research

Future research could include other personality measures and different training outcomes.

Additional research could explore whether employees' age would affect these findings.

Rogers, A., & Spitzmueller, C. (2009). Individualism /collectivism and the role of goal orientation in training. International Journal of Training and Development, 13(3), 185–201.

Participant Summary *(N=92)*

☐ *Participants from a multinational oil corporation; conducting engineering training*

☐ *33% U.S.; 25% Nigeria; 9% Canada*

☐ *Average job tenure of 3.9 years*

Results:

Graph: Motivation to learn (y-axis, 1 to 5) by Low PGO and High PGO (x-axis). Low collectivism (solid line) decreases from about 3.75 at Low PGO to about 2.4 at High PGO. High collectivism (dashed line) decreases from about 3.35 at Low PGO to about 1.2 at High PGO.

Chapter Exercises

Science: Replication and Extension

<u>Instructions:</u> Consider the Spotlight on Research summarized in this chapter. Address each of the following items by using two or three complete sentences on a separate sheet of paper.

1. What do you think were the strengths of this research?

2. What were the weaknesses?

PROPOSAL: If you conducted a follow-up study, what you would include in terms of:

- A sample of participants (whom would you study?)

- Variables you would include and hypotheses you would make (what would you test, specifically?)

Sequencing: Identify the Correct Order

<u>Instructions:</u> Consider the stages presented below. Label each one with a number (next to the stage), and describe why each is important on a separate sheet of paper.

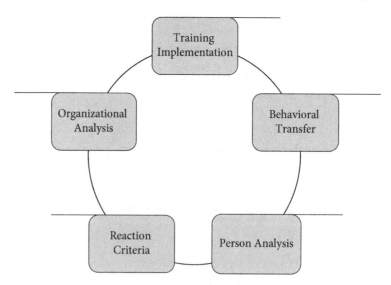

Short Essay Questions

<u>Instructions</u>: Please address the following essay questions concisely, writing in complete sentences on a separate sheet of paper.

1. Briefly describe the three major portions of a training needs assessment.

2. Describe the importance of the learning objective and how to write a good objective.

3. What are the advantages and disadvantages of any three training methods?

4. Describe the five major types of criteria for measuring training effectiveness.

5. Briefly describe any two theories of learning and provide a training application from each.

6. List and describe any three employee development activities.

Topics: Relate to Your Own Life

<u>Instructions</u>: Choose one of the topics below to write about a related experience from your own life. Use the space at the bottom of the page to document your experiences and opinions.

- Training at your organization. Describe the most recent training you have participated in:
  - what was the overall purpose?
  - what training method(s) were used?
  - which, if any, evaluation measures were taken?
- *Learning.* Which of the learning theories do you find most interesting, and why? How have your own learning experiences changed over time?
- *Employee Development.* Do you have any experiences with any of the methods described for employee development? If so, which ones? To what extent were development goals established and met?
- *Organizational Culture.* Would you say that your most recent place of employment had a continuous learning culture? Why or why not?

Index

References and Recommended Readings

Aguinis, H., & Kraiger, K. (2009). Benefits of training and development for individuals and teams, organizations, and society. *Annual Review of Psychology, 60,* 451–474.

Anderson, J. R. (1985). *Cognitive Psychology and Its implications.* New York: Freeman.

Arthur, W., Bennett, W., Edens, P. S., & Bell, S. (2003). Effectiveness of training in organizations: A meta-analysis of design and evaluation features. *Journal of Applied Psychology, 88,* 234–245.

Austin, J. T., & Vancouver, J. B. (1996). Goal constructs in psychology: Structure, process, and content. *Psychological Bulletin, 120*(3), 338–375.

Austin, J. T. (2008): A New Era of OBM. *Journal of Organizational Behavior Management, 28,* 214–217.

Christian, M., Bradley, J., Wallace, J., & Burke, M. (2009). Workplace safety: A meta-analysis of the roles of person and situation factors. *Journal of Applied Psychology, 94*(5), 1103–1127.

Baldwin, T., & Ford, J. (1988). Transfer of training: A review and directions for future research. *Personnel Psychology, 41*(1), 63–105.

Bandura, A. (1977). *Social Learning Theory,* Orville, OH: Prentice Hall.

Bandura, A. (1977). Self-efficacy: Toward a unifying theory of behavioral change. *Psychological Review, 84*(2), 191–215.

Belling, R., James, K., & Ladkin, D. (2004). Back to the workplace: How organisations can improve their support for management learning and development. *Journal of Management Development, 23*(3), 234–255. Retrieved April 6, 2009, doi:10.1108/02621710410524104

Bell, B. S., & Kozlowski, S. J. (2008). Active learning: Effects of core training design elements on self-regulatory processes, learning, and adaptability. *Journal of Applied Psychology, 93*(2), 296–316.

Boswell, W. (2006). Aligning employees with the organization's strategic objectives: out of "line of sight," out of mind. *International Journal of Human Resource Management, 17*(9), 1489–1511.

Brown, K. G. (2001). Using computers to deliver training: Which employees learn and why? *Personnel Psychology, 54*(2), 271–296.

Brown, K. G., & Sitzmann, T. (2011). Training and employee development for improved performance. In S. Zedeck, S. Zedeck (Eds.) *APA handbook of industrial and organizational psychology, vol. 2: Selecting and developing members for the organization* (pp. 469–503). Washington, DC: American Psychological Association.

Colquitt, J., LePine, J., & Noe, R. (2000). Toward an integrative theory of training motivation: A meta-analytic path analysis of 20 years of research. *Journal of Applied Psychology, 85*(5), 678–707.

Costa, R, and McCrae, R. (1992) Revised NEO Personality Inventory and NEO Five-Factor Inventory: Professional manual. Odessa: PAR.

Crowell, C. R. (2007). Of Rats and Humans. *Journal of Organizational Behavior Management, 27,* 37–64.

Davenport, R. (2005). Eliminate the skills gap. *Training and Development*, 26.

Davis, D., & Daley, B. J. (2008). The learning organization and its dimensions as key factors in firms' performance. *Human Resource Development International*, *11*(1), 51–66. doi:10.1080/13678860701782352

Furnham, A. and Stringfield, P. (1993) Personality and Work Performance. *Personality and Individual Differences, 14*, 145––53.

Garavaglia, P. (1995). *Transfer of Training: Making Training Stick. Practical Guidelines for Training and Development Professionals.* Reston, VA: American Society for Training and Development.

Gregory, J., Levy, P.E., & Jeffers, M. (2008). Development of a model of the feedback process within executive coaching. *Consulting Psychology Journal: Practice and Research*, 60, 42-56.

Hatala, J., & Fleming, P. (2007, March). Making transfer climate visible: Utilizing social network analysis to facilitate the transfer of training. *Human Resource Development Review*, *6*(1), 33––63.

Holton, E. F. III, Bates, R. A., & Ruona, W. E. A. (2000). Development of a generalized learning transfer system inventory. *Human Resource Development Quarterly, 11*, 333–360.

Hoover, A. L. (2008). Educational learning theories: Informing the fundamentals of instruction. *International Journal of Applied Aviation Studies*, *8*(2), 363–370.

Jeong, S., Lee, T., Kim, I., Lee, M., & Kim, M. (2007). The effect of nurses' use of the principles of learning organization on organizational effectiveness. *Journal of Advanced Nursing, 58*(1), 53–62.

Kaufman, D. (2003). Applying educational theory in practice. *British Medical Journal (International Edition), 326*, 213–217.

Keith, N., & Frese, M. (2008). Effectiveness of error management training: A meta-analysis. *Journal of Applied Psychology, 93*(1), 59–69.

Kim, H. (2004). Transfer of training as a sociopolitical process. *Human Resource Development Quarterly, 15*(4), 497–501.

Kirkpatrick, D. L. (1977). Evaluating training programs: Evidence vs. proof. *Training and Development Journal, 31*, 9–12.

Kirkpatrick, D. L., & Kirkpatrick, J. (2006). *Evaluating training programs: The four levels.* San Francisco: Berrett-Koehler.

Knowles, M. S. (1975). Adult Education: New Dimensions. *Educational Leadership, 33*(2), 85.

Kontoghiorghes, C. (2004). Reconceptualizing the learning transfer conceptual framework: Empirical validation of a new systemic model. *International Journal of Training and Development, 8*(3), 210–221.

Lewin, K. (1952). Group Decision and Social Change. In G. E. Swanson, T. M. Newcome, and E. L. Harley (Eds.), *Readings in Social Psychology*. New York: Holt.

Lim, D., & Morris, M. (2006). Influence of Trainee Characteristics, Instructional Satisfaction, and Organizational Climate on Perceived Learning and Training Transfer. *Human Resource Development Quarterly, 17*(1), 85–115.

Mayer, R. E. (1992). Cognition and instruction: Their historic meeting within educational psychology. *Journal of Educational Psychology, 84*, 405–412.

Myers, I. and McCaulley, M. (1985) Manual: A guide to the development and use of the Myers Briggs type indicator. Palo Alto, CA: Consulting Psychology.

Park, J., & Wentling, T. (2007). Factors associated with transfer of training in workplace e-learning. *Journal of Workplace Learning, 19*(5), 311–329. Retrieved April 3, 2009, doi:10.1108/13665620710757860

Pendry, L. F., Driscoll, D. M., & Field, S. T. (2007). Diversity training: Putting theory into practice. *Journal of Occupational and Organizational Psychology, 80*(1), 27–50.

Pierce, H.R., & Maurer, T.J. (2009). Linking employee development activity, social exchange, and organizational citizenship behavior. *International Journal of Training and Development*, 13, 139-147.

Noe, R. (2010). *Employee Training and Development* (5th Ed.) New York: Irwin McGraw-Hill.

Orem, S., Binkert, J., & Clancey, A. (2007). *Appreciative Coaching: A Positive Process for Change.* San Francisco: Jossey-Bass.

Schwoerer, C. E., May, D. R., Hollensbe, E. C., & Mencl, J. (2005). General and Specific Self-Efficacy in the Context of a Training Intervention to Enhance Performance Expectancy. *Human Resource Development Quarterly, 16*(1), 111–129.

Senge, P. (1990). *The Fifth Discipline: The Art and Practice of the Learning Organization.* New York: Doubleday.

Sitzmann, T., & Ely, K. (2010). Sometimes you need a reminder: The effects of prompting self-regulation on regulatory processes, learning, and attrition. *Journal of Applied Psychology, 95*(1), 132–144.

Sitzmann, T., & Ely, K. (2011). A meta-analysis of self-regulated learning in work-related training and educational attainment: What we know and where we need to go. *Psychological Bulletin, 137*(3), 421–442.

Skinner, B. F. (1953). *Science and Human Behavior.* New York: Macmillan.

Smith-Crowe, K., Burke, M., & Landis, R. (2003). Organizational climate as a moderator of safety knowledge-safety performance relationships. *Journal of Organizational Behavior, 24*(7), 861–876.

Thorndike, E. L. (1906). *The principles of Teaching Based on Psychology.* Syracuse, NY: Mason-Henry Press.

Tziner, A., Fisher, M., Senior, T., & Weisberg, J. (2007). Effects of trainee characteristics on training effectiveness. *International Journal of Selection and Assessment, 15*(2), 167–174.

Vancouver, J. B., & Kendall, L. N. (2006). When self-efficacy negatively relates to motivation and performance in a learning context. *Journal of Applied Psychology, 91*(5), 1146–1153.

Velada, R., and Caetano, A. (2007). Training transfer: The mediating role of perception of learning. *Journal of European Industrial Training, 31*(4), 283–296.

Velada, R., Caetano, A., Michel, J. W., Lyons, B. D., and Kavanagh, M. J. (2007). The effects of training design, individual characteristics and work environment on transfer of training. *International Journal of Training and Development, 11*(4), 282–294.

Watkins, K. E, and Marsick, V. J. (1999). *Dimensions of Learning Questionnaire.* San Francisco: Jossey Bass.

Wexley, K. N. and Latham, J. P. (2002). *Developing and Training Human Resources in Organizations.* Englewood Cliffs, NJ: Prentice-Hall.

Wilder, D. A., Austin, J., & Casella, S. (2009). Applying behavior analysis in organizations: Organizational behavior management. *Psychological Services, 6*(3), 202–211.

Vischer, J. (2007). The effects of the physical environment on job performance: Towards a theoretical model of workspace stress. *Stress and Health: Journal of the International Society for the Investigation of Stress, 23*(3), 175–184.

Zwick, T. (2006). The impact of training intensity on establishment productivity. *Industrial Relations, 45*, 26–46.

Employee Rewards:
Motivation, Compensation, And Benefits

5 Chapter Outline

Learning Objectives

The list of objectives below is your guide for organizing the content of this chapter. After you have read the chapter, you can test your proficiency by ensuring that you can address each of the objectives. Place a check in each box □ once you feel confident about your knowledge.

- ☐ Discuss the state of compensation research
- ☐ Compare and contrast tangible and intangible compensation
- ☐ Define motivation and its components
- ☐ Define how people choose to allocate effort according to Expectancy Theory
- ☐ Explain principles of fairness and applications of Equity Theory
- ☐ Discuss goal-setting theory and the conditions in which goals are effective
- ☐ Discuss job design and applications of the Job Characteristics Model
- ☐ Describe psychological flow and the concept of optimal motivation
- ☐ Describe Self-Determination Theory and its tenets of motivation
- ☐ Explain achievement goal orientations and their implications for the workplace
- ☐ Discuss various quality-of-life benefits and employee perks
- ☐ Describe how to set a valid salary structure
- ☐ Explain job evaluation and compensable factors
- ☐ Identify how organizational culture relates to external and internal equity
- ☐ Define different retirement plans
- ☐ Describe compensation legislation, including FICA, ERISA, COBRA, and HIPAA

Chapter Overview

This chapter is about the rewards that employees can receive from the workplace. There are a wide variety of these rewards, both monetary and nonmonetary, that have different values to different people.

Organizations can capitalize on these differences by creatively addressing employee motivation. Theories of motivation in workplace psychology provide a multitude of ideas for rewarding people. Motivational sources may be extrinsic, which are based on tangible rewards, or intrinsic, which are based on the activity itself being rewarding. Theoretical perspectives based on goal setting, fairness, job design, and cognitive choice can all be applied to provide motivational rewards for employees.

Appealing compensation and benefits programs increase the ability to attract and keep the best employees for the organization. These are of major concern for employees, as they are the basis for the exchange relationship in which employees provide their skills, effort, and productivity. The organization can balance this relationship by providing valued outcomes to employees. These outcomes can include both tangible compensation, such as wages and financial incentives for productivity, and intangible compensation, such as achievement and recognition.

The compensation system reflects the organizational culture and is formalized in its salary structure. The process of defining the salary structure is usually based on job analyses, labor market and economic conditions, and the compensable factors that the organization values. Deciding on the monetary value for a job is a process known as job evaluation. Using these methods to set compensation levels will result in a logical and fair pay system.

HR Professionals must be informed about rather complicated legislation regarding the administration of wages and benefits. This means compliance with congressional acts such as the Employee Retirement and Income Security Act (ERISA), the Health Insurance Portability and Accountability Act (HIPAA), and the Patient Protection and Affordable Care Act (PPACA). This chapter highlights some of the main purposes of these acts.

Different Things Are Rewarding to Different People ...

The State of Compensation Research

Workplace psychology has identified major gaps in compensation research. For instance, Cascio & Aguinis (2008) have noted the contrast between published articles and practitioner's needs. In fact, Deadrick & Gibson (2007) analyzed the difference between practitioner and academic interests and found that the largest gap was in compensation research.

In a review of the literature, Martocchio (2011) identified the biggest gap in research as being that scientists have not given attention to the psychological meaning of compensation and other rewards. Mitchell & Mickel (1999) have noted that there are symbolic meanings of money. The meanings given to money include: Achievement and Recognition, Status and Respect, Freedom and Control, and Power. Subsequent research (Furnham, Wilson, & Telford, 2012) identified four emotional associations of money (security, freedom, power, and love), and documented gender differences in these associations. The extent to which differing amounts of money convey these meanings undoubtedly depend on personality and culture. Further research is needed to identify these differences.

Research has shown that the link between salary and happiness is more complex than one might originally guess. Instead of a direct relationship between money and well-being, these associations level off after an income of $75,000. Researchers (Kahneman & Keaton, 2010) analyzed 450,000 survey responses to the Gallup-Healthways Well-Being Index (GHWBI). This survey included measures of life satisfaction, stress, worrying, sadness, and enjoyment. The data clearly showed a positive impact of income on well-being up to $75,000, but not beyond that income (even factoring in geographic location).

Other researchers (DeVoe & Pfeffer, 2009) have documented a positive relationship between compensation rate and happiness for employees who are paid on an hourly rate, but not for those who are salaried. Other factors such as the tradeoff between salary and leisure time are surely important. The Bureau of Labor Statistics (2004) presented data from a survey of life activities by income levels. They found that highly compensated employees spent significantly less time on leisure activities such as watching television or socializing with friends.

Many workers recognize that they would be willing to sacrifice a higher level of pay for better working conditions (Armstrong & Mitchell, 2008). The quality of these conditions can be easily raised with the material presented thus far in the book (e.g., good performance management, hiring, training, and employee development opportunities). A survey conducted by SHRM (2011) shows that most of the factors that positively influence employee engagement with work are not financial in nature. These include: relationships with coworkers and supervisor, the work itself, opportunities to use new skills, the meaningfulness of the job, and autonomy and independence.

This chapter will emphasize approaches to quality-of-life rewards based on motivation theories and employee-friendly benefits. It will then cover some of the "nuts and bolts" details of salary administration and related legal issues.

Basic Types of Rewards

Our review begins with indirect forms of compensation, which involve creative applications of motivation theories from workplace psychology. The next segment of the chapter deals with how direct monetary compensation can be formalized into a salary structure that is both logical and fair. Categories of each of these types of employee rewards will be elaborated below.

Tangible Compensation. Tangible, or direct, compensation refers to rewards having a monetary value for employees. This includes base pay such as salary or hourly wages. Other direct compensation includes pay differentials, which are wage payments that are made for work that goes beyond minimum job requirements. Pay differentials include overtime pay (typically 1.5 times the regular rate of pay, or "time and a half"), shift work, hazardous pay work, and on-call pay. Direct compensation also includes merit-based pay, incentive pay, and commission-based pay. Anything that provides money directly to the employee is considered tangible compensation. This is very important to employees when first considering their available job options.

Intangible Compensation. These are provided by the organization but do not provide direct financial outcomes to the employee. Intangible employee rewards can be very useful to the organization, if carefully packaged. These benefits can be just as useful in attracting and keeping good candidates. This group of compensation includes recognition, flexible work arrangements, and rewards that come from the work itself. Rewards that come from the work relate to motivation theories that have been proposed and studied in workplace psychology.

Intangible compensation = rewards are derived from reasons related to the task itself, such as achievement, enjoyment, and recognition

Rewards: Motivation Theories

Workplace psychology has a rich history of **motivation** theories that can be used to help design a rewarding work environment. Motivation is an unobservable construct that should not be confused with performance. Rather, motivation is a drive toward a task that is characterized by choosing the task (over other possible activities), exerting energy on the task, and persisting on it over time.

Motivation = the internal process that serves to direct attention, energize, and sustain goal-directed behavior over time

1. *Direction: the <u>choice</u> of behavior made*
2. *Arousal/intensity: the <u>energy</u> behind actions*
3. *Persistence: an individual's willingness to <u>continue</u> to exert effort over time*

These theories vary along with assumptions about what is actually rewarding to employees. For instance, McGregor's **Theory X** states that employees want the proverbial carrot and will be motivated to get it. **Theory Y** states that employees will desire challenging work environments and will be motivated by factors such as achievement.

Theory X = a managerial assumption that people are primarily motivated by tangible rewards

Although some motivation theories were proposed many years ago, their basic tenets have been supported by a multitude of research studies and are still being studied today. In addition, they suggest applications of employee rewards that do not necessarily require large expenses for organizations. A brief review of these ideas follows, with a highlight on implementations that can be followed by any organization.

Theory Y = a managerial assumption that people are primarily motivated by intangible rewards

Expectancy Theory (VIE Theory)

Expectancy Theory (Vroom, 1963) acknowledges that people have a multitude of tasks to choose from at any given time and will choose the course of action that maximizes their probability of obtaining a desired outcome.

Expectancy Theory is cognitive in nature, meaning that it relies upon the thought processes of people deciding between courses of actions. Expectancy Theory is composed of three components that are evaluated and combined by the employee. These components are:

Expectancy = a component of expectancy theory in which the employee links the probability of achieving a certain performance level if they give their effort to a particular task

- **Expectancy** = a perceived link between effort and performance. An employee may think: *If I try hard, will I do well at this task?*

- **Instrumentality** = a perceived link between performance and an outcome. *If I do well at the task, will I be rewarded for it?*

- **Valence** = the perceived value of that outcome. *How much do I want that reward?*

To decide between tasks, an employee combines evaluations of these three sources of information. The method of combining may differ, but if any of the three elements has a value that is low, the motivation to choose the task will be low. According to this theory, the task that has the maximum perceived payoff value will be chosen.

Applications. Applications of Expectancy Theory are based on understanding what employees value (valence). This can vary as a function of the cohort group of employees, so it is important for practitioners to have an awareness of what groups of employees actually value. This can be identified through industry reports or other studies, or by surveying current employees. The expectancy component was addressed in the training chapter with the concept of self-efficacy. Ongoing training and performance feedback will raise levels of expectancy. Instrumentality can also be addressed through performance management systems. It is important for employees to realize that there are consequences for their behaviors, and that they will benefit if they do well.

Equity Theory

Equity theory (Adams, 1963) posits that people are comfortable if they perceive fairness in the work exchange relationship, and uncomfortable (e.g., angry, upset, guilty) if they perceive unfairness. If unfair conditions are perceived, employees may react with negative behaviors such as theft, reduction of effort, or quitting. These reactions can be costly and turbulent for the organization.

Equity Theory is based on the idea that people evaluate what they receive relative to what they contribute and compare this ratio to that of other people (often coworkers). To make these evaluations, people first consider their own situation in terms of outcomes to inputs.

- *Outcomes.* Things that can be received, such as pay, benefits, interesting work, challenges, promotions.

- *Inputs.* Things that can be contributed, such as time, effort, skills, productivity, organizational citizenship behaviors.

Next, in determining whether the work environment is equitable, employees compare their own outcomes/inputs with what they perceive as the outcomes/inputs of other people. Equity theory predicts that perceived inequity may result in employees trying to correct the situation on their own (often with counterproductive work behaviors such as stealing or wasting time).

Instrumentality = a component of expectancy theory in which the employee links the probability of getting an outcome if they reach a certain performance level on a particular task

Valence = the value that an employee places on the outcome associated with performance on a particular task

Step 1 : Internal Equity Comparison

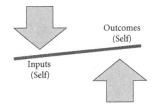

Outcomes
(Self)

Inputs
(Self)

Step 2 : External Equity Comparison

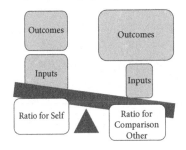

Research has generally been supportive of the notion that people respond poorly to perceived unfairness. In addition, research has shown that perceptions of inequity correlate positively with health-related complaints, emotional exhaustion, and cynicism (Taris, Kalimo, & Schaufeli, 2002; Cropanzano, Bowen, & Gilliland, 2007). Thus, there is a variety of practical reasons for organizations to invest in having an equitable system of rewards. However, there are individual differences in the tendency to keep track of who-is-getting-what. Research has documented **equity sensitivity** to describe how some people are more in tune to equity issues, whereas others are more benevolent even if they are not getting as much as others (e.g., Akan, Allen, & White, 2009).

Applications. Although it may seem childish, making comparisons with other people is a real phenomenon. An organization does not need to be concerned about trivial comparisons, but employee outcomes must be logically related to their inputs. Otherwise resentments and related problems will occur. Employees will behave more reasonably if they perceive a fair working environment. An essential application of this theory is to establish a logical pay structure (described later in the chapter). Although some organizations have tried to establish a "pay secrecy" policy, it often does not work. Therefore, it is not as desirable as simply having fairness in the distributions of rewards at work.

Goal-Setting Theory

Goal setting has been a topic of interest, in one form or another, for almost a century (for a review of all its manifestations throughout the decades, see Austin & Vancouver, 1996). In brief, the theory states that the use of specific, numeric performance goals will raise motivation and performance. This theory has been extensively developed in terms of the use of performance goals to increase motivation and performance (e.g., Locke & Latham, 1990; Locke & Latham, 2006). Goals function to direct attention, raise energy, and increase persistence. These effects can be applied at the individual and organizational performance management levels (Heslin, Carson, & VandeWalle, 2009).

Basic Goal-Performance Relationship

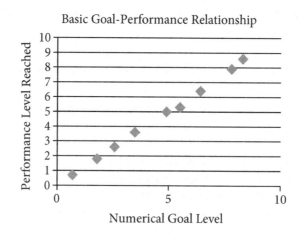

Basic Goal-Performance Relationship

For goal setting to be effective, it is necessary for the goal levels to be challenging and accepted by employees. Processes of self-regulation then take effect, where the employee compares their current progress relative to the desired state (achievement of the goal). For this to occur, performance feedback is necessary so that the employee can gauge goal progress. As part of this process, goal setting also positively influences self-efficacy and the development of strategies to reach the goal (e.g., Durham, Locke, Poon, & McLeod, 2000). The positive influence of goals has been shown in hundreds of studies in psychology, and has been applied to workplace productivity as well as sports and exercise (e.g., Weinberg, 2002). The use of goal setting may also be part of a bigger performance management system. As described in Chapter 2, it is essential to communicate the link between organizational goals, team goals, and individual goals. As a strategy, this approach is termed Management by Objectives, and has received considerable support as an organizational development technique (Yanagizawa, 2008).

All things considered, goal setting is a useful motivation technique that incorporates positive aspects of communication and performance management. However, the use of challenging numerical goals will not always work as intended. A rigid adherence to the "ends" has the potential to result in bad management practices if leaders and managers are inflexible with regard to goal progress (Bardes & Piccolo, 2010). For instance, it is not good practice to fire or otherwise punish an employee simply for failing to meet a performance goal. There may be valid reasons for not meeting the goal, and the appropriate response in this case is to meet to discuss what happened and to work together to overcome obstacles. Individual performance goals may also lead to competition in interdependent tasks (Mitchell & Silver, 1990). As with any workplace application, care should be taken to evaluate whether the implementation and results are effective.

Applications. The use of challenging performance goals raises motivation and performance for many situations. Overall, goals can be used as a motivational technique for clearly observable and well-learned tasks. The conditions for positive goal effects should be attended to. For instance, it is important for employees to accept the goal level. Thus, it is worthwhile to make certain that the goals are achievable if the employee works hard (e.g., a "stretch goal"), given the work environment. Another important condition surrounding individual goals is that they must not supersede team cooperation. When used properly, goals can be incorporated as a communication tool in a performance management system.

The Job Characteristics Model (Job Design)

Another approach to motivation is the use of **job design**, which concerns the manner in which the job is structured. The idea behind job design is that employees will find their work more rewarding if certain features are built into the work. An enduring theory of job design is the Job Characteristics Model (Hackman & Oldham, 1976; Oldham & Hackman, 2010). This theory states that people will find a job to be motivating and satisfying to the extent that it is built with certain features. These features are:

Conditions for Positive Goal Effects

Goal Level
- The level of the goal must be challenging but possible to attain

Goal Commitment
- The employee internalizes the goal

Feedback
- The employee is able to receive self-referent feedback about goal progress

Ability
- The employee has the ability/expertise to accomplish the task

Task Characteristics
- The task is easily observable and numerical goals can be easily understood

Job design = a technique to improve jobs by changing the number or responsibility level of tasks

- Autonomy = the freedom to control decision making about the way in which work is conducted

- Feedback = having knowledge of the results of one's work and how it is perceived

- Skill Variety = the opportunity to apply different skills by working on different tasks

- Task Significance = the impact of one's work on other important outcomes

- Task Identity = the sense of connection to the entire work output and process

The theory states that jobs should be designed to maximize these features. If this is done, psychological reactions to the workplace will be improved. This, in turn, will raise productivity, job satisfaction, and motivation. The theory takes into account that some people value challenging work more than others. A personality variable called Growth Need Strength (GNS) was included as a moderator of the effects. Specifically, the model will be more predictive for employees high in GNS, or the tendency to value opportunities for challenge and involvement. Research has generally supported the link between job characteristics and ratings of work motivation and job satisfaction (e.g., Hadi & Adil, 2010). Recent research has shown that a lack of autonomy and feedback is also related to employee burnout (Lambert, Hogan, Dial, Jiang, & Khondaker, 2012).

Applications. The Job Characteristics Model was designed with applications directly built into the theory. Clearly, cross training or job rotation can be used to raise skill variety. A good performance management system will function to raise feedback. Increasing employee contact with customers or clients will increase task identity and task significance. These are just a few of the many applications of this model. Over and above the applications proposed by the theory, it is up to wise practitioners within the organization to come up with creative ways to raise levels of autonomy, feedback, skill variety, task identity, and task significance. A potential controversy with job design is that it involves changing the fundamental requirements of the job and its responsibilities. As such, employees should be compensated for these extra assignments. Common sense should be used in "expanding" the job requirements for which a person was hired.

Psychological Flow

Of all the motivation concepts discussed thus far, the theory of **psychological flow** is perhaps the most Theory Y oriented. This theory describes a state of optimal motivation, such that a person becomes immersed in a task simply because they love the activity itself (Csikszentmihalyi, 1975). Characteristics of psychological flow include a sense of perfection, a loss of self-consciousness, and spontaneous creativity. It is also characterized by a distortion of time in

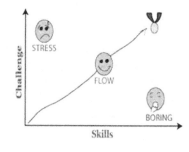

Psychological flow = a state of optimal motivation and immersion in an activity

which time passes very quickly. For psychological flow to arise, the challenges of the task must be appropriate for the person's skill level (e.g., Schiefele & Raabe, 2011).

Authors have discussed the application of psychological flow to the psychology of coaching (Wesson & Boniwell, 2007). In fact, the job of a life coach is to help clients discover their true passions and activities that create flow. In predicting the flow experience, recent research has documented that flow is significantly correlated with conscientiousness and emotional stability, but not with intelligence (Ullén, de Manzano, Almeida, Magnusson, Pedersen, Nakamura, Csikszentmihalyi, & Madison, 2012).

Applications. The biggest application of psychological flow is to hire people who have a proven track record of immersion in their field of choice. This can be demonstrated by a high level of productivity, as well as extra-role voluntary activities. From a job seeker's perspective, it is important to choose jobs that have features that allow for psychological flow (e.g., "working with other people" for extroverts). The use of the Myers-Briggs Type Indicator or career development/personality tests can be used to find good matches. When there is a good fit between employee work preferences and task characteristics, employee rewards should be present on a daily basis.

Self-Determination Theory

Another Theory Y approach warns of the dangers of using external rewards as a motivator for performance. Self-determination theory (Ryan & Deci, 2000) proposes that the major influences on motivation are based on the following intrinsic needs: the need for autonomy, the need for competence, and the need for relatedness. A reward structure that does not take these needs into account—or counteracts them—will not create a thriving workforce. This idea is supported by a recent survey (SHRM, 2012), in which 94 percent of respondents deemed autonomy and independence as important job features.

Importance of Autonomy and Independence

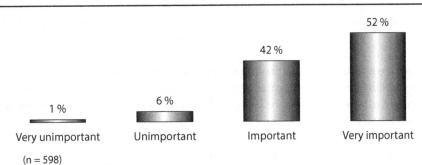

(n = 598)
Source: 2011 Employee Job Satisfaction and Engagement: A Research Report by SHRM

(Source: http://www.shrm.org/Research/SurveyFindings/Articles/Documents/11-0618%20Job_Satisfaction_Figures.pdf)

In fact, Self-Determination Theory suggests that anything that decreases perceptions of competence or autonomy will undermine intrinsic motivation. Even if the organization manages to keep people performing basic duties with transactional rewards, they will not engage in creativity, innovation, or citizenship behaviors. Research in the lab has demonstrated that offering monetary rewards for task performance actually decreases voluntary task behavior (Deci & Ryan, 1980). The authors concluded that, if a person attributed their task involvement to the receipt of money, they would not spend discretionary time on the task. Research in organizations has demonstrated that perceptions of autonomy and support from supervisors were related to performance evaluations and well-being (Baard, Deci, & Ryan, 2004).

Applications. This theory acknowledges that a large component of genuine motivation involves employee perceptions of control at their work environment. A loss of control is a big feature of workplace stress, covered in the following chapter. An example of such a loss of control would be "micromanaging" employees through highly detailed evaluations. According to Self Determination Theory, the following strategies will decrease intrinsic motivation: threats, deadlines, directives, competition, negative feedback, and performance-contingent rewards. By contrast, the following will increase intrinsic motivation: recognition of excellence, teamwork, autonomy, and positive feedback.

Achievement Goal Orientations

Achievement goal orientations describe the different views of success that people can have toward performance in either educational or workplace environments (Dweck, 1985; Nichols, 1979). These orientations toward success are considered to be partly a stable trait (a personality characteristic) and partly a function of the environment (such as cues about what is valued).

Research has shown that people may have varying levels of achievement orientation in terms of:

- Mastery goals = the focus is on demonstrating mastery of the topic by showing skill improvement and understanding of concepts. A favorable view of overall level of understanding is required for feelings of success.

- Performance goals = the focus is on demonstrating one's own performance level as being higher than that of others. A favorable view of oneself compared with others is required for feelings of success.

A **performance goal orientation** may consist of demonstrating high performance ("performance prove") or of avoiding failure ("performance avoid"). People with only this type of goal orientation tend to be threatened when they are faced with performance failures. The **mastery goal orientation**, however, is developmental in nature, and thus performance failures are not as much of a threat.

Applications. Achievement goal theory can be used to address the issue of employee rewards. Supervisors can highlight both types of achievement goal orientations by acknowledging the value of high performance as well as its developmental nature. This is particularly important if employees encounter failure or frustration on the job. During these situations, it is important for managers to provide encouragement and remind employees that successful performance is a function of practice. This will also help to create a Continuous Learning Organization, described in Chapter 4.

Thus far, the chapter has introduced several motivation theories that suggest ways to reward employees. It is important for organizations to work with these creative concepts, since budgets for payroll have been cut in the economic recession. Additional ideas for offering rewards in terms of Quality of Working Life are presented in the following section.

Rewards: Quality-of-Life Benefits

As mentioned at the beginning of the chapter, employees value direct compensation and are also interested in indirect rewards that improve their quality of life. A recent survey (SHRM, 2011) provides data on the relative frequency of indirect benefits. These results indicate that organizations are most willing to provide casual dress days, followed by flextime and telecommuting on a limited basis. A brief description of some of these benefits follows.

Flexible Working Benefits

	Offer the benefit	Plan to begin offering the benefit within the next 12 months
Casual dress day (one day per week)	55%	0%
Flextime [A]	53%	2%
Telecommuting on an ad-hoc basis [B]	45%	3%
Break arrangements [C]	42%	0%
Mealtime flex [D]	40%	1%
Casual dress (every day)	36%	*
Compressed workweek [E]	35%	1%
Telecommuting on a part-time basis	34%	0%
Casual dress (seasonal) [F]	24%	*
Telecommuting on a full-time basis	20%	0%
Shift flexibility [G]	18%	*
Seasonal scheduling [H]	16%	0%
Job sharing [I]	13%	1%
Alternating location arrangements [J]	5%	*
Results-only work environment (ROWE) [K]	2%	1%

(n = 592-600)

* Less than 1%.

[A] Allowing employees to choose their work hours within limits established by the employer.

[B] Telecommuting on an ad-hoc basis is defined as situations that may occur intermittently throughout the year or as a one-time event.

[C] Employees who generally can only take assigned breaks enter into an arrangement with their employer giving them more flexibility over when they take breaks (e.g., employees who need breaks for health reasons such as diabetics, nursing mothers, etc.).

[D] Making up time at some point during the day as a result of a longer meal break or allowing employees to leave early as a result of a shorter meal break.

[E] Allowing full-time employees to work longer days for part of the week or pay period in exchange for shorter days or a day off each week or pay period.

[F] Allowing casual dress for extended periods during the year (e.g., summer months, holidays, etc.).

[G] Allowing employees to coordinate with co-workers to adjust their schedules by trading, dropping or picking up shifts.

[H] Employees work only a certain number of months per year.

[I] Two or more employees share the responsibilities, accountability and compensation of one full-time job.

[J] Employees work part-year in one location and part-year in a second location (e.g., "snowbirds")

[K] Allowing employees to work wherever and whenever they wish as long as projects are completed on a timely basis.

Source: 2011 Employee Benefits: A Research Report by SHRM

(Source: http://www.shrm.org/Research/SurveyFindings/Articles/Documents/Emp_Benefits_Tables)

Accommodation Benefits: This category of benefits allows for reasonable accommodation of differences in life circumstances. This is particularly relevant for employees who are in a caregiver role for children, parents, or other family members. Minor differences in scheduling that do not affect the bottom line of organizations go a long way to improving quality of life.

- **Flextime** provides some flexibility in terms of the timeframe for arrival and departure from work. Core hours, often from 10:00 to 3:00, have required attendance, but the specific hours before and after that time are up to the employee. Flextime is associated with positive outcomes such as lower absenteeism (Baltes, Briggs, Huff, Wright, & Neuman, 1999), as it allows employees to deal with various life demands.

- **Telecommuting** allows employees to work at least two days per week from a remote location. It is important that the employee maintains a home office and is available via computer and/or phone.

- **Job Sharing** allows for two or more employees to split a traditional job. It is a very appealing option for working parents who want to maintain a professional position, but cannot dedicate to a full-time schedule. As reported in the SHRM survey, it is not offered as frequently because of potential difficulties with coordinating work, and the added expense related to employee financial benefits (e.g., health insurance).

Perks Programs. Other rewards can be offered in terms of employee perks or programs that promote healthy living. Although these do not provide direct pay to employees, they do provide benefits that may improve quality of working life.

- **Wellness programs** provide employees with access to health programs, facilities, or wellness experts (e.g., trainers or nutritionists). Online providers such as ComPsych can be used to access lifestyle resources such as behavioral health guidelines. These are addressed in more detail in Employee Assistance Programs (Chapter 6).

A recent survey (SHRM, 2012) shows the types of services organizations are offering in their wellness programs (see table). These data indicate that on-site flu shots are the most frequently offered service, followed by those involving a variety of healthy lifestyle interventions.

Most Frequent Employee Discount Offerings

• computer hardware/software	55%
• health programs outside of insurance	55%
• retail stores or sites	46%
• entertainment	46%
• organization's own goods and services	43%
• restaurants	35%

Preventable and Chronic Conditions?

Programs and Initiatives	Percentage
On-site seasonal flu vaccinations	64%
Health screening programs	42%
Health and lifestyle coaching	37%
Smoking cessation program	36%
Preventive programs specifically targeting employees with chronic health conditions	33%
Weight loss program	30%
Fitness center membership subsidy/reimbursement	30%
On-site fitness center	24%

(Source: http://www.shrm.org/Research/SurveyFindings/Documents/WellnessFlier_FINAL.pdf)

- **Employee discount programs** provide a reduced rate for goods and services. SHRM (2012) has reported that almost 60 percent of companies offer some type of employee discount.

The chapter thus far has emphasized the creative application of rewards for employees. Now, we turn to the more tangible rewards for employees: compensation and direct financial benefits. One of the most important things for an organization to be aware of is that their pay structure and pay scales communicate information about the organizational culture. The review of compensation starts with the development of the salary structure, and then moves to philosophical decisions the organization must make about administering rewards, and the implications for internal and external equity. The final section of the chapter covers some of the legislation surrounding these topics.

Setting a Valid Salary Structure

One of the most fundamental concerns regarding compensation is setting the base salaries. For purposes of example, this process is described as if starting from "scratch"—considering all the jobs in the company. This should not be done in a haphazard way because it is important to be able to attract strong, qualified job candidates. Fortunately, there are technical methods to help in salary decisions.

The formal positioning of salaries in an organization is known as a **salary structure**. Essentially, this is a systematic way to establish employee

Processes in Defining the Salary Structure

Consult or Conduct Job Analyses

↓

Identify Market Conditions: Price Jobs

↓

Identify Internal Compensable Factors

↓

Place Jobs in Pay Grades

↓

Implement Salary Structure

↓

Evaluate Salary Structure

Salary structure = the formal allocation of pay based upon position in the organization

Educational Requirements
- Degree of Specialization
- Degree of Difficulty

Skills
- Manual Labor Skills
- Problem Solving Skills
- Complex Mental Skills

Responsibility
- People's Well-Being
- Money; Accounting, Investments
- Materials or Equipment
- Safety or Security

Working Conditions
- Time Pressures
- Extreme Temperatures
- Extreme Noises

Factor comparison method = a highly detailed method of job evaluation that assigns a dollar value to each level of compensable factors prior to considering each job

Whole job ranking = a method of ordering jobs in terms of their value to the organization

direct compensation. It consists of two major components: pay grades and pay ranges. **Pay grades** are groupings of jobs based on their value to the organization. The **pay range** within each pay grade shows the minimum and maximum levels of pay within that grade, depending upon factors such as experience level and performance.

In ordering the pay grades, one can start with the job analyses. Chapter 2 introduced the job analysis as the process of defining job titles in terms of the work and performance responsibilities. This information can be used to price jobs in terms of their worth in national averages (e.g., Department of Labor) or by consulting industry salary surveys. In pricing jobs, one can also use other similar companies as benchmarks. These processes will ensure that the salary structure is sensible.

However, the needs of the organization might not perfectly align with external comparisons, so it is important that the relative salaries for jobs in the organization can be clearly justified. This will involve identifying the compensable factors through the process known as job evaluation.

Compensable Factors: Determining the Relative Worth of Jobs in the Organization

There are several different methods of **job evaluation**. Attempts to quantify the worth of jobs to the organization rely on the identification of **compensable factors**. Common factors, such as those put forth in the Equal Pay Act (1963) are skill, effort, responsibility, and working conditions. There are other models of compensable factors in the literature (see chart for an example of these factors).

The existence of these factors allows for assigning salaries to particular jobs. Two methods to accomplish this are the point factor and the factor comparison method. In the **point factor method**, each job is rated in terms how much the job requires performance on each of the factors. Then, the points are totaled (they may be summed, or weighted and then summed). The total points per job will reflect the relative ordering of the value of each job to the organization. In the **factor comparison method**, a dollar value is first assigned to each level of the compensable factor. The jobs are then rated on the factors, and the associated dollar value is summed (or weighted, and then summed).

There are also nonquantitative methods of job evaluation. For instance, for a small company or a start-up, one could use **whole job ranking**. This simply provides a ranking of the most valuable to the least valuable job, although it does not provide any numerical information such as points or dollars. If benchmark statements exist about the value of jobs (e.g., from other companies or industry standards), it is possible to use **job classification**. This relies on broad groupings of jobs that have approximately similar value to the organization. Finally, if there is an existing job evaluation or satisfactory pay structure, **job slotting** can be used. This process considers new jobs, or old jobs with new responsibilities, and simply "slots" them into the existing pay structure based on an appropriate comparison of their relative value.

This section has introduced applied concepts of the job analysis, job pricing, and job evaluation to set a valid salary structure. This structure should then be implemented and evaluated to determine its effectiveness. Obviously, the salary structure will need to be revisited as new positions are added and existing positions are revised. Another reason for making fundamental changes to the salary structure are when there are significant changes to the external labor or economic conditions. To be competitive in attracting the right people to do the jobs, the process will need to be addressed as needed. This will affect the ability to attract qualified employees, as well as employee perceptions of fairness. Other decisions must be made about how pay evolves over time (after the starting base salary). The following section covers these decisions in light of the organizational culture.

Organizational Culture and Compensation Approaches

Setting the salary structure in a way that is logical, fair, and consistent with the labor market and relative value of jobs is a great start to having a healthy organizational culture regarding pay. However, it is only a start. There are numerous other considerations that must be made in managing compensation. These include some fundamental philosophical issues in which the compensation system speaks directly to the organizational culture. The results of a SHRM survey indicate that being paid competitively within the local labor market was the most frequently chosen "very important" aspect of compensation.

Very Important Compensation Aspects

Note: Figure represents those who answered "very important." Percentages are based on a scale where 1 = "very unimportant and 4 = "very important." "Not applicable" responses were excluded.
Source : 2011 Employee Job Satisfaction and Engagement: A Research Report by SHRM

(Source: http://www.shrm.org/Research/SurveyFindings/Articles/Documents/11-0618%20Job_Satisfaction_Figures.pdf)

As mentioned above, The compensation system speaks to the culture of the organization and should be aligned accordingly. A compensation plan is a key component of a strategic business plan. It reflects where the organization fits in terms of its competition, and also reflects assumptions about employees and their performance over time. The following section covers some compensation philosophies. These policies and systems should make sense in light of the strategic vision for the organization.

1. **Exceeding the Market**. Organizations may choose to pay at a higher rate than the existing labor market. This choice may be based on prior profitability and ability to pay more. It may be a strategic choice to position the organization as a leader in the industry.

2. **Lagging the Market**. Some organizations are not able to offer as competitive a compensation package, but believe they can attract good employees with creative long-term benefits such as stock options or profit sharing. They also may choose to attract employees by offering more indirect compensation options and appealing to intrinsic motivation. Many not-for-profit organizations have this culture, and choose to highlight the nature of the work as a major source of employee rewards.

3. **Meeting the Market**. Many organizations choose to meet the market as a way to establish their ability to attract qualified candidates. This is a good conservative strategy, particularly if the organization can supplement the rewards for employees with creative measures that can be promoted during recruitment and hiring.

Market Conditions Fluctuate and Affect Internal Equity. At times, fluctuations in the labor market result in newer employees being paid more than those who have been with the organization for several years or more. This situation is known as **wage compression** and is a major source of perceptions of payment inequity. Organizations can address this by trying to make wage adjustments to bring all workers within appropriate ranges in the wage distribution, depending upon experience and performance.

It is also useful to have wage charts for each position to maintain awareness of employees' relative wages. A **compa-ratio** can be used to compare an employee's salary to the midpoint of the pay range. A **red circle** employee is one who is paid above the median for a salary range, whereas a **green circle** employee is one who is paid below the median. It is good practice to be sure that qualifications and performance data can justify why given employees are paid above or below an expected salary.

Internal Equity Approaches

A fundamental question the organization needs to address is how compensation is increased over time. Should it be a function of time and experience with the organization, linked to performance indicators, or both? The advantages and disadvantages of these approaches are reviewed below.

1. **Entitlement Philosophy**. This approach to compensation distributes compensation to employees in a way that is equal for all employees, or equal based on a seniority system. This is often the type of philosophy found in unionized organizations. An advantage to this system is that it does not encourage employees to compete with each other. Another advantage is

Wage compression = a pay discrepancy, wherein newer employees are paid more than senior employees due to changes in labor market conditions

Compa-ratio = the ratio of an employee's salary to the midpoint of the salary range

Red circle = a pay rate for an employee that is below the median of a salary range

Green circle = a pay rate for an employee that is above the median of a salary range

Entitlement philosophy = a system of distributing job outcomes (such as pay) on the basis of seniority

that it promotes loyalty to the organization. A disadvantage is that it does not motivate employees to be high performers.

2. **Equity Philosophy**. This approach distributes compensation to employees in a way that is intended to be directly proportional to their performance (i.e., pay-for-performance). One of the themes of Chapter 2 was the difficulty in defining performance factors and how to measure them. This problem is amplified when trying to implement pay for performance. A variety of motivation theories support the notion of using incentives; however, there is also research that cautions against this approach. Some believe that linking compensation to specific performance outcomes creates an inflexible work environment that is contrary to creativity and cooperation (see Chapter 2 for a review of OCBs). An advantage to this system is that it encourages employees to reach individual performance goals. A disadvantage is that it promotes competition, which can counteract teamwork. In addition, it may be risky in that it might lead to higher training and compensation costs than the benefits yielded in terms of organizational profit.

Equity philosophy = a system of distributing job outcomes (such as pay) on the basis of merit

3. **A Hybrid Entitlement/Equity Philosophy**. Given the potential problems associated with each of these "pure" approaches, it may be preferable to build a compensation system that combines the best features of each. For instance, the majority of pay could be based upon position and experience, and periodic bonuses could be awarded to employees who demonstrate clearly excellent performance that directly ties to organizational profitability (see Chapter 2). Announcing the necessary performance to achieve a future bonus could function to motivate all employees in a manner similar to that proposed by goal-setting theory and behavioral reinforcement principles.

Hybrid Entitlement/Equity Philosophy = a system of distributing job outcomes (such as pay) on the basis of seniority and merit based on future-oriented bonuses

Individual versus Group-Level Incentives

If the organization provides incentives for performance, an important consideration is whether the compensation will be based on individual or group performance, or both. The decisions about individual or group outcomes can affect how employees relate to each other. Individual incentives should be based on clearly published performance outcomes, and applied as a "bonus" for those who achieve the outcomes.

Team-based incentives will increase the extent to which individuals identify with group level performance (De Dreu, Nijstad, & Van Knippenberg, 2008). As the name implies, group-level incentives offer rewards for outcomes achieved at the work group or organizational level. Examples include gainsharing, profit sharing, and Employee Stock Ownership Plans (ESOPs). **Gainsharing** is a type of group-level incentive pay that occurs when work units set goals related to productivity improvement and share the financial rewards to the extent that bottom-line goals are met. The goals of these types of incentive systems are to encourage employees to think about the big-picture success of the work unit or organization. This should raise awareness of strategic objectives and encourage teamwork. Another strategy is to provide benefits in terms of stock options. These provisions guarantee employees the right to purchase stock at a future date at a certain monetary value. The idea behind stock options as a benefit is to

Gainsharing = a type of group incentive in which bonuses are shared at the team level if certain performance goals are met

Task interdependence = the completion of a task by one employee affects the task completion of another employee

encourage employees to feel a personal vested interest in the financial success of the organization.

Similar to the review of internal equity (above), research has supported the use of a hybrid reward system (Siemsen, Balasubramanian, & Roth, 2007; Pearsall, Christian, & Ellis, 2010). These authors note that work requiring **task interdependence** is well-suited to group rewards. However, it is important to maintain a component of individually based rewards to avoid problems with **social loafing** or reduced accountability. In a laboratory study, hybrid rewards led to higher levels of team performance than either individual or group rewards (Pearsall et al., 2010).

Social loafing = an occurrence where individuals in a group reduce their level of effort

The organizational strategy will indicate the appropriate compensation philosophy. From there, it is important for cohesive functioning that care is taken in managing the system. The chapter now turns to benefits that provide direct financial benefit to employees.

Direct Financial Benefits: Retirement, Health Care, and Paid Time Off

As mentioned above, there are many types of benefits an organization can provide for employees. This section will consider some of the most important discretionary benefits, such as retirement and health care. The employer benefit situation in the United States is interesting. It has unfolded in part due to a lack of adequate resources from Social Security retirement benefits and partly due to the tax breaks given to employers. This arrangement has been a "win-win" situation because it has provided significant tax benefits for both the organization and its employees. For instance, employees are able to set aside pre-tax income dollars toward their retirements. Organizations are allowed to claim tax deductions for matching employee contributions toward retirements. In fact, this has resulted in the majority of retirement benefits and health care benefits being funded by employers, a practice that has been referred to as "welfare capitalism" (e.g., Dulebohn, Molloy, Pichler, & Murray, 2009). However, the escalating costs of benefits (particularly health care) have led many organizations to cutback. A 2011 report from the Society of Human Resource Management indicated that benefit offerings have been negatively affected by economic changes.

To What Extent Have Benefits Offerings Been Negatively Affected by the Economy?

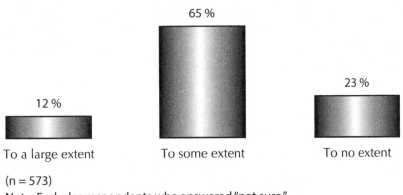

65 %

23 %

12 %

To a large extent   To some extent   To no extent

(n = 573)
Note: Excludes respondents who answered "not sure."
Source: 2011 Employee Benefits: A Research Report by SHRM

(Source: http://www.shrm.org/Research/SurveyFindings/Articles/Documents/Emp_Benefits_Figures.pdf)

Retirement

The Social Security Act was a major movement toward ensuring that the older population did not have to rely on family or charity for financial well-being. However, the extent to which retirement income from Social Security replaced wages earned averages less than 50%, and this number is projected to decrease due to longer life expectancy. Deferred compensation is often chosen to supplement retirement income. There are three major approaches to deferred compensation: defined benefit plans, defined contribution plans, and hybrid plans. Each plan is briefly addressed below.

Defined benefit plan. A defined benefit plan is one in which the employee is guaranteed a fixed monthly income during retirement. The employer is typically responsible for managing the account, matching employee contributions, and paying for insurance costs to make certain that retirement funds are available in the future. Because the amount paid out during retirement is guaranteed, the employer shoulders the risks associated with this type of benefit plan. The philosophy behind this plan is that the employee will remain with the employer for the duration of their working lives.

Defined contribution plan. A very common type of defined contribution plan is the 401k plan, named after section 401k of the tax code. In a defined contribution plan, the employer does not guarantee a certain amount of benefits upon retirement. Rather, plan benefits are expressed as an account balance, much like a typical banking account (e.g., savings account). This account balance only has a true value at the time it is withdrawn, however, so the actual value will fluctuate as a function of the investments made. These are often paid as cash balances upon termination of employment. The employer is responsible for setting up and managing accounts and making contributions to them; however, the investment risk is borne by the employees. In fact, a potential advantage touted by some is that the defined contribution plan puts the employee in charge of managing his or her own investment portfolio. Others, however, assert that many people do not have the training or experience to do so. Another risk to the employee is outliving the funds in their retirement accounts. To help avoid this risk, the employee may purchase a retirement annuity that provides them with a guaranteed fixed monthly income.

Hybrid plans. Hybrid benefit plans contain features of both defined benefit plans and defined contribution plans. These approaches all share with the defined contribution plan that a portion of the plan is based on investment. Therefore, it is not a guaranteed benefit, depending upon how the investment performs. An example is a target benefit plan, which is built upon a goal that the employee is trying to reach for a secure retirement. Based upon this, the plan sets aside a variable amount of income depending upon how the investments are doing, to help ensure a set retirement benefit. As mentioned above, there is no guarantee that the target will be exactly met (the funds may be above or below the target at the time they are drawn).

Health Insurance

The cost of health insurance in the United States has skyrocketed over the past decades. A recent study conducted by Milliman Consulting (2012) reports that annual costs for a family of four with workplace insurance will exceed $20,000. This figure includes costs paid by the employee such as premium payments and copayments, as well as the employer paid portion of the plan. This sets a new record in health care costs. People point to a variety of factors in the escalating costs of health care, ranging from profitable health insurance companies and medical salaries to the poor health of many U.S. citizens from lifestyle factors, including lack of exercise, poor eating habits, smoking, and drinking to excess.

For these reasons, health insurance is a benefit that most employees are keenly interested in. Note the results of the SHRM survey, suggesting that health care is the most frequently mentioned "very important" employer benefit.

Very Important Benefits Aspects

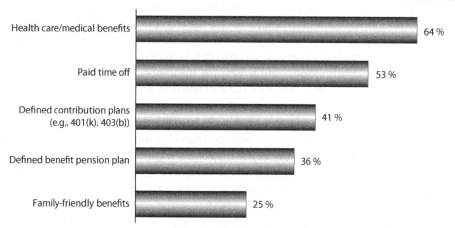

(n = 511-559)

Note: Figure represents those who answered "very important." Percentages are based on a scale where 1 = "very unimportant and 4 = "very important." "Not applicable" responses were excluded.
Source : 2011 Employee Job Satisfaction and Engagement: A Research Report by SHRM

(Source: http://www.shrm.org/Research/SurveyFindings/Articles/Documents/11-0618%20Job_Satisfaction_Figures.pdf)

The employer and the employee both benefit due to the tax breaks given to each party. The organization nevertheless must be careful to control costs related to health care. There are many options to accomplish this aim. One is to provide a self-funded health insurance program, paying for health care services as needed. This can be risky though, as it depends upon employees remaining healthy. If the employer tries this strategy, they may purchase a stop-loss insurance policy that will cover any health related costs beyond a predetermined amount. In this way, the organization would not be devastated by one or two very large claims. Legislation related to health insurance is covered in more detail below.

Paid Time Off

Another asset that provides direct financial benefit to employees is paid time away from work. This may include time for holidays, vacations, and sick days. The Bureau of Labor Statistics (2011) reported the following statistics related to employee access to paid time off. These data also reveal that such benefits are typically available to full-time workers at a much greater percentage than that of part-time workers.

	Paid Sick Leave	Paid Vacation	Paid Personal Leave
Private Industry	63%	77%	38%
Government	89%	60%	59%

Legal Issues in Compensation and Benefits

There is a variety of legal issues related to the administration of compensation and benefits. These issues have become increasingly complex, particularly due to the expansion and complexity of health care and related provisions. A very brief summary of employment law related to compensation and benefits is provided in the following sections.

Federal Insurance Contributions Act (FICA)

Prior to the Great Depression, income stopped as soon as a person stopped working, or if the worker became injured or too ill to work. Similarly, there were no health care provisions for these groups of people. The Great Depression highlighted fundamental problems for these groups, and led to the introduction of President Franklin Roosevelt's New Deal in the 1930s. FICA act was initiated to tax workers and companies in order to provide benefits for senior citizens, the disabled, and children of deceased workers. Its purpose was to ensure that those who were able could help provide basic needs for those who were unable. One aspect of the New Deal was the introduction of Social Security, which created payroll taxes to fund retirement, injury-induced disabilities, or disabilities one was born with. Medicare was added to FICA in the 1960s to help pay for health care for covered groups of citizens.

Fair Labor Standards Act (1938) and Related Amendments

The FLSA covers most employees (e.g., those of hospitals, federal and state agencies, private companies engaged in interstate commerce or grossing $500,000 in annual sales). One of the key aspects of this legislation was a minimum hourly wage. Technically, the issue of a minimum wage had already been addressed in the Davis-Bacon Act (1931), although this specifically dealt with paying a prevailing wage for people working within the construction industry who received federal contracts. For all other covered employees, the FLSA was the first to initiate a minimum hourly standard for employees. As of July 2009, the federal minimum wage was set to $7.25 per hour, although state and local laws may require a higher rate. The overtime provision set a maximum number of hours per week at 40, after which the employer is required to pay 1.5 times the regular rate of pay.

The overtime provision has serious ramifications for organizations and their compensation to employees. There are various types of exemptions from the FLSA. Some employees are deemed exempt from the act because of their ongoing critical role in business processes and/or their salary level. Position exemptions from FLSA can fall into one of four categories: administrative, professional, creative, or executive. The salary level that exempts coverage for these positions is $455/week or $23,660 annually.

At times organizations do not correctly categorize employees in terms of exemption status. This situation could mean that the organization owes all employees in that job category overtime pay. For instance, Wal-Mart paid almost $5 million in back wages and penalties for violations of FLSA's overtime provisions.

Safe Harbor Provisions. However, if payroll makes a simple error (e.g., non-systematic) regarding FLSA, the employer is not held in violation if the organization corrects the error, ensures that they will follow regulations in the future, and communicates a clear policy and complaint system for employees to follow.

The Portal-to-Portal amendment (1947) helped clarify what counted as compensable time and when overtime was required. The key issue is whether the employee is free to spend the time as they please (and therefore the time is not compensable) or if their time is optionally spent. For instance, commuting time is not compensable because it is an employee option how far they choose to live from work. However, employees who must remain on the work site waiting for an assignment are entitled to pay because they cannot freely control their time.

Employee Retirement Income Security Act (ERISA; 1974)

This act was put into place to protect benefits of employees in the private sector, as well as protection for their beneficiaries. These laws were passed to prevent situations in which employees would not receive promised benefits due to mismanagement of the benefit plan. The Pension Benefit Guaranty Corporation (PBGC) was established to function as an insurance company against this type of occurrence.

ERISA requires payment of funds when employees reach retirement age, and also covers the beneficiaries of these benefits. This law also mandates detailed explanations of the plan to its recipients so that they are informed of their benefit rights. To limit malfeasance, this law establishes fiduciary responsibility to plan administrators, plan advisers, or anyone who manages the plan or its assets.

Consolidated Omnibus Budget Reconciliation Act (COBRA; 1985)

This act focused on extending access to group health care rates negotiated by employers. It covers employees and their families (spouse and children) upon a **qualifying event** that causes the loss of employer-covered health care. There is a long list of qualifying events. Examples for employees include voluntary or involuntary turnover (except for cases of gross misconduct) or becoming ineligible for coverage due to a major reduction in work hours. Examples for family members include divorce, the employee's death, or a child ceasing to be a covered dependent due to age.

Under these circumstances, the employee is eligible to purchase health care for self and family members at the group health plan rate for a limited time. The American Recovery Act of 2009 further helped people maintain healthcare by providing subsidies of 65% of the cost of health care coverage.

Health Insurance Portability and Accountability Act (HIPAA; 1996)

The main purpose of this act is to enforce continued health care benefits and to ensure that people are not denied coverage due to preexisting health conditions. Another major portion of this act was administrative simplification. This was enacted to encourage the movement of health care toward digital record storage, with guidelines for protecting patient privacy.

A preexisting health condition is one for which a diagnosis or medical advice was received during the six-month period prior to the health care enrollment date. HIPAA mandates that these conditions may only be excluded from coverage for twelve months.

Patient Protection and Affordable Care Act (PPACA; 2010)

In another attempt to address the health care crisis, the Patient Protection and Affordable Care Act (often referred to as Obamacare) was passed in 2010. This legislation sought to encourage a greater percentage of U.S. citizens to carry health insurance. It adopted a "multi-payer" approach, in which health care costs will be covered by several different groups (payments from employers, individuals, and government tax dollars). In recognition that many citizens cannot afford health insurance, the act expanded Medicaid eligibility, increased the age of dependents (children) to 26, and established statewide insurance exchanges to help people shop for low-cost insurance options.

The act also includes fees in the form of taxation if certain conditions are not met. The "individual mandate" means that the uninsured will be subject to an annual tax if they elect to carry no coverage by 2014 (although citizens near the federal poverty level are eligible to receive federal subsidies on a sliding scale). Organizations that employ more than 50 people also will be subject to a penalty if they do not provide health insurance coverage and their employees seek federal assistance. In an effort to control health care costs, the Medical Loss Ratio was included in the act to require insurance companies to spend 80-85% of insurance premiums on the provision of health care (not on administrative costs).

The penalty aspects of the act were viewed by some as unconstitutional; however, it was reviewed by the Supreme Court on June 28, 2012 and upheld as constitutional because the various incentives and fees were treated as taxation issues and therefore under the purview of the federal government.

This chapter has covered a wide range of concepts and laws related to employee rewards. These include financial pay and benefits, as well as intangible rewards related to motivation and recognition. A survey conducted by SHRM (2011) categorized the types of pay and benefit options noted as "most important" (i.e., the top value of the scale). The table shows the ordering in terms of percentages and significant differences between groups.

Comparison of Select Very Important Aspects of Compensation and Benefits

	Overall	Differences Based on Gender	Differences Based on Tenure	Differences Based on Age	Differences Based on Job Level	Differences Based on Organization Staff Size	Differences Based on Race
Health care/medical benefits	64%	—	—	—	Nonexempt hourly employees (62%), professional nonmanagement employees (74%), middle-management employees (65%) > executives (39%)	—	—
Paid time off	53%	Female (58%) > male (49%)	—	—	—	25,000+ employees (67%) > 1 to 99 employees (44%)	African American (78%) > Caucasian (52%)
Define contribution plans	41%	—	—	—	—	—	African American (67%) > Caucasian (41%)
Defined benefits plan	36%	—	—	Baby Boomers (45%) > Generation X (27%)	—	2,500 to 24,999 employees (49%), 25,000+ employees (45%) > 1 to 99 employees (27%)	African American (66%) > Caucasian (34%)
Opportunities for variable pay	32%	Female (36%) > male (28%)	—	—	—	—	—
Family friendly benefits	25%	Female (29%) > male (21%)	—	—	—	—	—

Note: Dash "-" indicates that there were no significant differences in this category.
Source: 2011 Employee Job Satisfaction and Engagement: A Research Report by SHRM

(Source: http://www.shrm.org/Research/SurveyFindings/Articles/Documents/11-0618%20Job_Satisfaction_Tables.pdf)

As mentioned above, health care was most frequently identified as the most important issue. Paid time off was next in terms of frequency, and this was mentioned as more important by women and African Americans. Retirement benefits were mentioned next most often, with African Americans and baby boomers providing significantly higher ratings. Opportunities for variable pay and family-friendly benefits were also among the most important issues, with women rating them more important than did men.

There is a wide variety of monetary and nonmonetary approaches to rewarding employees. Part of the goal of the hiring system (Chapter 3) is to match people to jobs that they will find to be engaging. Organizations can use motivation theories from workplace psychology to create reward systems to which employees will respond favorably. Similarly, there are many types of benefits that can be offered to instill commitment to the organization and its ongoing success. Those in Human Resources and management should invest the energy to ensure that the base salary structure and variable compensation are sensible and beneficial to the organization and its employees.

Putting it All Together

Considering the material in this chapter, here are a few "take-home" ideas for making sure you have a good system of Employee Rewards:

- There is a wide variety of monetary and nonmonetary ways of rewarding employees.

- Know your employees! What makes them feel rewarded for their contributions to the organization? Have enough flexibility to value different preferences without encumbering the system.

- Motivational theories provide a great source for setting creative rewards. Use job design to raise the intrinsic appeal of the work, and psychological flow theories to match employees to the work they love.

- Some motivation theories highlight ways to appropriately use extrinsic rewards. Set specific, numerical goals for tasks that provide self-referent feedback and allow for independent work.

- Be careful! Many employees will compare their rewards with that of other employees and respond poorly if the compensation system is not fair and consistently administered.

- The system for rewarding employees should be consistent with organizational culture. Be aware of the organization's purpose, mission, vision, and client base in establishing a compensation philosophy.

- Use a **pay-for-performance** system carefully. It must be fair and be perceived as such. The system can also be viewed as controlling.

- To ensure that the pay system is fair, use a systematic approach to setting the salary structure. It should be based on the job analyses, market and labor conditions, and rewarding valued job components.

- Use job evaluation to establish how you want to place a dollar value on these job components. Job evaluation methods show how this can be done in a logical manner.

- There are many employment laws related to the administration of compensation and benefits. Those in Human Resources must be aware of these and be detail oriented in payroll responsibilities.

Spotlight On Research

Castilla, E. J., & Benard, S. (2010). The paradox of meritocracy in organizations. *Administrative Science Quarterly, 55,* 543–576.

Participant Summary

☐ MBA Students (N=101)

☐ 39 women; 62 men

☐ Mean age = 30 years (s.d. = 3.5)

☐ Prefer jobs with supervisory responsibility: yes = 72%; not sure = 24%; no = 4%

Results

	Meritocratic Condition	Updated Non-meritocratic Condition
Female	$374.02	$401.66
Male	$420.10	$399.66

Meritocracy and Gender Bias

Introduction

Meritocracy = a system (such as a compensation system) founded on the notion that rewards will be given on the basis of merit.

Those who espouse meritocracy believe that it is the fairest system because everyone has equal access. This should not allow for discriminatory factors.

However, workplace inequalities exist when meritocracy systems are in place. Field studies show a 25 percent bigger bonus for men when awards are given at the manager's discretion. Could these systems trigger schemas of bias?

Research Question:

Do compensation systems based on meritocracy result in gender bias against women?

Method

Participants were offered an optional class exercise (a management simulation) as part of the educational unit.

A "Values" handout either **did** or **did not** emphasize a meritocracy system. Part of the meritocracy manipulation was that "raises and bonuses are based entirely on the performance of the employee."

Task: Participants were asked to role play the manager in charge of three employees. They were asked to read performance reports and assign bonuses to each of the hypothetical employees.

The dependent variable of interest was the amount of bonus assigned to the hypothetical male and female employees.

Results

There was a main effect, with men awarded a larger bonus.

There was an interaction, such that this gender difference was only observed in the meritocracy condition (see graph).

Ironically, participants rated the meritocracy organization as having a fairer system.

Discussion: Directions for Future Research

Other studies should examine whether these results would apply to other demographic characteristics such as ethnicity.

The conditions for establishing meritocracy and maintaining fairness should be examined in the real world.

Chapter Exercises

Science: Replication and Extension

<u>Instructions</u>: Consider the Spotlight on Research summarized in this chapter. Address each of the following items by using two or three complete sentences on a separate sheet of paper.

1. What do you think were the strengths of this research?

2. What were the weaknesses?

   PROPOSAL: If you conducted a follow-up study, what you would include in terms of:

3. A sample of participants (whom would you study?)

4. Variables you would include and hypotheses you would make (what would you test, specifically?)

Sequencing: Identify the Correct Order

<u>Instructions</u>: Consider the stages presented below. Label each one with a number (next to the stage), and describe why each is important on a separate sheet of paper.

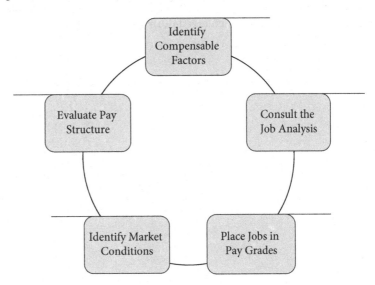

Short Essay Questions

<u>Instructions</u>: Please address the following essay questions concisely, writing in complete sentences on a separate sheet of paper.

1. Identify the difference between tangible and intangible rewards, and give examples of each.

2. Briefly describe the three major components of Expectancy Theory (VIE theory).

3. Explain the principles of fairness described by Equity Theory and any two organizational applications.

4. What are any two compensation philosophies, and a potential advantage and disadvantage of each?

5. Briefly describe the Consolidated Omnibus Budget Reconciliation Act (COBRA) and what it means for employees and their families.

6. Identify any three employee benefits that relate to quality of life.

Topics: Relate to Your Own Life

<u>Instructions</u>: Choose one of the topics below to write about a related experience from your own life. Use the space at the bottom of the page to document your experiences and opinions.

- *Motivation.* Describe an activity that you are genuinely motivated to do. What is the activity, and how do you feel while doing it? How does this differ from other activities?

- *Compensation.* Which of the compensation philosophies do you most closely agree with, and why?

- *Benefits.* Consider all the tangible and intangible benefits that an organization can offer. Which are most important to you, and has this changed during your working life?

Index

References and Recommended Readings

Adams, J. S. (1963). Toward an understanding of inequity. *Journal of Abnormal and Social Psychology, 67*, 422–436.

Akan, O. H., Allen, R. S., & White, C. S. (2009). Equity sensitivity and organizational citizenship behavior in a team environment. *Small Group Research, 40*(1), 94–112.

Austin, J. T., & Vancouver, J. B. (1996). Goal constructs in psychology: Structure, process, and content. *Psychological Bulletin, 120*(3), 338–375.

Baard, P. P., Deci, E. L., & Ryan, R. M. (2004). Intrinsic Need Satisfaction: A Motivational Basis of Performance and Well-Being in Two Work Settings. *Journal of Applied Social Psychology, 34*(10), 2045–2068.

Baltes, B. B., Briggs, T. E., Huff, J. W., Wright, J. A., & Neuman, G. A. (1999). Flexible and compressed workweek schedules: A meta-analysis of their effects on work-related criteria. *Journal of Applied Psychology, 84*, 496–513.

Bardes, M., & Piccolo, R. F. (2010). Goal setting as an antecedent of destructive leader behaviors. In B. Schyns, T. Hansbrough, B. Schyns, T. Hansbrough (Eds.) *When leadership goes wrong: Destructive leadership, mistakes, and ethical failures* (pp. 3–22). Greenwich, CT: IAP Information Age Publishing.

Castilla, E. J., & Benard, J. (2010). The paradox of meritocracy in organizations. *Administrative Science Quarterly, 55*, 543–576.

Cropanzano, R., Bowen, D., & Gilliland, S. (2007). The management of organizational justice. *The Academy of Management Perspectives, 21*, 34-48.

Csikszentmihalyi, M. (1975). *Beyond boredom and anxiety*. San Francisco: Jossey-Bass.

Csikszentmihalyi, M. (1990). *Flow: The psychology of optimal experience*. New York: Harper & Row.

Csikszentmihalyi, M. (1999). If we are so rich, why aren't we happy? *American Psychologist, 54*, 821–827.

Deadrick, D. L., & Gibson, P. A. (2007). An examination of the research-practitioner gap in HR: Comparing topics of interest to HR academics and HR professionals. *Human Resource Management Review, 17*, 131–139.

DeVoe, S. E., & Pfeffer, J. (2009). When Is Happiness About How Much You Earn? The Effect of Hourly Payment on the Money-Happiness Connection. *Personality and Social Psychology Bulletin, 2009; 35* (12).

Diener, E., & Seligman, M. E. P. (2004). Beyond money: Toward an economy of well-being. *Psychological Science in the Public Interest, 5*, 1–31.

Dulebohn, J. H., Molloy, J. C., Pichler, S. M., & Murray, B. (2009). Employee benefits: Literature review and emerging issues. *Human Resource Management Review, 19*, 86–103.

Durham, C. C., Locke, E. A., Poon, J. L., & McLeod, P. L. (2000). Effects of group goals and time pressure on group efficacy, information-seeking strategy, and performance. *Human Performance, 13*(2), 115–138.

Furnham, A., Wilson, E., & Telford, K. (2012). The meaning of money: The validation of a short money-types measure. *Personality and Individual Differences, 52*, 707-711.

Hackman, J. R., & Oldham, G. R. (1976). Motivation through the design of work: Test of a theory. *Organizational Behavior and Human Performance, 16*, 250–279.

Hadi, R., & Adil, A. (2010). Job characteristics as predictors of work motivation and job satisfaction of bank employees. *Journal of the Indian Academy of Applied Psychology, 36*(2), 294–299.

Heslin, P. A., Carson, J. B., & VandeWalle, D. (2009). Practical applications of goal-setting theory to performance management. In J. W. Smither and M. London (Eds.), *Performance management: Putting research into action* (pp. 89–114). San Francisco: Jossey-Bass.

Katsikea, E., Theodosiou, M., Perdikis, N., & Kehagias, J. (2011). The effects of organizational structure and job characteristics on export sales managers' job satisfaction and organizational commitment. *Journal of World Business, 46*(2), 221–233.

Kossek, E., & Michel, J. S. (2011). Flexible work schedules. In S. Zedeck (Ed.), *APA handbook of industrial and organizational psychology, vol. 1: Building and developing the organization* (pp. 535–572). Washington, DC: American Psychological Association.

Lambert, E. G., Hogan, N. L., Dial, K., Jiang, S., & Khondaker, M. I. (2012). Is the job burning me out? An exploratory test of the job characteristics model on the emotional burnout of prison staff. *Prison Journal, 92*(1), 3–23.

Locke, E. A., & Latham, G. P. (1990). *A theory of goal setting and task performance.* Englewood Cliffs, NJ: Prentice Hall.

Locke, E. A., & Latham, G. P. (2006). New Directions in Goal-Setting Theory. *Current Directions in Psychological Science, 15*(5), 265–268.

Martocchio, J. J. (2011). Strategic reward and compensation plans. In S. Zedeck, S. Zedeck (Eds.) *APA handbook of industrial and organizational psychology,* (pp. 343–372). Washington, DC: American Psychological Association.

Mitchell, T. R., & Silver, W. S. (1990). Individual and group goals when workers are interdependent: Effects on task strategies and performance. *Journal of Applied Psychology, 75*(2), 185–193.

Oldham, G. R., & Hackman, J. (2010). Not what it was and not what it will be: The future of job design research. *Journal of Organizational Behavior, 31*(2-3), 463–479.

Pearsall, M. J., Christian, M. S., & Ellis, A. P. J. (2010). Motivating interdependent teams: Individual rewards, shared rewards, or something in between? *Journal of Applied Psychology, 95*, 183–191.

Schiefele, U., & Raabe, A. (2011). Skills-demands compatibility as a determinant of flow experience in an inductive reasoning task. *Psychological Reports, 109*(2), 428–444.

Siemsen, E., Balasubramanian, S., & Roth, A. (2007). Incentives that induce task-related effort, helping, and knowledge sharing in work groups. *Management Science, 53*, 1533–1550.

Taris, T. W., Kalimo, R., & Schaufeli, W. B. (2002). Inequity at work: Its measurement and association with worker health. *Work & Stress, 16*(4), 287–301.

Ullén, F., de Manzano, Ö., Almeida, R., Magnusson, P. E., Pedersen, N. L., Nakamura, J., & Csikszentmihalyi, M., & Madison, G. (2012). Proneness for psychological flow in everyday life: Associations with personality and intelligence. *Personality and Individual Differences, 52*(2), 167–172.

Weinberg, R. S. (2002). Goal setting in sport and exercise: Research to practice. In J. L. Van Raalte, B. W. Brewer (Eds.), *Exploring sport and exercise psychology (2nd ed.)* (pp. 25–48). Washington, DC: American Psychological Association.

Wesson, K., & Boniwell, l. (2007). Flow theory: Its application to coaching psychology. *International Coaching Psychology Review, 2*(1), 33–43.

Yanagizawa, S. (2008). Effect of goal difficulty and feedback seeking on goal attainment and learning. *Japanese Psychological Research, 50*(3), 137–144.

Risk Management
Occupational Stress, And Safety

6 Chapter Outline

Learning Objectives

The list of objectives below is your guide for organizing the content of this chapter. After you have read the chapter, you can test your proficiency by ensuring that you can address each of the objectives. Place a check in each box ☐ once you feel confident about your knowledge.

☐ Define terms related to occupational health, stress, and risk management

☐ Identify categories of workplace risks

☐ Define risk management and discuss approaches to handling risk

☐ Explain why organizations should conduct HR audits

☐ Identify the appropriate conduct of workplace investigations

☐ Explain why occupational stress has consequences for organizations

☐ Define stressors, stress, and strain

☐ Explain the role of cognitions in occupational stress

☐ Identify job demands and other aspects of work that are perceived as stressors

☐ Explain how role-related problems are stressful for employees

☐ Define bullying, the forms it may take, and its prevalence

☐ Describe some of the physiological and psychological responses to a stressor

☐ Describe the breakdowns that employees can have under prolonged stress

☐ Discuss stress management techniques: primary, secondary, and tertiary

☐ Identify both employee and organizational variables linked to safety outcomes

☐ Define ergonomics and how it can be used to reduce workplace injuries

☐ Explain the benefits of establishing a safety climate within organizations

☐ Explain the Occupational Safety and Health Act and its requirements

Chapter Overview

There are many potential risks for people at the workplace—for instance, injuries, accidents, and occupational stress. These risks have potential costs to the organization and the well-being of employees. The identification of work-related risks and the decisions of how to deal with them are known as risk management. This chapter will provide an overview of risk management tactics, workplace stress, and employee safety. The overarching goal of studying these topics is to increase occupational health.

The impact of risks on the organization can be minimized by anticipating and managing them. Industry experts should be consulted during this process. Other tools that can be used include the establishment of emergency management plans, Standard Operating Procedures, HR audits, and workplace investigations.

Occupational stress occurs when the demands of work exceed employees' perceived ability to cope. In and of itself, this can be distressing, and under certain intense or prolonged conditions it can lead to a breakdown. The breakdown might involve destructive behavior such as drug/alcohol addiction or violence against self or others. Theories of occupational stress have been developed to help understand why it occurs and how to handle it. A "primary approach" to stress management involves changing the stressor so that stress is not experienced. Sometimes this is not possible, and other approaches may be employed. For instance, the organization may provide referral services or an Employee Assistance Program (EAP) to help.

Another major risk factor is employee safety. It is important to ensure a workplace free of unnecessary hazards and known health risks. The Occupational Safety and Health Act (1970) is federal legislation that mandates safety principles and mandatory reporting of certain injuries and accidents. Injuries and accidents can be addressed using ergonomic principles. The field of ergonomics is based upon designing the workspace to maximize efficiency and safety. Organizational culture also plays a role in a safe environment. Research has documented that a safety climate yields positive outcomes for the organization and its employees.

Risk Management

Risk management is the strategic process of risk identification and reduction. Here, we will consider a few of the risks associated with the workplace and the approaches an organization may take to dealing with them.

Categories of Workplace Risks

There is a large number of potential workplace risks. A brief list of risk categories follows.

Biological. This category of risks deals with those that are alive, or thrive on a life source. These include molds, fungi, bacteria, viruses, and mildew. Specific examples of biological hazards that have posed threats to human safety are the blood-borne pathogens such as the Human Immunodeficiency Virus (HIV) and the Hepatitis B Virus (HBV).

Chemical. Some employees work with chemical substances such as heavy metals (e.g., mercury, lead) or various types of acids/bases that pose both immediate and long-term dangers. Any organization that deals with hazardous chemicals is required by federal law (Occupational Safety and Health

Act, 1970) to follow safety procedures and diligent product management. Specific rules are in place for dealing with the proper disposal of chemical waste to reduce societal risks.

Physical/Kinesthetic. There are many jobs that are hazardous to employees because of the physical environment. This may include repetitive motions that cause strain on the body, noise levels that can lead to hearing loss, or dangerous activities that could lead to falling or other accidents.

Financial. Risks to organizations occur in terms of the available financial resources and the ability to compete within a given industry. Risks in this category include new competitors, patent infringement, product replacement, changes to technology, or global and local economic conditions.

Security. Increases in data transmission and digital storage have led to increased risks of security. This can relate to violations of privacy, loss of data, and identity theft, among other security issues.

Stress Related. Increases in workload and related pressures have led to increased stress reactions among employees. In fact, the psychological and physical issues pertaining to stress are the fastest growing type of ADA claim filed.

Risk Management Approaches

The specific risks to an organization vary as a function of occupational type and legal environment. Identification of risk factors should be conducted by a specialist on the prevalence and costs associated with different industries. Such a specialist may be hired on a consulting basis, or the organization may invest in a full-time position for a person with such a background. Either way, it is an important investment for a company, as it can potentially ward off very large expenses associated with risks.

The first step in risk management is **risk assessment**. This process is used to generate a list of possible risks to the organization. Next, an assessment is made of the likelihood that these risks will actually occur. Part of the assessment process is ranking the urgency level of each risk identified and deciding upon the organizational approach to it.

There are four basic approaches to forecasting and warding off potential threats: risk transfer, risk acceptance, risk mitigation, and risk avoidance. If the threat is probable and costly, the organization may choose **risk transfer**. This assigns the risk to another organization, typically an insurance company. For instance, Employment Practices Liability Insurance (EPLI) can be used to shift Human Resources risks. This type of insurance is very important, as it protects the organization from the threat associated with lawsuits from current and former employees. If the probability and costs associated with a risk are low, the organization may choose **risk acceptance**. This means there will be no significant action to address the risk. If the probability of the risk is moderate, or if the costs are significant, the organization may choose **risk mitigation** to significantly reduce the risk. This would be the case if the work was redesigned or improved equipment was purchased. If the probability of the risk and/or if the costs are high, the organization may choose to eliminate the risk with **risk avoidance**. An example would be ceasing to use a particular process or

The Management of Risks

chemical that has been shown to cause health problems. In other words, the organization "gets rid of" the risk.

Techniques for Risk Management

In addition to a formal assessment of risks in terms of probabilities and costs, there are strategic tools to help prevent or prepare for risks. A brief description of some of these tools follows.

HR Audits

An application of risk management to human resources is the **HR audit**, which allows for the identification of risks associated with Human Resources practices. HR audits are careful examinations of current policies and practices to ensure that they are working effectively and are in compliance with employment law.

Categories of practices to be addressed during the HR audit include recruitment, selection, wage administration, discrimination and employee rights, occupational safety, and delivery of performance feedback. As with most data-based approaches, HR audits involve interviews, examinations of workplace documents, and observations of work practices. The key is to document practices and flag areas that could create risks to the organization. These areas can be improved upon to minimize or eliminate those risks.

Sample questions that could be addressed when checking the safety environment in an HR audit are included below.

- Have employees been trained to promptly report potential safety risks?

- Is a systematic process for investigating accidents and injuries being followed?

- What security measures are in place in the event of a hostile trespasser?

- Is fire safety equipment readily available?

- Are minors prohibited from performing hazardous work, as stipulated in the Fair Labor Standards Act?

HR audit = careful examination of Human Resources practices and policies to ensure that they are functioning well and not creating risks to the organization

Emergency Management Plans

Organizations should prepare for emergency situations. Some of these preparation tactics, such as an evacuation plan, are required by OSHA (described later in this chapter). Others should be created to the extent that they are implicated as having a reasonable probability of occurrence. Some categories of **emergency management plans** are listed below.

Emergency Action Plan. As part of the attempt to prepare for the event of an emergency, organizations should create an emergency action plan. The plan consists of evacuation procedures with a destined meeting area and a way to account for employees. It is important to have an alarm system or other method of communication so that employees can be quickly informed in the event of an

Emergency management plans = a risk management tool in which the organization prepares for various emergency situations.

emergency. It is also important to practice evacuation procedures periodically so that the process is well known to employees.

Emergency Response Plan. Whereas the emergency action plan is used to prepare people for how to cope with an emergency, the emergency response plan is created to plan out how the business intends to resume operations following an emergency. Much of the emergency response plan involves delegating authority for the return to normal business processes.

The role of the HR department in emergency management plans is shown in the chart below. A survey conducted by SHRM (2005) indicates that the primary role is for communication, coordination, and training about the plans.

Other HR Functions Related to Disaster Preparedness

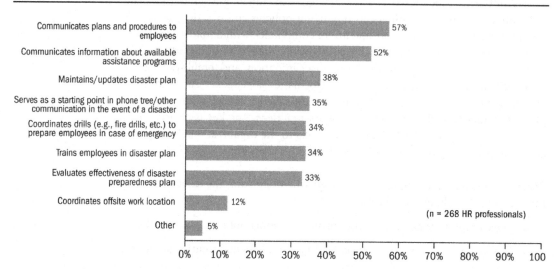

Note: Percentages do not total 100% because multiple responses were allowed.

Source: SHRM 2005 Disaster Preparedness Survey Report

(Source:http://www.shrm.org/Research/SurveyFindings/Articles/Documents/2005%20Disaster%20Preparedeness%20Survey%20Report.pdf)

Standard Operating Procedures

Another major tool for reducing workplace risks is the development of Standard Operating Procedures (SOPs). These are detailed and comprehensive descriptions of safe methods for conducting workplace procedures or operating equipment. All employees should be trained in SOPs, and on-the-job behavior should be observed periodically to ensure that the procedures are being followed correctly.

Workplace Investigations

If an accident, injury, or any type of allegation is made against employees of the organization, it is important to conduct a **workplace investigation** to find out what happened. As a rule, the organization should initiate the investigation immediately following the incident.

One of the most important features of the investigation is to have a neutral person in charge of conducting it. This might be a specialist in HR, or in some situations, it may be better to contract with someone outside the organization. The investigator should not have, or be perceived to have, a vested interest in the outcome of the investigation. Like any formal study, a careful plan should be developed and followed. It is imperative that detailed documentation be made throughout the investigation.

The investigator will start by developing a blueprint for the investigation, including time line, the people who need to be talked to, and any other physical evidence or medical evaluations that must be gathered. For the interviews, a list of questions should be developed and pilot tested for thoroughness and clarity. Prior to the interviews, it should be made clear that there will be no retaliation as a result of participation in the investigation. Interviews should be recorded, with utmost care being given to the security of these recordings. Following the completion of the data collection, the investigator should prepare a formal report of the findings. If an employee has been shown to violate organizational policy or to commit an otherwise criminal action, the organization is obligated to initiate the appropriate response (ranging from communication to dismissal).

Conducting an unbiased, formal investigation will help to ensure that policies are being applied fairly. The information gathered can be used to make changes to help ensure that the incident does not happen again. In addition, if any subsequent legal action is taken against the organization, it will be well prepared with documentation.

Thus far, this chapter has described various categories of risks to the organization, and why it is important to be prepared to manage them. The discussion now turns to occupational stress, which has been well documented in the workplace psychology literature. An input-process-outcome model will be presented to explain the many factors that can be involved in occupational stress.

Occupational Stress: Stressors, Stress, and Strain

Occupational stress is a very prevalent problem at the workplace. According to the U.S. Department of Labor, one out of every six working Americans reports being "extremely stressed at work on a regular basis," and the National Institute for Occupational Safety and Health places these estimates at one out of every three working Americans (http://www.cdc.gov/niosh/doc). The estimated cost associated with high levels of stress (e.g., missing work, low-quality work, turnover, drug/alcohol abuse, workers' compensation) is $200 billion per year. Workplace psychology has documented stress in terms of characteristics of the workplace and the ways that employees perceive and react to it.

Workplace investigation = a systematic, immediate, and unbiased study of alleged incidents at work

Example of the Stressors/ Stress/Strain Process

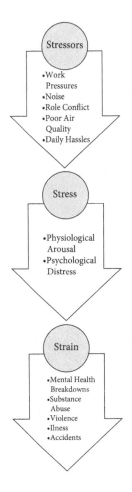

To fully understand the psychology of stress and how it can create risks for organizations, it is necessary to define a few key terms. The model in the flowchart differentiates between three related concepts: Stressors, Stress, and Strain. **Stressors** are aspects of the work environment that may be perceived as a threat. **Stress** is the psychological and physiological reaction to a potential stressor if it is perceived as a threat that cannot be coped with. **Strain** is a reaction to prolonged exposure to stress, characterized as a breakdown of a medical, behavioral, and/or psychological nature. The following sections will provide an overview of some of the variables involved with the Stressors-Stress-Strain process. It is important to recognize the cyclical nature of this process. Strain outcomes such as substance abuse or accidents can then turn into a stressor (threat) to the individual, thereby creating an ongoing chain of stress and strain reactions.

The Role of Cognitions

It is important to note that stressors will not lead to stress or strain unless they are perceived as a significant threat to the employee. The socio-cognitive model (e.g., Lazarus & Folkman, 1984) explains that stress occurs as the result of a cognitive appraisal of the stressor and of coping resources. **Primary appraisal** is an assessment of whether the stressor constitutes a threat (e.g., to safety, ego, or attainment of goals). **Secondary appraisal** is an assessment of one's coping resources to deal with the threat. Coping resources include problem-solving skills, social support, positive beliefs, health and vigor, material resources, or money. If the resources are deemed insufficient, stress occurs. Cognitive reappraisals occur over time as circumstances evolve.

The challenge-hindrance model merges the concept of cognitive stress appraisal with motivational reactions described in Chapter 5 (Lepine, Podsakoff, & Lepine, 2005). This model defines how the nature of the appraisal activates Expectancy Theory concepts (expectancy, instrumentality, and valence). Specifically, the initial assessment of the stressor will lead to it being characterized as a hindrance or a challenge. In the case of a hindrance, the employee has low Expectancy Theory evaluations and is more likely to exhibit poor performance and strain. In the case of a challenge appraisal, the employee has high Expectancy Theory evaluations and is more likely to exhibit problem solving and better performance, without showing strain. The positive experience resulting from a potential stressor has also been referred to as **eustress.**

Stressors

Not everyone will agree on what comprises a stressor – what is threatening to one person is not a problem for someone else. Typical characteristics of a stressor include novelty, unpredictability, a perceived threat (to something important), and a perceived inability to cope with the threat. Some commonly noted stressors are covered in the following list.

- *Job Demands.* According to the Demands-Control Model, there are two primary influences on work-related stress: **job demands** and

Primary appraisal = the first cognitive reaction to a potential stressor in which a person evaluates whether or not it is a threat

Secondary appraisal = a cognitive evaluation of whether available resources can adequately cope with a stressor

Eustress = a positive stress reaction that is characterized by a heightened state of physical arousal and a perception of facing a challenge

Job demands = work pressures that can burden the resources of employees

control (Karasek, 1979; Häusser, Mojzisch, & Schulz-Hardt, 2011). Job demands include workload, time pressures, role-related pressures, or intellectual requirements. Control is a function of the autonomy at work and discretion for using different skills. The Demands-Control Model includes a measurement of the levels of demands and control (assessed with the Job Content Questionnaire, or JCQ). These measures provide indicators of imbalance and specific directions for changing the job, typically by providing more control over the workspace.

Control = the extent to which an employee has autonomy at work

This model was expanded into the Job Demands-Resources Model to include **social support** as a moderator (Karasek & Theorell, 1990). In other words, the effects of high job demands without control are less likely to exert themselves if the employee has social support. Research has demonstrated the link between job demands and burnout, and job resources to employee engagement (Van den Broeck, Vansteenkiste, De Witte, & Lens, 2008). Other research has documented that job demands affect employees' willingness to follow safety procedures, a topic that will be addressed later in the chapter (Turner et al., 2012).

Social support = the network of friends, family, or colleagues who provide assistance and help reduce negative effects of stress

- *Hassles.* **Daily hassles** include irritating and frustrating demands that characterize everyday experience (Lazarus & Cohen, 1977). Examples of daily hassles include traffic, paying bills, chores, and parking. A measure specific to workplace hassles has been developed, the Daily Hassles at Work Scale (DHAWS; Vanitha & Husain, 2011). Studies have shown a correlation between daily hassles and physical and mental health problems (e.g., Flett, Molnar, Nepon, Hewitt, 2012).

- *Air Quality.* Both outdoor and indoor air pollution have an impact on the cardiovascular system and overall feelings of well-being. Major sources of indoor air pollution include particulates from tobacco or combustion-based sources, construction materials, pesticides, and naturally occurring radioactive particles such as radon gas. A buildup of such particles associated with poor ventilation has been referred to as **Sick Building Syndrome,** or SBS (World Health Organization, 1983). It can be documented through the presence of environmental toxins and is implicated when employees feel sick at the workplace and healthy when they leave. Research has shown that SBS correlates with a variety of physical complaints such as headache and nausea (Kinman & Griffin, 2008). It has also been correlated with employee absences and burnout (Redman, Hamilton, Malloch, & Kleymann, 2011).

Sick Building Syndrome = a set of physical and psychological complaints, wherein the employee feels ill at work and fine upon leaving the building

- *Multitasking.* Multitasking refers to a juggling act of numerous tasks at one time, and has become a way of life for many working people. **Multitasking** makes it very difficult to pay attention to your current environment. Kirsh (2000) has listed many of the costs associated with multitasking as a cause of cognitive overload, including making mistakes, wasting time, and increased safety risks. For instance, recent research has demonstrated that multitasking led to decreased accuracy in a computer task (Adler, & Benbunan-Fich, 2012). Related research has demonstrated a positive association between the use of numerical goal setting and multitasking behavior (Strickland & Galimba, 2000), wherein pursuing goals led to more frequent switching between tasks.

- *Role-related problems.* The Role Stress Model was built around the idea that employees have a variety of different expectations to meet while at work (Ilgen & Hollenbeck, 1991). A **role** can be thought of as a part in a play, where people are acting according to a particular script. **Role conflict** occurs when a person feels torn in different directions due to role demands. This may occur if the employee has different bosses or clients who issue incompatible demands for a project. It is also common for working parents who want to be a good parent as well as a good employee. A related concept is **role overload**, which is the existence of too many roles and a feeling of being overwhelmed. This is a common occurrence for people who are given a lot of varied work to do and asked to multitask through the different assignments. These types of stressors all involve having too much on one's plate. A different type of occupational stressor occurs if there is a lack of clarity about work roles. This is called **role ambiguity**. It occurs when someone is uncertain of role assignments and feels confused about where they fit in the organization.

- *Bullying.* **Bullying** is persistent intimidating or insulting behaviors directed at an individual, causing that person to feel threatened or vulnerable. Bullying has been linked to stress-related symptoms similar to Post-Traumatic Stress Disorder (Bond, Tuckey, & Dollard, 2010). A recent study (SHRM, 2012) revealed that over half of surveyed organizations had instances of workplace bullying over the previous year. Most bullying incidents occurred between peers (82 percent), followed by supervisor to employee (56 percent). The types of bullying behaviors reported by human resource managers include:

  - Verbal abuse, including shouting, swearing, name calling, and malicious sarcasm—73%

  - Malicious gossip, rumors, and lies—62%

  - Threats and intimidation—50%

  - Cruel comments and teasing—47%

  - Ignoring and excluding—43%

  - Unduly harsh or constant criticism—41%

  - Aggression—38%

  - Abuse of authority—36%

  - Unjustified interference with work performance—25%

  - Use of technology for bullying—19%

  - Physical assaults—16%

Role conflict = a job stressor where an employee perceives incompatible demands

Role overload = a job stressor where an employee perceives too many demands

Role Ambiguity = a job stressor where an employee is uncertain of responsibilities

Organizations have counteracted the prevalence of bullying by creating zero-tolerance policies for bullying and reporting procedures for handling allegations of it (see Workplace Investigations section above). Another approach to minimizing the influence of bullying is to provide training sessions directed at the topic.

Stress

Early researchers of the effects of stress on the body demonstrated some of the fundamental <u>physical</u> processes that occur when encountering a stressor. Walter Cannon (1932) is associated with the **Fight or Flight response**. In these situations, stressors activate the endocrine system and the sympathetic nervous system (SNS), producing increased heart rate, respiration, and stress hormones such as adrenalin. Adrenaline increases blood flow to the heart, increases oxygen intake to the lungs, stimulates the liver to release glucose, and dilates pupils to improve vision. Initially, these types of changes function to improve decision making and physical performance. However, chronic activation leads to wear and tear on the body.

To further understand how the physiological effects of stress can lead to strain, it is important to consider the General Adaptation Syndrome. Hans Selye was an endocrinologist who placed animals under extremely stressful conditions and then conducted autopsies on them when they died. He noted (1956) that stress can cause major physiological systems to fail, and is attributed with identifying the **General Adaptation Syndrome** stages of dealing with stress (depicted in the flowchart).

In the alarm stage, the fight-or-flight physiological reactions are triggered to help cope with the immediate demands of the stressor. In the resistance phase, the person maintains arousal levels to deal with the stressor, but the physiological by-products build up and major bodily systems tire. In the exhaustion phase, physiological components in the body's system start to break down. Selye believed there is a finite amount of energy to adapt to stress. Three causes for a breakdown are a loss of potassium ions, a loss of adrenal glucocorticoids, and weakening of vital organs.

In addition to the effects on physiological systems, stress can also impact <u>psychological</u> processes in a way that creates distress for the employee, and ultimately leads to strain-related breakdowns. Rather than meet the stressor as a challenge and engage in problem solving to address it, some people engage in **catastrophic thinking** (McKay, 2005). This means that they blow the stressor out of proportion and become preoccupied with how terrible things are. This type of reaction can lead to **rumination**, or a tendency to have obsessive thoughts about the stressor, essentially reliving it, even if it is no longer a threat (e.g., Roger, de Scremin, Borril, & Forbes, 2011). Psychological processes such as these are experienced as stressful to employees and can create strain.

Fight or Flight response = the physiological mobilization of the body when faced with a potentially threatening situation

Three Causes of Breakdown

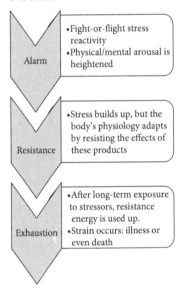

Alarm	• Fight-or-flight stress reactivity • Physical/mental arousal is heightened
Resistance	• Stress builds up, but the body's physiology adapts by resisting the effects of these products
Exhaustion	• After long-term exposure to stressors, resistance energy is used up. • Strain occurs: illness or even death

Catastrophic thinking = exaggerating a problem by imagining the worst-case scenarios

As noted above, prolonged exposure to stress can lead to negative health consequences associated with **exhaustion**. Workplace psychology has also implicated chronic stress as a factor in a variety of occupational outcomes, including health problems, burnout, drug and alcohol use, psychological problems, and violence.

Exhaustion = the physical breakdown of the body's systems under prolonged exposure to stress

Health Problems

To consider the potential for wear and tear on the major systems in the body, consider what the body endures under prolonged stress in terms of various muscle groups (e.g., Kjellber & Wadman, 2007; Chandola, Heraclides, & Kumari, 2010):

The skeletal muscles brace, resulting in

- Headache
- Backache and muscle pain
- Temporomandibular-joint (TMJ) syndrome

Cardiac muscle strains, resulting in

- Chest pains
- Heart palpitations
- Heart attack

Smooth muscles tense, resulting in

- Excessive stomach acids; ulcers
- Stomachaches
- Irritable bowel syndrome

These examples only pertain to muscle groups, but long-term health consequences exist for virtually every major physiological system. The list of negative health consequences associated with prolonged exposure to stress is extremely long. A partial list of these effects includes a link to a metabolic syndrome related to diabetes (Chandola, Brunner, & Marmot, 2006), immune system dysfunction (Segerstrom & Miller, 2004), chronic high blood pressure (Jones, Conner, McMillan, & Ferguson, 2007), and obesity (Pervanidou, & Chrousos, 2011).

Burnout

A stress-related topic that is particularly relevant to occupational health is that of **burnout**. Burnout is a term that can be overused to describe minor mood ailments; however it is actually a more serious condition characterized by extreme emotional exhaustion, depersonalization, and low personal accomplishments (Maslach & Jackson, 1981). Burnout is also typified by feeling sad, helpless,

Burnout = a type of job strain characterized by extreme exhaustion, depersonalization, and cynicism

and as though one's work is lacking in meaning. It is particularly prevalent in occupations for which an employee originally held many idealistic notions about helping others, such as in the health or educational fields. Research has demonstrated that occupational burnout can affect interpersonal relationships outside of work (e.g., Bakker, 2009).

The psychological opposite of burnout is **work engagement**. Work engagement is characterized as a positive, fulfilling, work-related state of mind that is comprised of three components: vigor, dedication, and absorption (Schaufeli, Salanova, Gonzalez-Roma, & Bakker, 2002). An engaged employee has a sense of energetic and effective connection with their work activities, and they see themselves as able to deal completely with the demands of their job (Schaufeli et al., 2002). This research demonstrated that work engagement is related to a variety of positive work outcomes, including job satisfaction, low absenteeism, low turnover, and high organizational commitment.

Work engagement = a high level of involvement with work, characterized by vigor, absorption, and dedication

Substance Use and Abuse

Research has proposed a "tension reduction" hypothesis as far as the use of drugs and alcohol to cope with job stressors (e.g., Liu et al., 2009). This means that some employees who experience stress at work will use drug substances to try to escape from the work-related tension. Substance use is recognized as a risk factor for workplace accidents (e.g., Christian, Bradley, Wallace, & Burke, 2009).

Substance abuse occurs when an employee cannot control the intake of drugs and/or alcohol, and its use threatens physical, social, and financial well-being. The prevalence of substance use and abuse at the workplace is widespread. The Occupational Safety and Health Administration (2005; osha.gov) cites that 75 percent of illicit drug users in the United States have jobs. A recent large-scale survey (Frone, 2012) revealed that 60 percent of those surveyed said they could use alcohol or drugs at work, and 23 percent reported having been exposed to an impaired coworker during the previous year.

Substance abuse = a pattern of use of drugs or alcohol in a way that exceeds societal norms and creates financial, medical, or social problems for the user

Psychological Problems

Workplace stresses can result in psychological breakdowns such as **anxiety** or **depression**. The specific symptoms for these mental health disorders can be found in the Diagnostic and Statistical Manual of Mental Disorders (e.g., DSM-5 to be published in 2013), reviewed and published by the American Psychiatric Association. Therapists and psychiatrists attempt to categorize psychological problems through the frequency and severity of symptoms.

In general, anxiety is characterized by a negative mood state, persistent worry, and an impending sense of dread (Beck et. al, 1996). Depression is characterized by deep sadness, recurring thoughts of suicide, hopelessness, and a low energy level similar to extreme fatigue (Beck, Steer, & Garbin, 1988). Both of these psychological states correlate with other life challenges, such as interpersonal/family problems, appetite problems, and sleep disturbances.

Although psychological problems often stem from other sources (e.g., genetic or family background), they also fall into the arena of strain-related breakdowns

Anxiety = a distressing psychological state characterized by a pervasive sense of dread and unease

Depression = a distressing psychological state characterized by negative mood, hopelessness, and despair

in workplace psychology. In fact, the Equal Employment Opportunity Commission (EEOC) receives approximately 3,000 psychology-related claims per year, making this the largest category of claim brought under the Americans with Disabilities Act.

Workplace Violence

For some people, stressful situations escalate into violence. Research has shown that some instances of **workplace violence** are a direct consequence of stress, and that there are approaches to replacing this behavioral option with more prosocial ones (Bowen, Privitera, & Bowie, 2011). Incidents of workplace violence receive a lot of media attention, perhaps due to their shocking or unexpected nature. However, according to a 2011 study conducted by the U.S. Department of Justice, workplace violence constitutes approximately 15 percent of the total national incidences of violence. The number of acts of nonfatal workplace violence has fallen steadily since 1993 (when it was 75 percent higher than in 2009). However, other forms of workplace violence do occur in large numbers, with an estimated 6 million employees being threatened with violence at work (Wagner & Hollenbeck, 2009).

In terms of fatal workplace incidents, the use of guns accounted for 80 percent of workplace homicides. Approximately 70 percent of workplace homicides were committed by strangers/robbers, compared to approximately 20 percent work associates or former coworkers. These 20 percent receive much attention in the psychological community. Attempts to provide a profile of employee homicidal behavior most often paints a picture of a male employee, often middle aged, who believes that he has been wronged by a person or persons at the workplace. People who engage in violence unfortunately believe that it is possible to "correct" the injustice by lashing out against others at work.

Interventions regarding these strain-related outcomes can be difficult because the employee needs to admit to experiencing strain before he or she can receive help. An insightful supervisor will be able to notice early signs of a problem and can initiate a conversation under the guise of performance management. During that conversation, the employee and supervisor can work together to generate ideas for overcoming stress and strain at work.

Organizations must prepare formal policy statements against workplace bullying and violence. Situations of escalating conflict should be reported and followed by a thorough workplace investigation. Policies should be implemented to immediately cease the aggressive behavior. The employees who were involved should be referred to community counseling. If a termination of employment has occurred, all access cards and keys should be taken from the fired employee. Organizational personnel and security should be informed that this person should not be on the grounds of the organization, and provided with a contact number to report any sightings. Zero-tolerance policies (toward violence and carrying weapons at work) should be written and posted throughout the worksite. As seen in the results of an SHRM survey (2006), organizations with a formal policy against weapons at the workplace often include a zero-tolerance policy.

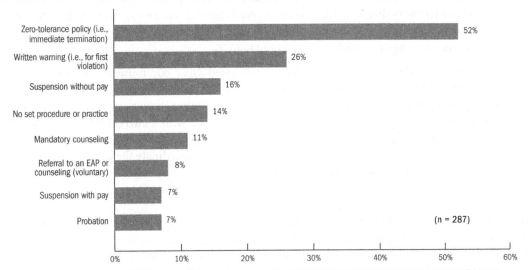

Note: Percentages do not total 100% due to multiple response options. HR professionals from organizations without weapons policies were excluded from this analysis.

Source: SHRM 2006 Weapons in the Workplace Survey Report

(Source: http://www.shrm.org/Research/SurveyFindings/Documents/2006%20Weapons%20In%20The%20Workplace%20Survey%20Report.pdf)

Stress Management

The chapter has introduced models of the stress process that have applications to improve employees' working lives. To some extent, the management of stress is the responsibility of the employee, but there are things that organizations can do to help. Research in **stress management** has identified three categories of approaches. These are primary, secondary, and tertiary prevention strategies to attempt to break the stress process at each stage.

Primary prevention strategies involve tactics to reduce or eliminate stressors from the work environment. An example would be improving job design so work processes function more smoothly. Job design tactics described in Chapter 5 such as job enrichment and job rotation can be used to provide relief from task-related stresses. Another instance of a primary prevention strategy would be improving equipment to be more effective and comfortable for its operators. Basically, primary strategies include anything that progressively deals with the potential stressors in a way that stops the stress process. Some specific examples based on stress theories are listed below.

- The Demands/Control/Support Model provides a measurement tool for assessing perceived job demands. This information will suggest certain avenues for reducing or sharing job demands. It also provides directions for empowering the employee to be able to control these demands. Finally, applications of this model include building a support network to help buffer the negative effects of a demands/control mismatch. Supervisors should be trained to provide support to employees, and groups of coworkers can also provide support in a formal or informal manner.

- One of the most direct applications of the cognitive models (Socio-Cognitive and Challenge-Hindrance) is to cultivate a culture of continuous learning. This will reduce the number of on-the-job stressors that are experienced as threats, and create an expectation that challenges are expected and welcomed. A team-centered culture can also provide coping resources to address the challenge in a problem-centered manner.

- Role-related conflict demonstrates that people need clear communications about what is expected of them. Role-related problems can be addressed with unambiguous performance management. A supervisor should have clear communication about performance expectations and provide support to employees. This can be provided with a current job description and clear performance feedback from a supervisor (such as that described by after-event reviews). Similarly, managers who work together on a project must coordinate the assignments they give to employees. Role stressors also suggest the need for flexibility in working arrangements for some employees who have demanding care-giving assignments.

Secondary prevention strategies do not attempt to change the stressor. Rather, these tactics are aimed at modifying the responses to those stressors. This category is what most people think of when they hear "stress management programs." These programs include lifestyle choices, time management, nutrition or fitness programs, relaxation, or cognitive restructuring (changing self-talk).

- Meditation. Meditation is the process of purposely deepening attention and awareness to a focal point and gaining more control over unnecessary mental activity.

- Exercise: The Surgeon General recommends 30–60 minutes of moderate physical activity each day. This would use approximately 150 calories daily or 1000 calories weekly. Exercise helps offset the stress response, and reduces the risks of premature disability. Exercise has the following effects:
  ° Contracting and relaxing tense muscles
  ° Utilizing the energy mobilized during the stress response in a productive way
  ° Shifting our attention away from our problems and onto something we enjoy

- Cognitive Restructuring (Ellis & Harper, 1975). These authors noted that much of our stress in modern life is determined by the way we view the world. They created Rational Emotive Behavior Therapy to help people recognize illogical beliefs and replace them with more rational thoughts. Harper & Ellis created an ABCDE technique to help people challenge their beliefs and change their outcomes:
  ° **A**ctivating event = stressor
  ° **B**elief system = illogical beliefs
  ° **C**onsequences = negative effects
  ° **D**ispute = challenge beliefs
  ° **E**ffects = were consequences changed?

Tertiary prevention strategies are those that involve healing the negative effects of stressors once stress has already occurred. The goal here is to stop strain from happening. The category of organizational options usually falls under the heading **Employee Assistance Programs** (EAPs). These may provide on-site counseling services or may provide referral services for a wide variety of life problems such as divorce, bankruptcy, or other legal assistance. EAPs can also provide help for people who have interpersonal problems or who are struggling with drug or alcohol addiction. These programs are designed to maintain employee confidentiality, and it is important to respect the need for privacy on these personal matters.

Employees will often try to hide psychological problems for fear of the stigma associated with them. In fact, it may be considered as intrusive and unprofessional to expect supervisors or employees to openly discuss mental/emotional states. A defining characteristic of addiction is that the user tries to hide their behaviors. Organizations should establish clear policies regarding drug and alcohol use and communicate these during new employee orientation and ongoing communication (such as visible signs and training). However, organizations should be prepared to provide referral services for counseling, if requested. Organizations that can afford to invest more substantially in their employees' well-being may have counseling services as part of an Employee Assistance Program.

Workplace Safety

This section of the chapter covers issues related to employee safety at work. Accidents and injuries at the work site are numerous and very costly. The Bureau of Labor Statistics has reported information that, in 2010, there were over 3 million recorded cases of workplace injuries/illnesses and over 4,000 workplace fatalities. The Liberty Mutual Research Institute for Safety (2005) estimated workers' compensation costs for the most disabling injuries to be $48 billion dollars. Jobs with the highest risk factors in terms of fatalities are in the following industries: fishing, logging, transportation, farming, mining, law enforcement, and construction. The chart from the Bureau of Labor Statistics provides specific injury data.

NONFATAL INJURIES, PRIVATE INDUSTRY (2010)

Total recordable cases: 3,063,400

Cases involving days away from work: 933,200

Cases involving sprains, strains, tears: 370,130

Cases involving injuries to the back: 185,270

Cases involving falls: 208,470

FATAL WORK-RELATED INJURIES

Total fatal injuries (all sectors): 4,547

Total fatal injuries (private industry): 4,070

Highway incidents (private industry): 837

Falls (private industry): 598

Homicides (private industry): 423

Flow Chart of Employee Variables that Influence Safety Outcomes

Individual Variables
- Safety Motivation
- Safety Knowledge
- Conscientiousness
- Attitudes toward safety
- Drug/Alcohol Addiction

Safety Performance
- Safety Compliance
- Safety Participation

Safety Outcomes
- Accidents
- Injuries
- Fatalities

Research in Workplace Safety

One of the interesting problems in studying workplace safety as a dependent variable is trying to decide what to measure. It is clear that accidents, injuries, and workplace fatalities are outcomes that create a major risk for organizations and employees. In an ideal world, these outcomes would be so well-understood that their occurrence could be virtually eliminated. However, authors in workplace psychology have noted that many accidents/injuries are a function of factors outside the control of the organization or the employee, such as Acts of Nature or risks inherent to the job (Kaplan & Tetrick, 2011).

Recognizing this, researchers have attempted to define important variables that are under a person's control (e.g., Christian, Bradley, Wallace, & Burke, 2009; Neal & Griffin, 2006). At the level of the employee, there are two types of safety performance variables: safety compliance and safety participation. **Safety compliance** refers to adherence to safety procedures and wearing protective equipment. **Safety participation** refers to going beyond basic safety procedures and actively reporting safety issues, as well as whistle-blowing if unsafe work environments are observed. There are a number of employee variables, such as safety motivation, that can be used to predict safety performance, as indicated in the flowchart.

This model portrays only a tiny piece of the puzzle regarding workplace outcomes such as accidents, injuries, and fatalities. These variables only include those most proximally affecting individual processes. There are a host of other variables at the group and organizational level. These will briefly be reviewed in list form below.

A considerable amount of research has investigated workplace safety issues related to accidents on the job. Some of these have already been reviewed, such as occupational stress and employee training (specifically safety training). The following section of the textbook will review additional predictors of workplace accidents by categorizing them in terms of organizational variables, scheduling, social variables, and ergonomic variables.

- **Organizational Variables.** The stance that executive-level leaders take toward safety has direct results on the psychosocial safety climate. Investments that are made in proper equipment and training also reduce the occurrence of accidents (e.g., Katsakiori et al., 2010). The creation and communication of clear policies and procedures regarding occupational health and safety directly influences the safety climate. The provision of incentives for following safe procedures has been shown to positively affect the adherence to safety policies, although there is a concern that incentives for safety may result in underreporting of accidents (Kaplan & Tetrick, 2011).

- **Work Scheduling Variables.** It is important to design work processes to minimize employee fatigue, which is a major factor in workplace accidents (e.g., DeArmond & Chen, 2009). Scheduling practices that tend to increase fatigue include shift work, particularly the graveyard shift or the use of rotating shifts. Jobs that are very repetitive or boring in nature also create fatigue. Finally, the lack of appropriate rest breaks will increase the incidences of accidents on the job.

- **Physical Environment Variables**. Many of the variables that were implicated as workplace stressors have also been linked to workplace accidents. Essentially, anything that creates a distraction or leads to discomfort on the job has the potential to create an unsafe work environment. Examples include extremes of temperature, extremely loud environments, poor illumination, or environmental pollutants. Any job that requires working with environmental hazards or heavy equipment will increase the risk for injuries and accidents (Kaplan & Tetrick, 2011).

- **Social Psychological Variables**. These variables include the dynamics that social psychology brings to safety. These include group norms for safe behavior, group morale, and communication about safe behaviors. A feature of the workplace that has received considerable research validation is safety climate . Safety climate describes the level of commitment to safe work behaviors pervasive in the workplace environment. It can range from complete disregard to safety to a strong emphasis on it. It can be characterized in terms of shared perceptions of organizational policies, practices, and procedures aimed at the protection of worker health and safety (stemming largely from management practices).

In a strong safety climate, the value placed on occupational safety is something that is well known and shared by employees (e.g., Hofmann & Stetzer, 1996). Research has demonstrated the link between safety climate, safe work behaviors, and safety outcomes (e.g., Clarke, 2010). Other research has demonstrated that traditionally effective leadership behaviors (such as transactional and transformational leadership) were only effective when the safety climate was strong (Kapp, 2012). In addition, a strong safety climate can buffer the negative effects of workplace bullying (Bond et al., 2010). Research has shown the correlation between psychosocial safety climate and occupational health measures (Law, Dollard, Tuckey, & Dormann, 2011).

- **Ergonomics**. Ergonomics is an entire field dedicated to improving workplace efficiency and safety. It covers all aspects of workspace and equipment design, including controls, displays, warnings, computer interfaces, and the work itself. It is the study of the physical and mental characteristics of people and tasks for the purpose of designing appropriate environments. In fact, ergonomics serves the broader interests of improving any environment where humans interact with machines, tools, or equipment. Its goals are to make activities safer and enhance people's well-being. Research has supported the link between ergonomics and occupational safety (e.g., Niu, 2010).

Ergonomics = the study of the interaction between worker and the workplace with a view to making improvements to equipment or processes

The demand for ergonomics was recognized during World War II to improve the designs of airplane cockpits. At that time, the controls and displays were not grouped together logically, and some of the more important feedback instruments were not in the line of

- What are the sight lines for visual information you receive?

- How is your posture affected by the tasks?

- How far, and how often, do you have to reach for necessary tools or equipment (e.g., the "reach envelope")?

sight. In addition, the control knobs were too similar in size and feel, leading to confusion during high-stress situations. Ergonomic principles were implemented to make improvements to these designs.

Many people have encountered ergonomic principles in terms of the layout and arrangements of their office desks, chairs, and computer. The term **ergonomic analysis** is an inspection of the workspace to eliminate injury risk factors such as unnecessary reaching, lifting, and body postures that lead to back strain. Ergonomics can be used to emphasize work design and improve the equipment or furniture of the workspace. This, in turn, improves productivity and minimizes the likelihood of injuries.

The chapter thus far has introduced a number of factors that relate to workplace safety performance and safety outcomes. These include factors at the individual level such as safety knowledge, motivation, and attitudes. At the work environment level, there are other influential factors like ergonomics, scheduling, training, and safety climate. The following section summarizes some of the approaches organizations can take in managing risk related to safety.

Approaches to Safety Management

Clearly, the organization would like to minimize incidences of injuries, accidents, fatalities, and their associated costs. There are many different approaches that can be taken to increase workplace safety, as indicated in the diagram. The personnel approach focuses on hiring and training safe behaviors. The rewards approach uses performance management, feedback, and contingent rewards to raise safety. The job design approach focuses on arranging the job itself to minimize risk factors such as repetitive motions or fatigue-inducing job requirements.

Applications. There are many interventions that can be implemented to reduce the risk of accidents at the workplace. One of the most important things that Human Resources can do to help accomplish this goal is to engage in practices that support the safety climate. To create a safety climate, organizations need to develop specific safety plans and follow through with them. Activities that should be conducted start with a clear statement of company policy that is emphasized during hiring and throughout the organization. It is important to have full support of management, who lead by example and rhetoric about safety. Care should be taken to identify the costs/benefits of following safe procedures, and communicating why the benefits outweigh the costs. Employees should be encouraged to report safety problems. Contact information should be clearly displayed for safety administration at the organizational level as well as outside the organization (e.g., OSHA posters). There should be a clear process for reporting safety concerns that rewards rather than punishes employees. Careful inspections and record keeping about safety should be made, and fall clearly under the responsibility of division managers.

Organizational Approaches to Safety:

Personnel Approach	•Hire based on proven track record of safety •Provide new employee session dedicated to safety •Dedicate ongoing training resources to safety
Rewards Approach	•Communicate the benefits of safety at work •Use Reinforcement Theory to measure and reward safe behaviors •Display group or organizational progress relative to safety goals
Job Design Approach	•Modify tasks or equipment to improve efficiency and reduce injury •Design the flow of work to reduce fatigue

It may be worthwhile to schedule a meeting with an ergonomics consultant to tour the organization. During this discussion, knowledge of the state of the industry can be used to identify specific improvements to workspace design. Another part of an on-site tour may include a visual observation of work in progress. This may give the ergonomic specialist a clear view of ways in which the workplace can be improved. As mentioned above, ergonomic improvements are not only to address ongoing injuries, they are also to improve the flow of work. In fact, there may be a host of beneficial outcomes from having an ergonomic analysis.

Legislation: The Occupational Safety and Health Act (1970)

A comprehensive federal law was passed in 1970 to establish guidelines for safe work environments. The Occupational Safety and Health Act, also known as the Williams-Steiger Act, applies to virtually all private companies and many public agencies as well.

The essence of this act is that U.S. workers have a right to be safe at work, which means they have a right to be protected from known serious hazards at the workplace. This act charges employers with identifying and eliminating all such hazards that could result in death or serious harm. This is known as the **General Duty Standard**. If it is not possible to eliminate the hazard, the employer must reduce the hazardous risk by informing and training employees about safe-handling of the hazards. The employer also must monitor the impact of the hazard, such as via air testing or medical testing. For the employee's part, he or she must conform to safety standards put in place for their own well-being.

National Institute of Occupational Safety and Health. The OSH Act included the creation of a federal agency called the National Institute of Occupational Safety and Health (**NIOSH**). The purpose of this organization is to sponsor and conduct health and safety-related research. It also is responsible for using this knowledge to recommend actions to eliminate or reduce the impact of workplace hazards and stressors.

Occupational Safety and Health Administration. Part of the OSH Act included the creation of a federal agency called the Occupational Safety and Health Administration. This agency is responsible for investigating claims of unsafe working conditions (violations of the act) and may also issue citations or impose fines if violations are found. Allegations of unsafe workplaces may be made by employees known as whistle-blowers, or by others in the community. Once a claim of OSHA violations has been made to the agency, an agent will first attempt to resolve the issue by contacting the employer. If it is not clearly resolved, a work-site inspection will be made. This will include various types of data collection, such as visual inspection of work processes, chemical sampling, and interviews with employees. The investigation will conclude with a written report and possible citations or fines. Listings of major fines and the most frequently cited violations are posted online at www.osha.gov. OSHA keeps track of the causes of workplace fatalities and injuries and their causes. The most frequent causes of workplace deaths involve motor vehicles, falls, drowning,

General Duty Standard = a mandate that organizations attempt to identify and eliminate serious hazards to employee safety and health

National Institute for Occupational Safety and Health (NIOSH) = an agency created as part of the Occupational Safety and Health Act to research and provide safety recommendations for workplaces

electrocution, fire, and poisoning. Injuries overlap these categories, including motor vehicles, falls, overexertion and strain, and exposure to hazardous chemicals.

Developing Plans for Safety. OSHA requires that organizations be forward thinking and develop and communicate plans that relate to employee safety. These plans include a fire emergency plan, emergency action plan, and safety and health management plan. These plans also help organizations minimize their risks for harm to the employees and risks of delayed business functioning.

Record Keeping and Material Safety Data Sheets. Other employer responsibilities include keeping detailed records. Obviously, records must be kept of all work-related injuries and illnesses, and formal reports must be written in every case that involves medical treatment beyond first aid, or involves the employee needing to miss work to recover. More serious incidents must be investigated, such as those involving hospitalization of more than three employees or any work-related fatality. Other mandatory records that must be kept include Material Safety Data Sheets (MSDS). These records include the proper labeling of substances and the known risks that they pose. The MSDS provides employees and emergency personnel (e.g., firefighters) with procedures for safe handling, use, and disposal.

Safety Communication. At a minimum, the organization must prominently position safety posters and incident summaries on site. Posters must be clearly displayed according to color-coded guidelines, regardless of the size of the organization. Organizations with more than 11 employees are also required to post summary information about workplace accidents and injuries; those with fewer numbers are not required to do so. For example, Form 300A is an annual summary of all logged safety information that must be certified by a company executive and posted during every February following the calendar year of record.

Employee Rights. Employees have many rights to take an active role in ensuring the safety of their work environments. They can inform their employer and/or OSHA about safety violations or unsafe conditions, they can confidentially request an OSHA inspection of apparently unsafe areas, and they have the right to not be retaliated against for these actions. If the employee thinks there has been such retaliation, they have the right to file a formal complaint with OSHA within 30 days of the incident.

Criticisms of OSHA. The federal attempt to increase safety at the workplace has not gone without criticism. Many of these critiques are typical of those aimed at federal employment legislation. These ideas range from OSHA being just another bureaucracy that increases unnecessary paperwork, to it not having enough staffing or punitive power to make any real changes to the work environment (see Silverstein, 2008). However, data from the Bureau of Labor Statistics show that, since the passage of OSHA, workplace fatalities have dropped by 60 percent, and injury rates have fallen by 40 percent.

Putting it All Together

Considering the material in this chapter, here are a few "take-home" ideas for managing stress, safety, and other risks.

- There are many types of risks at the workplace. An organization must be proactive to identify and minimize these risks.

- Some techniques for managing risks include HR audits, emergency management plans, standard operating procedures, and workplace investigations.

- Occupational stress is very prevalent in today's workforce and results in many workers' compensation and disability claims.

- To understand the process of occupational stress, it is important to consider stressors, stress, and strain.

- Research in psychology has identified stressful job demands and other characteristics of the workplace.

- Bullying has become fairly commonplace at work, and organizations should develop formal policies against it.

- Stress breakdowns include health problems, burnout, substance abuse, mental health issues, and violence.

- There is a variety of stress management tactics that can be employed by organizations or by the individual.

- Workplace safety outcomes include accidents, injuries, and fatalities and are very costly to organizations.

- Employees are directly responsible for safety performance. To raise performance, they should have the correct safety knowledge, skills, attitude, and an attention to detail.

- Safety outcomes are associated with implementation of a safety climate, training, scheduling, and ergonomics.

- Other tactics organizations can employ to manage safety risks include: hiring people with a proven safety record, establishing safety goals, and using job design principles.

- The Occupational Safety and Health Act (1970) was instituted to mandate safe working environments.

Spotlight On Research

Work Stress and Alcohol Use

Lui, S., Wang, M., Zhan, Y., & Shi, J. (2009). Daily work stress and alcohol use: Testing the cross-level moderation effects of neuroticism and job involvement. Personnel Psychology, 62, 575–597.

Participant Summary *(N=37)*

☐ *Participants from companies in Beijing*

☐ *14% women; 86% men*

☐ *29.7% managers; 21.6% engineers; 18.9% office staff; 10% other*

☐ *Average age of 31 years (sd = 8)*

☐ *Average tenure of 4.9 years (sd = 6.3)*

Results

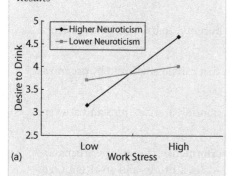

(a)

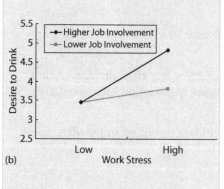

(b)

Introduction

Work Stress = a fundamental evaluation of distress at work.

Alcohol use is correlated with: various types of cancer, hypertension, injuries, accidents, liver cirrhosis, and violence.

Research Question:

Is there a link between job stress and the desire to drink alcohol, and does this relationship depend on neuroticism or job involvement?

Method

A recruitment announcement for the study was distributed at four companies in Beijing. Inclusion criteria included that the employee was full time and drank alcohol.

Initial Assessment. Participants responded to surveys of:

☐ Neuroticism (α=.83).
   Self-identification with eight words such as *"moody."*

☐ Job Involvement (α=.84) Agreement with five items such as *"To me, my job is a very large part of who I am."*

Ongoing Assessment over a Month. Daily telephone measures of:

☐ Alcohol Consumption. Number of alcoholic drinks consumed in terms of a standard consumption unit (e.g., can of beer).

☐ Desire to Drink Alcohol. *"I feel like I can really use a drink."*

☐ Stress Level Checklist. Occurrence of eight stressful events such as, *"A coworker criticized me today."*

Results

There was an association between self-reported work stress and the desire to drink alcohol.

There was an interaction, such that the link between stress and desire to drink was stronger for those high in neuroticism (see graph).

There was also an interaction (depicted in the graph), such that the link between work stress and desire to drink was stronger for those with high job involvement.

Discussion: Directions for Future Research

Additional research could assess alcoholism over the lifespan and its relationship with job stress.

Future studies could include other individual differences that influence the relationship between stress and alcohol cravings.

Chapter Exercises

Science: Replication and Extension

<u>Instructions:</u> Consider the Spotlight on Research summarized in this chapter. Address each of the following items by using two or three complete sentences on a separate sheet of paper.

1. What do you think were the strengths of this research?

2. What were the weaknesses?

PROPOSAL: If you conducted a follow-up study, what you would include in terms of:

- A sample of participants (whom would you study?)

- Variables you would include and hypotheses you would make (what would you test, specifically?)

Sequencing: Identify the Correct Order

<u>Instructions:</u> Consider the stages presented below. Label each one with a number (next to the stage), and describe why each is important on a separate sheet of paper.

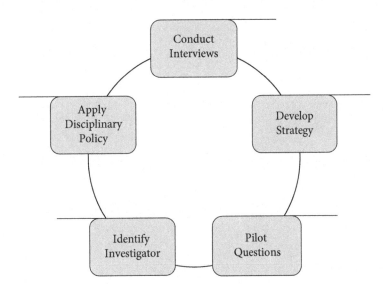

Instructions: Please address the following essay questions concisely, writing in complete sentences on a separate sheet of paper.

1. Briefly describe any three techniques that organizations can use in risk management.

2. List and briefly describe any three steps involved in a workplace investigation.

3. List and briefly describe the components of the stress process in terms of: stressors, stress, and strain.

4. Explain any two theoretical approaches to studying stress.

5. Describe three organizational influences on employee safety.

6. Describe OSHA and how it functions to regulate occupational safety.

Topics: Relate to Your Own Life

Instructions: Choose one of the topics below to write about a related experience from your own life. Use the space at the bottom of the page to document your experiences and opinions.

- *Risk Management.* Are you aware of the approaches your workplace has taken to risk management? If so, what are they? Have you participated in any emergency preparation activities, and if so which emergencies do you feel prepared to handle?

- *Safety.* Does your workplace have the features of a safety climate? Provide specific examples to explain your answer.

- *Stress.* Consider the stress theories and concepts covered in the chapter. Which best captures your life experiences with stress, and why?

Index

References and Recommended Readings

Adler, R. F., & Benbunan-Fich, R. (2012). Juggling on a high wire: Multitasking effects on performance. *International Journal of Human-Computer Studies, 70*(2), 156–168.

Bacharach, S. B., Bamberger, P. A., and Sonnenstuhl, W. J. (2002). Driven to drink: Managerial control, work-related risk factors, and employee problem drinking. *Academy of Management Journal, 45,* 637–658.

Bakker, A. B. (2009). The crossover of burnout and its relation to partner health. Stress and health: *Journal of the International Society for the Investigation of Stress, 25,* 343–353.

Beck, A. T., Epstein, N., Brown, G., & Steer, R. A. (1988). An inventory for measuring clinical anxiety: Psychometric properties. *Journal of Consulting and Clinical Psychology, 56,* 893–897.

Beck, A. T., Steer, R. A., & Garbin, M. G. (1988). Psychometric properties of the Beck Depression Inventory: Twenty-five years of evaluation. *Clinical Psychology Review, 8,* 77–100.

Bond, S. A., Tuckey, M. R., & Dollard, M. F. (2010) Psychosocial safety climate, workplace bullying, and symptoms of posttraumatic stress. Organization Development Journal, *28,* 38–56.

Bowen, B., Privitera, M. R., & Bowie, V. (2011). Reducing workplace violence by creating healthy workplace environments. *Journal of Aggression, Conflict, and Peace Research, 3,* 185–198.

Chandola, T., Brunner, E., & Marmot, M. (2006). Chronic stress at work and the metabolic syndrome: Prospective study. *British Medical Journal, 332,* 521–525.

Chandola, T., Heraclides, A., & Kumari, M. (2010). Psychophysiological biomarkers of workplace stressors. *Neuroscience and Biobehavioral Reviews, 35,* 51–57.

Christian, M., Bradley, J., Wallace, J., & Burke, M. (2009). Workplace safety: A meta-analysis of the roles of person and situation factors. *Journal of Applied Psychology,94,* 1103–1127.

Clarke, S. (2010). An integrative model of safety climate: Linking psychological climate and work attitudes to individual safety outcomes using meta-analysis. *Journal of Occupational and Organizational Psychology, 83,* 553–578.

DeArmond, S., & Chen, P. Y. (2009). Occupational safety: The role of workplace sleepiness. *Accident Analysis and Prevention, 41,* 976–984.

Ellis, A., & Harper, R. A. (1975). *A new guide to rational living.* Oxford, England: Prentice-Hall.

Flett, G. L., Molnar, D. S., Nepon, T., & Hewitt, P. L. (2012). A mediational model of perfectionistic automatic thoughts and psychosomatic symptoms: The roles of negative affect and daily hassles. *Personality and Individual Differences, 52*(5), 565–570.

Folkman, S., & Lazarus, R. S. (1985). If it changes it must be a process: Study of emotion and coping during three stages of a college examination. *Journal of Personality and Social Psychology, 48*(1), 150–170.

Ford, M., & Tetrick, L. (2008). Safety motivation and human resource management in North

America. *The International Journal of Human Resource Management, 19*(8), 1472–1485.

Frone, M. R. (2006). Prevalence and distribution of alcohol use and impairment in the workplace: A U.S. national survey. *Journal of Studies on Alcohol, 76,* 147–156.

Frone, M. R. (2008). Are work stressors related to employee substance use? The importance of temporal context in assessments of alcohol and illicit drug use. *Journal of Applied Psychology, 93,* 199–206.

Frone, M. R. (2012). Workplace substance use climate: Prevalence and distribution in the U.S. workforce. *Journal of Substance Use, 17*(1), 72–83.

Grant, A., Christiansen, M., & Price, R. (2007). Happiness, health, or relationships? Managerial practices and employee well-being tradeoffs. *Academy of Management Perspectives, 21*(3), 51–63.

Griffin, M. A., & Clarke, S. (2011). Stress and well-being at work. In S. Zedeck, S. Zedeck (Eds.), *APA handbook of industrial and organizational psychology,* (pp. 359–397). Washington, DC: American Psychological Association.

Häusser, J., Mojzisch, A., & Schulz-Hardt, S. (2011). Endocrinological and psychological responses to job stressors: An experimental test of the Job Demand-Control Model. *Psychoneuroendocrinology, 36*(7), 1021–1031.

Holmes, T. H., & Rahe, R. H. (1967). The Social Readjustment Rating Scale. *Journal of Psychosomatic Research, 11,* 213–218.

Jones, F., Conner, M., McMillan, B., & Ferguson, E. (2007). Impact of daily mood, work hours, and strain variables on self-reported health behaviors. *Journal of Applied Psychology, 92,* 1731–1740.

Kaplan, S., & Tetrick, L. E. (2011). Workplace safety and accidents: An industrial and organizational psychology perspective. In S. Zedeck,

S. Zedeck (Eds.), *APA handbook of industrial and organizational psychology,* (pp. 455–472). Washington, DC: American Psychological Association.

Kapp, E. A. (2012). The influence of supervisor leadership practices and perceived group safety climate on employee safety performance. *Safety Science, 50*(4), 1119–1124.

Katsakiori, P., Kavvathas, A., Athanassiou, G., Goutsos, S., Manatakis, E. (2010). Workplace and organizational accident causation factors in the manufacturing industry. *Human Factors and Ergonomics in the Manufacturing and Service Industries, 20,* 2–9.

Kendall, E., & Muenchberger, H. (2009). Stress at work: Using a process model to assist employers to understand the trajectory. *Work: Journal of Prevention, Assessment & Rehabilitation,32*(1), 19–25.

Kinman, G., & Griffin, M. (2008). Psychosocial factors and gender as predictors of symptoms associated with sick building syndrome. *Stress and Health: Journal of The International Society for the Investigation of Stress, 24,* 165–171.

Kirsh, D. (2000). A Few Thoughts on Cognitive Overload. *Intellectica, 30,* 19–51.

Kjellberg, A., & Wadman, C. (2007). The role of the affective stress response as a mediator of the effect of psychosocial risk factors on musculoskeletal complaints. *International Journal of Industrial Ergonomics, 37,* 367–374.

Lazarus, R. S., & Folkman, S. (1984). *Stress, appraisal, and coping.* New York: Springer.

Law, R., Dollard, M. F., Tuckey, M. R., & Dormann, C. (2011). Psychosocial safety climate as a lead indicator of workplace bullying and harassment, job resources, psychological health, and employee engagement. *Accident Analysis and Prevention, 43,* 1782–1793.

Liu, S., Wang, M., Zhan, Y., & Shi, J. (2009). Daily work stress and alcohol use: Testing the cross-level moderation effects of neuroticism and job involvement. *Personnel Psychology, 62,* 575–597.

McKay, D. (2005). Studies in cognitive processing during worry. *Cognitive Therapy and Research, 29,* 359–376.

Nakata, A. (2011). Effects of long work hours and poor sleep characteristics on workplace injury among full-time male employees of small- and medium-scale businesses. *Journal of Sleep Research, 20,* 576–584.

Niu, S. (2010). Ergonomics and occupational safety and health: An ILO perspective. *Applied Ergonomics, 41,* 744–753.

Pervanidou, P., & Chrousos, G. P. (2011). Stress and obesity/metabolic syndrome in childhood and adolescence. *International Journal of Pediatric Obesity, 6,* 21–28.

Redman, T. H., Malloch, P., & Kleymann, H. B. (2011). Working here makes me sick! *Human Resource Management Journal, 21,* 14–27.

Roger, D., de Scremin, L., Borril, J., & Forbes, A. (2011). Rumination, inhibition and stress: The construction of a new scale for assessing emotional style. *Current Psychology: A Journal for Diverse Perspectives on Diverse Psychological Issues, 30*(3), 234–244.

Schaufeli, W., & Bakker, A. B. (2004). Job demands, job resources, and their relationship with burnout and engagement: A multi-sample study. *Journal of Organizational Behavior, 25.*

Schaufeli, W., Salanova, M., Gonzalez-Roma, V., & Bakker, A. B. (2002). The measurement of engagement and burnout: A two-sample confirmatory factor analytic approach. *Journal of Happiness Studies, 3,* 71–92.

Segerstrom, S. C., & Miller, G. E. (2004). Psychological stress and the human immune system: A meta-analytic study of 30 years of inquiry. *Psychological Bulletin,* 601–630.

Selye, H. (1956). Stress and psychobiology. *Journal of Clinical & Experimental Psychopathology, 17,* 370–375.

Selye, H. (1956). *The stress of life.* New York: McGraw-Hill.

Silverstein, M. (2008). Getting home safe and sound: Occupational Safety and Health Administration at 38. *American Journal of Public Health,98*(3), 416–423.

Turner, N., Stride, C. B., Carter, A. J., McCaughey, D., & Carroll, A. E. (2012). Job Demands-Control-Support model and employee safety performance. *Accident Analysis and Prevention, 45,* 811–817.

Van den Broeck, A., Vansteenkiste, M., De Witte, H., & Lens, W. (2008). Explaining the relationships between job characteristics, burnout, and engagement: The role of basic psychological need satisfaction. *Work & Stress, 22,* 277–294.

Vischer, J. (2007). The effects of the physical environment on job performance: Towards a theoretical model of workspace stress. *Stress and Health: Journal of the International Society for the Investigation of Stress, 23,* 175–184.

Vanitha, B. B., & Husain, A. (2011). Daily hassles among school teachers. *Journal of the Indian Academy of Applied Psychology, 37,* 240–245.

World Health Organization (1983). Indoor air pollutants exposure and health effects. Copenhagen: Regional Office for Europe.

Labor and Employee Relations

7 Chapter Outline

Learning Objectives

The list of objectives below is your guide for organizing the content of this chapter. After you have read the chapter, you can test your proficiency by ensuring that you can address each of the objectives. Place a check in each box ☐ once you feel confident about your knowledge.

☐ Define terms related to labor relations and unionization

☐ Identify labor practices directed toward both the employer and the employee

☐ Describe the Worker Adjustment and Retraining Notification Act

☐ Define sexual harassment, its forms, related legislation, and outcomes of it

☐ Explain the Family and Medical Leave Act and how it benefits employees

☐ Identify labor practices that benefit employers

☐ Describe major historical events and legislation in unionization

☐ Discuss the stages of the unionization process

☐ Identify appropriate organizational actions during a union drive

☐ Describe labor relations breakdowns and related activities

☐ Define negotiation and terms related to finding a settlement

☐ Identify the mind-sets that may be brought to negotiation, and research findings

☐ Define organizational conflict and categories of conflict

☐ Explain dispute resolution strategies

☐ Define Employee Relations and the use of employee involvement techniques

☐ Describe organizational commitment and job satisfaction, and why these are important to organizations

Overview

One of the greatest areas of controversy in workplace psychology concerns the actual working conditions in terms of workers' rights and the rights of employers. These topics, collectively, are termed labor relations, and include the nuts-and-bolts that affect all workers, such as wages, hours of employment, personnel decisions, and grievances. The United States has a very long history of legislation and common law doctrine that govern expectations about working experiences. These laws and doctrines sometimes benefit the employee, sometimes the employer, and sometimes both.

To provide a unified voice on these issues for workers, labor unions have emerged. Labor unions engage in collective bargaining to gain favorable working conditions for its members. Many of the desired outcomes relate to compensation, so management often tries to keep these requests for improved labor conditions in check. A variety of employment laws have been enacted by Congress over the years to help maintain a balance between the rights of workers and the rights of employers.

The process of bargaining between labor unions and management is formally called negotiation. There is an established body of psychological research on the topic of negotiation. This research includes the different approaches to it, the effectiveness of these approaches under different conditions, and the influence of individual differences such as personality and gender.

A broader topic in workplace psychology is that of conflict, wherein one party perceives its goals to be frustrated by another. When this happens, the organization may choose to manage the conflict by bringing in a third party process such as arbitration or mediation. It is in the organization's best interest to have a proactive conflict management system in place. In a worst-case scenario, conflict can erupt into workplace violence. Organizations must be prepared to manage these events as well.

A related concept is employee relations, which covers the entire range of how employees relate to each other, management personnel, and just about everything else in the working environment. Building positive employee relations sets an organizational culture of trust among employees and managers. There are many techniques that can be implemented to positively affect culture, and also influence the performance of the organization.

Views of those Opposed to Labor Unions ...

" ... SO, AFTER THE UNION WON A 35 HOUR WEEK I SAID, 'WHY DON'T WE NOW TRY FOR A ZERO HOUR WORK WEEK.'"

Basic Working Conditions

There is a long and interesting history of congressional acts related to the practices involved in labor relations. Employers and employees have rights in terms of the exchange relationship. These have been influenced by the legislative process, court decisions, and organizational practices that have evolved over time. Influences on labor relations have created expectations for working conditions in the United States in terms of what the employees and the employer will contribute. These issues will be covered briefly in the following section.

Protections for both Employer and Employee

At-will Employment

At-will employment means that either the employee or the employer may terminate the employment relationship at any time for any lawful reason. Thus, this common expectation of work means that the employment relationship should not be assumed to be indefinite. Both parties are free to end the relationship for reasons they see fit (excluding certain exceptions that are covered under "wrongful termination" below). At-will employment makes it much easier for either party to make employment changes.

At-will employment = either the employer or employee may end the working relationship for any lawful reason

Good-Faith and Fair Dealing

Organizations and employees will benefit to the extent that both parties are acting with good faith and attempting to deal fairly with each other. This means that both are genuine in their interest in accomplishing agreed-upon work goals of a high quality.

Due Process

In employment, **due process** means that employment actions will be taken according to established procedures. Due process expectations include having a voice in decisions, and having the right to an impartial appeal of these decisions. Due process through legal channels is also granted to either party if named as a defendant in an employment-related lawsuit. Although the system is not perfect, due process helps with basic fairness.

Due process = employment actions follow established procedures to ensure fairness

Protections for Employees

Restrictions around Child Labor

A provision of the Fair Labor Standards Act was to put a series of restrictions around child labor as a function of the age of the child, the working conditions, and the time of year. For instance, those aged 14 and 15 may only work eighteen hours during a school week and no more than 40 hours per week during a non–school week. Children under the age of 18 are not allowed to work in mines or in other environments that pose a significant health risk, such as working with hazardous chemicals.

Wrongful Termination

Although the majority of cases of an employee leaving the organization fall under at-will employment, there are some situations that classify as **wrongful termination**. For instance, an employer may fire someone due to a prejudice against the employee's skin color or religion. Other examples include firing an employee for serving on jury duty, for whistle-blowing against financial fraud, filing a concern about safety, filing a workers' compensation claim, or for being

Wrongful termination = an unlawful end to the employment relationship that violates a contract or violates employment law

called from reserve to serve military duty. Another type of wrongful termination involves breach of contract. This is clearest in situations where there is a signed employment contract, although contracts may be implied verbally and can be upheld if corroborated by a witness.

Another case of wrongful termination is **constructive discharge**. In this situation, an employer makes the working conditions so intolerable that an employee feels forced to resign. Examples would include public belittling, bullying, or withdrawing all support that is necessary to do the job (e.g., *Turner v. Anheuser Busch*, 1994).

Worker Adjustment and Retraining Notification Act (1988)

Workers have the right to notice if there will be impending mass layoffs or plant closings. The **WARN Act** requires employers to notify employees 60 days prior to the date of an upcoming mass layoff so that they may plan accordingly. A **mass layoff** is defined as one such that, in a 30-day period, 33 percent of employees or 500 employees (whichever is greater) will lose their jobs. A **plant closing** occurs if a facility is shut down for six months or more, or if 50 or more employees lose their jobs in 30 days.

This act applies to employers of more than 100 employees, who may be full time or part time employees working a combined 4,000 hours or more per week. However, there are several situations in which WARN does not apply. These include natural disasters, unforeseeable business situations, and a faltering company that is seeking additional investment funding.

Sexual Harassment (Title VII of the Civil Rights Act of 1964)

Employees have the right to work in an environment that is free from harassment that inhibits their ability to successfully do their jobs. Sexual harassment is defined as behavior that demeans or humiliates someone based on sex (Berdahl, 2007). Although such behavior is often sexual in nature, it may instead be based on intolerance or hostility.

Basic forms of sexual harassment include quid pro quo and hostile environment. **Quid pro quo harassment** is typically committed by a boss. The harassment takes the form that a **Tangible Employment Action** (TEA: such as hiring, firing, or promotion) is dependent upon the employee agreeing to sexual requests.

The **hostile work environment** is a different type of harassment that is the aggregate of a series of individual behaviors that might not seem injurious if considered independently (e.g., sharing of lewd jokes, touches, suggestive comments, or sexual pictures). This type of sexual harassment is more controversial in nature because what is offensive and intimidating to some is not perceived as such by others.

The Equal Employment Opportunity Commission has defined aspects of the hostile work environment that constitute harassment. For instance, behaviors are harassing to the extent that they create an inability to conduct work or the creation of an intimidating environment. In practice, the courts consider the severity and the frequency of the alleged harassing behaviors, as well as the

Constructive discharge = an unlawful end to the employment relationship that is based on a manager creating intolerable working conditions for an employee

WARN Act = Congressional legislation passed in 1988 that mandates communication with employees in the event of a mass layoff or plant closing

Quid pro quo harassment = a form of sexual harassment typically perpetrated by a supervisor who indicates that conditions of employment will be based on acquiescence to requests

organization's awareness and response to the behaviors. The U.S. Supreme Court has ruled on several landmark cases in an attempt to clarify the legality of harassment. These are described briefly below.

Meritor Savings Bank v. Vinson (1986). This landmark case indicated that sexual harassment is a violation of Title VII of the Civil Rights Act of 1964. Furthermore, it held that the employer has the burden of proof in demonstrating a clear antiharassment policy and training regarding this policy.

Harris v. Forklift Systems (1993). This case helped to bolster the validity of the hostile work environment interpretation of harassment. The courts found that behavior need not be proven to be physically or psychologically injurious. Rather, it was decided that offensive and frequent abusive behavior is a violation of Title VII because it creates an intolerable work situation for a reasonable person.

Faragher v. City of Boca Raton (1998). This case held that an organization may be held liable for the harassing actions of its supervisors. This ruling reinforced that the organization's distribution and enforcement of clear antiharassment policies and training will be considered in evaluating whether or not a violation of Title VII has occurred.

Oncale v. Sundowner Offshore Services (1998). The ruling in this case was that sexual harassment that leads to a hostile work environment can be created by same-sex perpetrators, and is still a violation of Title VII.

Research on Sexual Harassment

A substantial amount of research in psychology has attempted to measure the prevalence and consequences of sexual harassment. This is a difficult task because people do not agree on what constitutes sexual harassment, and men and women do not necessarily experience the same behaviors as harassment (e.g., Rotundo, Nguyen, & Sackett, 2001). Current views on the meaningful measurement of sexual harassment include an appraisal of whether the behaviors were perceived as positive (e.g., funny), negative (e.g., embarrassing), as well as an appraisal of whether there was a positive outcome (e.g., work-related benefit) or negative outcome (e.g., work-related harm).

A meta-analysis (Ilies, Hauserman, Schwochau, & Stibal, 2003) studied the prevalence rates of sexual harassment by context. This study reported the following levels of incidence: military (69%), academic (58%), private industry (46%), and government (43%). These numbers do not mean that the respondents had been targeted or suffered negative outcomes; simply that they had seen harassing behaviors at work.

A separate meta-analysis has demonstrated the correlation between sexual harassment and a variety of work-related outcomes (Willness, Steel, & Lee, 2007). These authors demonstrated negative correlations between sexual harassment and productivity, job satisfaction, and justice perceptions. There were significant positive associations between sexual harassment and job stress, burnout, and mental health problems.

Applications. It is clear that sexual harassment has detrimental outcomes that affect the individual and the organization. In fact, the Equal Employment Opportunity Commission reported that they handled 14,000 charges of sexual harassment, at costs estimated above $37 million (E.E.O.C., 2005). Thus, fiscally it is important that organizations create an antiharassment policy, and to include this as part of new employee orientation, the employee handbook, signs posted at the workplace, and ongoing training. In terms of enforcing the policy, the organization should have dedicated resources to conducting investigations following allegations of sexual harassment. Employees should be made aware of whom to contact in the case of harassment.

Family and Medical Leave Act (1993)

Major legislation was enacted in 1993 to allow people to take up to 12 weeks of unpaid leave to deal with significant life changes. These changes include: a serious health condition, new parenting responsibilities (including adoption and foster care), care for a family member with serious health conditions, or for situations related to covered active duty (part of the Supporting Military Families Act of 2010).

There are four requirements for an employee to be eligible to take FMLA leave. They must have worked for the employer for 1250 hours over the last year, have worked for 12 months, work for a covered employer, and work for a company that has 50 or more employees within 75 miles.

However, there are situations in which an employer is not required to reinstate the employee in exactly the same position. If the leave would create a grievous business loss that could threaten the functioning of the organization, a new hire may be made during the time of the leave. This is known as the key employee exception.

Protections for Employers

The previous section has described some basic features of the workplace that have been established to protect employees. There are also legal and financial protections for employers surrounding the work environment.

Employee Diligence

Employee diligence = an employment expectation that employees will work conscientiously in the best interest of the organization

A helpful feature for the employment exchange relationship is **employee diligence**. This means that an employee is expected to act with reasonable care and skill in the course of doing the job. A related idea is the **duty of obedience**, which means that an employee is expected to respect the division of authority in the organization. This employer protection has less of an impact in today's U.S. workforce because many organizations have removed lines of authority by restructuring the organization and by implementing practices such as self-managing teams. Thus, this expectation is not as prevalent as it once was in the United States. However, it is still relevant in certain organizations such as the U.S. military, and to some extent workers are expected to accept the existing lines of authority in organizational decision making.

Duty of obedience = an employment expectation that employees will respect the chain of command within the organization

Nondisclosure Agreements

Nondisclosure agreement = a formal, legally binding document in which an employee agrees not to discuss any trade secrets or other confidential material

Employers may require new employees to sign a **nondisclosure agreement**, which means that the employee is forbidden to communicate any business-related information outside of work. It is intended to protect proprietary information such as patents and trade secrets. These agreements define confidentiality and what is covered by it.

Noncompete Agreements

Employers may require that employees do not go to work for a rival company if the employment relationship is terminated for any reason and thus require a **noncompete agreement**. Organizations that provide specialized training may view employment as an investment and wish to restrict employees from using them as a stepping stone to other career opportunities. A related idea is a non-solicitation agreement, which prohibits employees from seeking customers and clients with company resources.

Sample Noncompete Agreement

For good consideration and as an inducement for_____(Company) to employ_____(Employee), the undersigned.

Employee hereby agrees not to directly or indirectly compete with the business of the Company and its successors and assigns during the period of employment and for a period of _____ years following termination of employment and notwithstanding the cause or reason for termination.

The term "not compete" as used herein shall mean that the Employee shall not own, manage, operate, consult, or be an employee in a business substantially similar to or competitive with the present business of the Company or such other business activity in which the Company may substantially engage during the term of employment.

The Employee acknowledges that the Company shall or may in reliance of this agreement provide Employee access to trade secrets, customers, and other confidential data and goodwill. Employee agrees to retain said information as confidential and not to use said information on his or her own behalf or disclose same to any third party.

This agreement shall be binding upon and inure to the benefit of the parties, their successors, assigns, and personal representatives.

Signed this _____ day of _____ 20____.

_____
Company

_____
Employee

This sample Noncompete Agreement was provided by Kinsey Law Offices (Kinsey 2007). It is intended as general information only and is not intended to serve as legal advice or as a substitute for legal counsel.

Mandatory Arbitration for Dispute Resolution

Another form of protection for employers is to require employees to sign an agreement that they will enter into legally binding arbitration to resolve any disputes arising out of work. This requirement as a condition of employment was upheld by the Supreme Court (Circuit City Stores, Inc. v. Adams, 2001). It is controversial because arbitrators typically find for the employer. However, in *EEOC v. Waffle House* (2002), the Supreme Court ruled that the EEOC may bring suit against an employer even if such an agreement was signed. The rationale is that the commission is an independent agency that did not agree to the arbitration agreement.

The previous sections have examined some terms and legislation related to basic working conditions and protections to employees as well as employers. These provisions, however, do not address all of the expectations surrounding labor relations. Tensions between the interests of employers and workers have led to the development of employee unionization and collective bargaining. These topics have been such a hotly contested part of the U.S. workplace that a multitude of related legislation and specialized jargon has evolved. These topics are also a major part of the PHR examination. The field of workplace psychology has tended to examine the processes of conflict and negotiation as broader constructs; these will be reviewed at the end of the chapter.

Unionization

The word "union" has become a shorthand way of referring to a labor union, or collective of employees who bargain for working rights together. Some people have favorable views of unionization and collective bargaining as necessary for workers' rights (e.g., Western & Rosenfeld, 2011). Others see them as leading to a privileged attitude toward working that negatively affects productivity and inhibits currency in work processes (e.g., Rau, 2012).

The Prevalence of (and Opinions about) Unions in the United States

Union membership has declined over the past few decades, particularly in the private sector. A study reports these numbers as decreasing from the early 1970s from 34 percent to 8 percent for men and 16 percent to 6 percent for women (Western & Rosenfeld, 2011). In terms of the overall percentage of the U.S. workforce that is unionized, rates fell from 32 percent in 1950 to 13 percent in 2005 (Panagopoulos & Francia, 2008). These authors report the results of large national surveys (Gallup and Pew) that show some interesting trends in attitudes. The majority of respondents approved of unions overall (60%), but the majority also did not believe that government workers should be allowed to strike (70%). An additional question revealed that respondents would initially tend to side with a union against "a company." These data suggest that public opinion supports the need for unions to protect workers' rights in the private sector (where there exists very little union representation).

Employment Law Related to Unionization

Congress has enacted several laws over the past century to try to find a good balance between union rights and employer rights to avoid abuses from either side. A brief review of these laws follows.

Sherman Antitrust Act (1890). The purpose of this legislation was to ensure that businesses could not create monopolies, and thereby restrict free trade. However, pressure from employers on the courts resulted in this being used to limit union efforts under the guise that unions monopolized labor resources.

Clayton Act (1914). This act clarified that the Sherman Antitrust Act was not intended to restrict unionization. Thus, unions were exempt from its coverage.

Norris-LaGuardia Act (1932). This act established the rights of labor unions to organize and to strike, and limited the use of court injunctions in labor disputes. It also made illegal the use of **yellow dog contracts**. These had been used as an employer tactic to block unions by making new employees agree that they did not (and would not) join a union.

National Labor Relations Act (1935), aka the Wagner Act. This was known as the "Labor Bill of Rights." It protected concerted activities during collective bargaining. Section 7 of the act acknowledged the rights of employees to unionize and seek collective bargaining. The following section of the NLRA made it illegal for employers to interfere with this process in any way. Another important provision was the establishment of the National Labor Relations Board (NLRB). This is a bipartisan committee charged with enforcing the provisions of the NLRA, including investigating claims of unfair labor practices, and monitoring union elections.

Labor Management Relations Act (1947), aka the Taft-Hartley Act. Over a decade later, Congress enacted legislation aimed at restraining union power. This act identified Unfair Labor Practices (ULPs) on the part of unions. Examples include **featherbedding** and **hot cargo agreements**. Featherbedding required that union members be paid wages whether or not their work was actually needed. Clearly, this is not in the best interest of the organization and is, in fact, a type of extortion. In a "hot cargo agreement," union members would refuse to handle or process any work done by a company that was not unionized. The LMRA (1947) also provided government the power to issue an injunction against a strike if it threatened national interests.

Labor Management Reporting and Disclosure Act (1959), aka the Landrum-Griffin Act. This act was initiated on the grounds that union leaders had misappropriated funds, and that union representatives had behaved in a violent manner. To address this issue, this legislation enforced greater accountability for unions, particularly in terms of financial matters. The act mandated an annual financial report to the Department of Labor, and included a union member bill of rights such as free speech and periodic elections for union officials.

The Process of Unionizing

The legislation reviewed above indicates the importance of finding a balance between employer and worker rights. Unions are known for advocating for worker rights in a manner that is more powerful than could be achieved by individuals. There are a formal set of steps involved in the process of unionization. These are described briefly below.

1. Employee Interest in Collective Bargaining. There are many reasons that workers may become interested in unionization. They may want a more unified voice in workplace negotiations, they may find management personnel or practices to be unfair, or they may compare their work environment unfavorably with others who have unionized. Research has shown that economic conditions do predict unionization, but so do perceptions

Yellow dog contract = an illegal employer tactic of requiring employees to promise not to join a labor union

Featherbedding = an unlawful practice in which a labor union required wage payments to its members even if their work was not needed

Hot cargo agreements = an unlawful practice in which members of a labor union refuse to handle goods produced by a nonunionized company

of workplace justice and social identification with the union (e.g., Blader, 2007).

2. Authorization Cards. Once sufficient interest has been generated, union organizers will send **authorization cards** to employees. There is support to proceed with a union election if 30 percent or more of the eligible employees sign the authorization cards. Essentially, the authorization card contains a written, signed, and dated verification of the employee's support of a union election.

3. Request for Recognition. At this point, a union organizer will issue a formal written statement to the organization, requesting that the union be recognized as the bargaining agent for employees. Often, however, the organization does not recognize the union at this stage and ensures a campaign and formal certification vote.

4. Petitioning the National Labor Relations Board. If voluntary recognition is not given, the NLRB will be petitioned to authorize an election. The board is also responsible for ensuring that the signatures on the authorization cards are sufficient and valid.

5. Preelection Conference. The NLRB will then schedule a meeting with representatives from the employer and the union, clarifying issues such as who will be in the collective bargaining unit, and the time and location of the election. The employer must provide the union organizers with an **Excelsior list**, which is a list of the names and addresses of all employees who are eligible to vote in the election. This list must be provided by the organization within seven days of the NLRB scheduling the election date.

6. Campaign. Both sides will initiate campaigns to influence voters. Legitimate campaigning activities involve communication about the advantages and disadvantages of forming a union, such as that done via meetings or leafleting. Another major tactic during this time is the use of picketing, in which a group of employees march with signs, slogans, or handouts at the entrance to the organization. The media may also be invited to cover the campaign to garner public support for either side. During this time, representatives of both sides must avoid Unfair Labor Practices that may interfere with the legitimacy of the process. This includes anything that may be construed as coercion or bribery.

7. Union Election. At the specified time and location, the election will be held. The outcome of the election is determined by a simple majority of those who vote.

Actions of the Organization during a Unionizing Drive

Organizations may perceive major drawbacks to having a unionized workforce. These include the potential for slowing down work changes and processes (such as those suggested by job design implementations) and an inability to continue with employment-at-will. During collective bargaining, unions typically fight

---

Authorization cards = a signed document that indicates whether an employee is interested in being represented by a labor unions

Excelsior list = a list providing the names and addresses of all employees who are eligible; this list must be provided by the employer to the organizing union

Regardless of whether the union is certified (voted in) or not, the NLRB will typically put a **statutory bar** in effect for the year following the vote. The assumption is that the vote does, in fact, represent the majority opinion and too many elections will lead to business instability.

against changes to performance management practices and negotiate aggressively for higher pay for workers.

If interest in a union begins, management is completely within its rights to publicize and distribute a clear rationale for why the workplace is better without the union. It is important, however, to follow the **TIPS guideline** to avoid charges of unfair labor practices (and associated investigations). These letters represent activities that management *must not* engage in, including **T**hreaten, **I**nterrogate, **P**romise, or **S**py on employees or union organizers.

Another approach is to graciously accept and welcome the union. Research has shown that job satisfaction, supervisory effectiveness, occupational identity, and community support all benefit from employee commitment to both the organization and to the union (Carson, Carson, Birkenmeier, & Toma, 2006). This research warns against pressuring employees to choose either the union or the organization.

Union Security Clauses

Unions are stronger when they have a large membership. This increases union dues and creates a stronger presence in the organization and in the community. However, it is unwise to alienate those who would rather not join and/or pay dues. Some states have **Right to Work** laws, which allow people to join the workplace but do not require them to join the union.

The Bargaining Unit and Collective Bargaining

Unions engage in collective bargaining to establish the working conditions for employees in a bargaining unit. The bargaining unit is based on geographical proximity, the extent to which the workforce is already organized, and work interests.

Collective bargaining is the process of negotiating an employment contract. Negotiation will be discussed in greater detail in the following section. Mandatory subjects during collective bargaining include wages, work hours, benefits, performance management, grievances, and union security. Permissible subjects are those that are agreed upon by both parties, including organizational restructuring, hiring procedures, and modifications to benefits. Unlawful subjects include anything not formally agreed upon by both parties, and any type of collusion among the parties.

Labor Relations Breakdowns

At times management personnel and union representatives are unable to agree about fundamental aspects of working conditions. When this happens, the organization may engage in a **lockout**, which means that union members are kept from the premises and therefore restricted from working. Conversely, union members may refuse to engage in working through various means such as a **strike**.

Some different approaches to union membership include:

- Open shop clause = employees may choose whether or not to join the union; the only legal union security clause in "right to work" states.

- Agency shop clause = employees may choose whether or not to join the union, but must pay union dues regardless.

- Maintenance membership clause = those who join the union are required to pay union dues for the duration of the employment contract.

- Union shop clause = employees must join the union, although they have 30 days to do so.

- Closed shop clause = an employer may only hire those who belong to the union; made illegal by Taft-Hartley.

There are two different types of legal strikes: those over unfair labor practices and those over economic matters. Economic strikes are conducted to obtain a concession during collective bargaining. A major activity during a strike is organizational **picketing**, in which union members walk or stand near the organization with signs, slogans, and chants about the labor dispute. In some cases, union members may engage in a **sympathy strike**, which means that they choose not to cross a picket line in support for striking workers.

Sympathy strike = an expansion of the impact of a strike by refusing to cross the picket line of another union engaged in a strike

Negotiation

Negotiation is the process of attempting to find a mutually agreeable solution to the needs of two or more parties. Research in workplace psychology has recognized the complex nature of negotiation (e.g., Gelfand, Fulmer, & Severance, 2011). It involves the emotions, thoughts, and behaviors of individuals, as well as group level processes such as power struggles, politics, and social influence. It also occurs in broader organizational and national cultures. This overview will cover some basic terms in the negotiation process and possible stances that parties can take in engaging in negotiation.

In negotiation, two (or more) sides communicate to make a deal. Negotiations are typically characterized by six features (Gelfand et al., 2011).

1. The negotiating parties perceive a conflict of interest.

2. Parties are in communication.

3. Compromises are possible.

4. Parties exchange offers and counteroffers.

5. Negotiated outcomes are determined together.

6. There are mixed motives: (a) to further self-interests; and (b) cooperate to reach a solution.

Settlement range = a negotiation outcome that is less than the target point but acceptable

In approaching a negotiation, each side has a **target point**, which is what they are trying to promote during the discussion. Below the target point is an acceptable **settlement range**, which represents something less than ideal but still appealing enough to agree to. Below the settlement range is an area of **impasse**, in which proposals will be deemed unacceptable. Impasse represents negotiation breakdowns.

Impasse = a negotiation breakdown in which the parties cannot collaborate to reach a mutually agreeable solution

Negotiation Mind-Sets

The mind-sets that the parties in negotiation adopt can direct the entire process. These stances can be a function of personality, an ingroup-outgroup mentality, or expectations about the other party.

Distributive bargaining = a type of negotiation that is based on a "win-lose" mentality

Distributive Bargaining. The mindset of **distributive bargaining** is one of "win-lose." Another name for this approach is Positional Bargaining, which emphasizes an adversarial approach to the process. A negotiator with this mind-set believes that the resources under discussion are limited, and must be distributed between sides. This implies that any amount that one side achieves will result in less for the other side.

Integrative Bargaining. The mind-set here is "win-win." In this mindset, if both parties work together, it is possible to ensure that the needs of both parties are met. Related to **integrative bargaining** is the notion of interest-based negotiations. Here, the approach is to recognize that each side has common interests and to emphasize these goals. Other issues may be less important and/or easier to compromise about if the fundamental mutual interests can be agreed upon.

Negotiation Research

Workplace psychology has documented the role that negotiation plays in labor relations. Research has demonstrated that labor management cooperation can result in beneficial outcomes for both management and union employees (e.g., Ospina & Yaroni, 2003). These authors describe how cooperation emerges when there is free information flow and a mutual desire to improve the organization's functioning. Other research has described how interest-based negotiations were used to reach agreement during large-scale collective bargaining (McKersie, Sharpe, Kochan, Eaton, Strauss, & Morgenstern, 2008).

Research has shown that negotiators are prone to make the same types of cognitive errors in perception and decision making introduced in Chapter 2. Negotiators are often influenced by the "framing" created by an initial offer or by a preconceived notion. These create an anchoring from which the negotiator will be hesitant to deviate. Research has demonstrated an interesting interaction between personality and negotiation mind-set (Dimotakis, Conlon, & Ilies, 2012). Using the Big Five personality model, these researchers found that agreeable people functioned better within integrative bargaining, whereas disagreeable people achieved better outcomes in distributive bargaining. Other research has demonstrated that negotiators are less likely to cooperate on values-based issues than interest-based issues (e.g., Wade-Benzoni, 2002).

Thus far, this chapter has focused on basic working conditions and the dynamic between the rights of employees and employers. Special attention was given to the process of unionization and collective bargaining. Collective bargaining involves a broader process of negotiation, which can sometimes break down if the interested parties cannot agree on a mutual solution. In this case, conflict has occurred. Due to the long-evolving nature of union/management conflict in the United States, some of the parameters of conflict resolution have been established with congressional and common law. In organizations that are not unionized, however, it is important to think ahead about how to manage conflict at the workplace.

Addressing Conflict

Psychologists define **conflict** as a state when an individual or group is deprived of a desired state due to another person or group (e.g., De Dreu, 2011). There are several categories of conflicts in organizations.

- Relationship conflicts. This category can emerge from personality clashes, romantic relationships gone awry, and gossip. It can also be created if group members compete for resources or over a certain role in the group. Research has also documented relationship conflicts that emerge over workplace diversity and the tendency to engage in in-group/out-group behavior (e.g., van Knippenberg, De Dreu, & Homan, 2004).

- Task conflicts. This type can emerge when there are limited resources such as equipment, staffing, or space. Group members may disagree about who has access to these resources, or how a task should best be accomplished. This is likely to occur if training has been inadequate, and people accomplish the task in different, arbitrary ways.

- Process conflicts. This category of conflict is about the flow of work, communication, and the exchange of work outcomes in interdependent environments. This type of conflict is most likely to occur in disagreements about work boundaries and delegation of tasks. Social psychology has documented the extent to which people can engage in non-cooperative behavior in order to achieve personal outcomes (e.g., Weber, Kopelman, & Messick, 2004).

At first glance, conflict is seen in strictly negative terms, such as interfering with work performance and team cohesiveness (Raver & Barling, 2008). Workplace psychology acknowledges that conflict can be beneficial for organizations in certain situations. For instance, conflict that is constructive in nature and accepted as part of the organizational culture can be used to challenge assumptions and foster innovation.

However, conflict can be detrimental. It can interfere with work functioning and even lead to violence. In fact, it is well known in psychology that frustration of goals can lead to aggression (the well-researched frustration-aggression effect; Dollard, Doob, Miller, Mowrer, & Sears, 1939). If left alone, conflict has a tendency to escalate when employees perceive that someone else is trying to harm them (Baron, 1997) or become involved in expanded power struggles (Winter, 2007). When these situations occur, it is best to follow a formal process of dispute resolution. The dispute should be handled like any workplace investigation (as described in Chapter 6). Many organizations have opted for formalizing the dispute resolution process.

Organizational Dispute Resolution

Given the potential disruption of conflict, many organizations have implemented formal systems for handling complaints, grievances, and allegations of misconduct (Olson-Buchanan & Boswell, 2008). **Organizational Dispute Resolution** (ODR) may take several different forms, with varying levels of formality and in terms of the number of people who are involved. For instance, many organizations have reporting systems that initially proceed through the chain of immediate supervision. If necessary, the dispute may require formal investigations and filing associated paperwork with Human Resources.

At times the standard organizational procedures are not sufficient to resolve the conflict, and a third party must be brought in to manage and resolve it. This is sometimes referred to as **Alternative Dispute Resolution** (ADR), because it is an alternative to the typical, less formal routes that can be handled by a manager. These approaches include conciliation, mediation, or arbitration. Each approach follows a process of fact finding and suggestions for resolution. They differ in that only in arbitration is the proposed resolution legally binding.

Conciliation. **Conciliation** is the least formal approach and has a goal of smoothing over conflict. It starts with the designation of a neutral person conducting a fact-finding mission. Some organizations have a designated party who hears and attempts to resolve conflict; this person is often known as an **ombudsman** or **ombudsperson**. Another attempt to use neutral third-party dispute resolution with organizational members is the **peer review panel**. This panel consists of managerial and nonmanagerial staff who listen to both sides of the conflict and make recommendations.

Mediation and Arbitration. There are circumstances, however, where the conflict cannot be resolved through communications between the two parties. This may require bringing in a third party from outside the organization to manage the conflict. This process may include **mediation** or **arbitration**. The difference between these approaches is that, whereas a mediator will hear all the evidence and recommend a solution, the arbitrator will hear all evidence and reach a solution that is legally binding.

Regardless of the approach to conflict resolution, there are several tactics that will improve the likelihood of resolving the dispute. It is important that the third party used in Alternative Dispute Resolution is, in fact, neutral (meaning that he or she has no vested interest in the outcome). Another necessary feature is to conduct an honest investigation to gather the relevant facts, and to organize these facts in a way that minimizes distractions. The neutral party should employ **active listening** to ensure correct representation of each side of the conflict. During discussions, weight should be given to facts that can be supported with documentation. Another approach to bring each side together is known as **constructive confrontation**. In this approach, a cooperative mind-set is achieved by agreeing on smaller topics before focusing on the bigger issues. The neutral party should be flexible and creative in finding a resolution that is agreeable to both parties in the conflict.

The chapter thus far has reviewed the nature of the working relationship. This process can be viewed in terms of an exchange relationship, in which the employee gives their time, effort, and skills in exchange for outcomes from the organization. These outcomes include wages and benefits, and the relationship may be strengthened by the use of additional measures to encourage perceptions of fairness and involvement. Some organizational strategies to improve employee relations are reviewed below.

Employee Relations

As mentioned throughout the textbook, workplace psychology acknowledges the exchange relationship that exists between employees and employers. Employee relations are concerned with maintaining a positive exchange relationship and fostering an organizational culture of trust. Much of the work surrounding employee relations concerns performance management (covered in Chapter 2) and employee rewards (Chapter 5).

Conciliation = a type of dispute resolution strategy based on meetings with peers with a goal to smoothing the conflict

Peer review panel = an attempt at conflict resolution based on meetings, often with a group of coworkers

Active listening = a communication technique of reflecting meaning back to a speaker to ensure that understanding has taken place

Constructive confrontation = a resolution strategy to agree on smaller items of dispute prior to addressing the more complex items

There are several additional tactics for building positive employee relations. Some specific techniques to address employee relations that have not been discussed elsewhere in this book are: (a) recognition and appreciation programs; (b) raising employee involvement; and (c) addressing employee attitudes such as job satisfaction and organizational commitment. A review of these ideas follows.

Employee relations strategies must be carefully implemented. Workplace psychology has documented the **perils of participation**. This describes a net negative effect on employee relations if input is sought from employees, but then ignored. As with all applied topics in workplace psychology, employee relations programs should fit specifically with strategic objectives. Each program should be associated with detailed goals that can be evaluated in terms of their effectiveness and managed by people who will be held accountable for the program results.

Recognition and Appreciation Programs

To show appreciation for employees, the organization may provide formal recognition programs and company appreciation events. These programs can communicate that employees are personally regarded, and that the workplace has a social element as well as a productive one.

A survey conducted by SHRM (2011) revealed the extent to which organizations invest in various appreciation programs. The most frequently used approaches were holiday parties, milestone gifts (such as birthdays or years of service), and company picnics.

Other Benefits

	Offer the benefit	Offer the benefit but have plans to reduce or eliminate the benefit within the next 12 months	Do not offer the benefit but have plans to do so within the next 12 months
Holiday parties	79%	10%	1%
Milestone rewards[A]	68%	6%	1%
Company picnic	56%	9%	2%
Noncash companywide performance awards[B]	47%	6%	1%
Community volunteer programs	40%	5%	1%
Discount ticket services[C]	37%	6%	*
Company-purchased tickets[C]	32%	14%	*
Take your child to work day	25%	0%	*
Pets at work	6%	0%	0%
Take your parent to work day	1%	0%	*
Take your pet to work day[D]	1%	0%	*

(n = 532)
* Less than 1%
A For example, lunch on birthday, gift certificate recognizing years of service, etc.
B For example, gift certificate, extra day off.
C For example, sporting events, cultural events, theme parks, etc.
D Once a year as opposed to pets at work generally.
Source: 2010 Employee Benefits (SHRM, 2010)

(Source: http://www.shrm.org/Research/SurveyFindings/Articles/Documents/10-0280%20Employee%20Benefits%20Survey%20Report_Tables.pdf)

Employee Involvement Techniques

Another approach to raise employee relations consists of attempts to increase employee involvement with work processes. Approaches to job design such as the Job Characteristics Model (covered in Chapter 5) can be used to raise employee involvement. Other employee involvement techniques include brown-bag lunches with formal or informal employee presentations. These provide a forum for employees to be publicly accountable for their work and stay more connected with each other.

Some approaches to employee involvement can be addressed through supervision and leadership. Communication can be raised through a healthy performance management system, wherein managers provide ongoing feedback (described in After-Event Reviews, Chapter 2). This is also related to a management philosophy called **management by walking around** (MBWA), wherein managers are directly involved and available during daily work. This is similar to the concept of adaptive leadership (Yukl & Mahsud, 2010), in which an effective leader is one who actively solicits employee input about role expectations.

In addition, employees often have good ideas about improving work processes or services. To tap into this resource, it is necessary to gather information through focus groups or employee surveys. Another way to gather this information is to include formal or informal employee suggestion programs. A 2011 survey of 745 Human Resources professionals (SHRM, 2011) revealed that 80 percent of companies had such programs.

Other survey findings revealed that:

- 57 percent of persons surveyed make workplace suggestions regularly; 27 percent claim to make more than 20 suggestions annually.

- 30 percent of employees made more than 10 suggestions but fewer than 20.

- Women were more likely than men to make more than 10 workplace suggestions annually (61 percent and 46 percent, respectively).

- Workers age 55 and older were more likely than those age 25 to 34 to make 10 or more suggestions (76 percent and 51 percent, respectively).

- Salespeople and HR professionals tend to make the most suggestions (50 percent and 28 percent, respectively).

- Management and corporate executives were most likely to offer more than 20 suggestions per year.

- 6 percent offer no workplace suggestions.

- The number of suggestions made does not vary by company size

(Source: http://www.shrm.org/Publications/HRNews/Pages/AnyoneListening.aspx)

To avoid the perils of participation, it is important to dedicate resources to using employee input. A plan should be put in place to summarize the results and tell employees how those results will be used.

Attitudes that have been widely researched in workplace psychology include organizational commitment and job satisfaction. These employee attitudes are important because they translate into desirable outcomes such as performance (Judge, Thoresen, Bono, & Patton, 2001) and ethical behavior (Kish-Gephart, Harrison, & Trevino, 2010).

Organizational commitment is an attitude that addresses the extent to which the employee intends to remain with the organization. Low organizational commitment is directly related to employee turnover. Research has supported three main types of organizational commitment (Meyer & Allen, 1997):

1. Affective commitment = the extent to which the employee identifies with organizational values and cares about the organization's success

2. Normative commitment = the extent to which the employee feels obligated to stay with the organization because of the expectations of others (e.g., coworkers, family members)

3. Continuance commitment = the extent to which the employee plans to stay with the organization because there are not many alternatives

When unemployment is high, continuance commitment becomes more important to employees in terms of predicting whether they plan to look for other employment. Although the specific reasons were not assessed, a survey (SHRM, 2010) revealed that 70 percent of employees were unlikely or very unlikely to seek alternative employment.

Likelihood of Looking for a Job in 2010 Outside of Current Organization

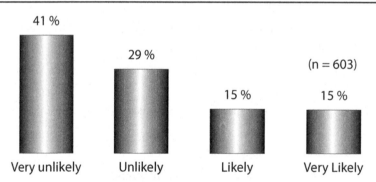

Source: 2010 Employee Job Satisfaction (SHRM, 2010)

(Source: http://www.shrm.org/Research/SurveyFindings/Articles/Documents/10-0252_Figures.pdf)

Job satisfaction is defined as the affective reaction to the job and the extent to which it allows for the fulfillment of important values. Job satisfaction is often considered in terms of facets such as: pay, coworkers, supervision, opportunities for promotion, and the job itself. Job satisfaction is one of the most often studied variables in workplace psychology in academic settings (Cascio, 2008).

An interesting contrast exists between the science and practice of workplace psychology regarding job satisfaction. Whereas academic studies of job satisfaction virtually always use validated surveys (such as the Job Descriptive Index or the Minnesota Satisfaction Questionnaire), practitioners often use other sources of information to gain information about job satisfaction. Note that most of this information is gained during exit interviews, followed by speaking directly to employees, either directly or during performance evaluations. Although formal surveys and focus groups are used by organizations, other "proxy" measures such as turnover data, word of mouth, and complaints are also used.

How Organizations Determine Employee Job Satisfaction

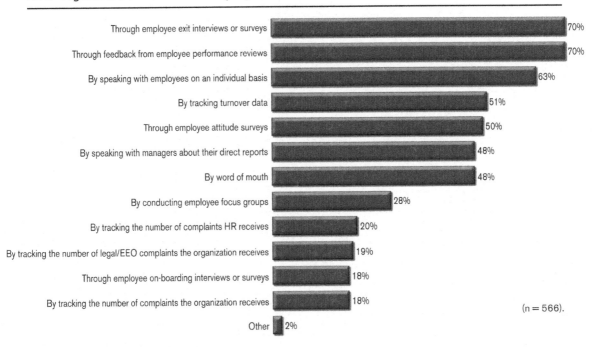

Through employee exit interviews or surveys	70%
Through feedback from employee performance reviews	70%
By speaking with employees on an individual basis	63%
By tracking turnover data	51%
Through employee attitude surveys	50%
By speaking with managers about their direct reports	48%
By word of mouth	48%
By conducting employee focus groups	28%
By tracking the number of complaints HR receives	20%
By tracking the number of legal/EEO complaints the organization receives	19%
Through employee on-boarding interviews or surveys	18%
By tracking the number of complaints the organization receives	18%
Other	2%

(n = 566).

Note: Percentages do not total 100% due to multiple response options.
Source: 2010 Employee Job Satisfaction (SHRM, 2010)

(Source: http://www.shrm.org/Research/SurveyFindings/Articles/Documents/10-0252_Figures.pdf)

The review of employee relations has presented a brief overview of some ideas related to employee recognition, involvement, and attitudes. In fact, most of the material in this textbook can be used to enhance employee relations. To think about this topic in a general sense, imagine that the organization is running a campaign to be a desirable place to work. Any of the HR practices that value employees will be perceived positively if managed correctly. Organizations must be fair in their development and implementation of HR policies and be creative in their valuation of the hard work that employees put forth.

Putting it All Together

Considering the material in this chapter, here are a few "take-home" ideas for labor relations and employee relations.

- The nature of the employment relationship has evolved over time, creating both legislation and common-law doctrine to protect the interests of employees and employers. These include at-will employment, good faith and fair dealing, and due process.

- Protections for employers include employee diligence, nondisclosure agreements, noncompete agreements, and mandatory arbitration.

- Protections for employees include measures against wrongful termination, the WARN Act, dealing with sexual harassment, and the Family and Medical Leave Act.

- Employee unions are groups who form for the purposes of bargaining about working conditions. There is a large amount of employment law related to union activities.

- Employers are fully entitled to discourage union formation through the presentation of information and persuasion, but they may not threaten or bribe employees.

- Bargaining about working conditions is a subset of the topic of negotiation. Negotiation research has identified different mind-sets for bargaining representatives, which will direct their behaviors.

- Negotiators are also prone to typical judgment errors identified in cognitive and social psychology.

- Workplace conflict can be resolved smoothly if the organization has a proactive resolution strategy in place.

- If left alone, workplace conflict can lead to a destructive environment.

- Employee relations strategies can be used to create a working atmosphere that is based on shared appreciation and trust.

- Organizations should dedicate resources to their employee relations strategies; otherwise these strategies are unlikely to have the intended impact.

Spotlight On Research

Gender and Negotiation

Introduction

Negotiation = a fundamental bargaining process in which two parties attempt to agree upon an outcome.

Research has suggested that men typically receive better outcomes.

"Double whammy" for women: If women conform to sex role expectations (e.g., accommodating), they will negotiate less. If they use an assertive negotiating style, they violate sex role expectations and suffer negative social costs (e.g., exclusion).

The gender dyad must be examined, as it creates expectations of both the self and other during negotiations.

Research Question:

Are there gender differences in persistence in negotiation among different gender dyads?

Method

Participants were recruited through a research website and offered $5 for participation.

Task: Participants took part in a negotiation simulation for a purchase price on a four-bedroom home and were given a report on the amenities and comparable sales. They were provided with a target price as well as a "walk-away" number.

A research confederate/negotiator asked for an offer and then countered with one $25,000 away, and was unwilling to budge.

The negotiation concluded when the participant gave up.

Negotiation persistence was rated on a seven-point scale. *"I stood my ground"; "I compromised easily"; "I was as accommodating as possible."*

Results

There were gender differences in negotiation persistence and strategies.

There was an interaction such that the negotiation process depended on the gender dyad (see graph).

Discussion: Directions for Future Research

Studies should assess real-world negotiation strategies.

Future research should include nonverbal behavior and its effectiveness as a function of gender.

Bowles, H., & Flynn, F. (2010). Gender and persistence in negotiation: A dyadic perspective. Academy of Management Journal, 53(4), 769–787.

Participant Summary

☐ *Undergraduate Students (N=77)*

☐ *48 women; 29 men*

☐ *Average age = 20 years*

☐ *Asian (37%), White (28%), Hispanic (18%), Black (10%)*

Results

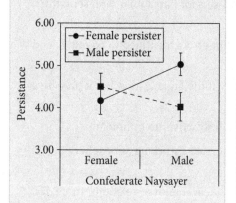

Chapter Exercises

Science: Replication and Extension

<u>Instructions:</u> Consider the Spotlight on Research summarized in this chapter. Address each of the following items by using two or three complete sentences on a separate sheet of paper.

1. What do you think were the strengths of this research?

2. What were the weaknesses?

    PROPOSAL: If you conducted a follow-up study, what you would include in terms of:

3. A sample of participants (whom would you study?)

4. Variables you would include and hypotheses you would make (what would you test, specifically?)

Sequencing: Identify the Correct Order

<u>Instructions:</u> Consider the stages presented below. Label each one with a number (next to the stage), and describe why each is important on a separate sheet of paper.

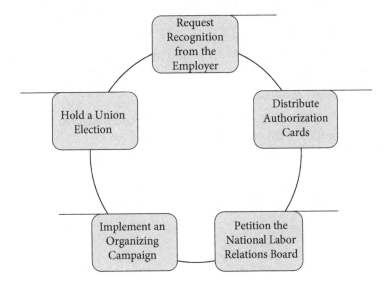

Short Essay Questions

<u>Instructions</u>: Please address the following essay questions briefly, writing in complete sentences on a separate sheet of paper.

1. Explain any three terms that relate to employment protections for <u>employees</u>.

2. Explain any three terms that relate to employment protections for <u>employers</u>.

3. Describe the sequence of steps used in the process of unionization.

4. Define any three types of Unfair Labor Practices (union or employer).

5. Describe three types of dispute resolution strategies.

6. Define negotiation and the different mind-sets that can be brought to it.

Topics: Relate to Your Own Life

<u>Instructions</u>: Choose one of the topics below to write about a related experience from your own life. Use the space at the bottom of the page to document your experiences and opinions.

- Employer and Employee Work Protections. Do you think there is a good balance between the rights of workers and employers in the United States? Why or why not?

- Unionization. Do you have any experiences working in a union environment, or does anyone from your family? Would you describe the union as having a positive or negative presence, both, or neither?

- What approaches, if any, does your workplace use to build positive employee relations?

- Workplace conflict. Describe your most recent encounter with conflict at work.

    If directly involved:

    What started the conflict? Was it at the individual or group level? What did you do to resolve it, and was your attempt successful?

    If not directly involved:

    How did it affect your work? Was it appropriately handled in terms of organizational policy and communication? Why or why not?

Index

References and Recommended Readings

Barsade, S., & Gibson, D. (2007). Why does affect matter in organizations? *Academy of Management Perspectives, 21*(1), 36–59.

Blader, S. L. (2007). What leads organizational members to collectivize? Injustice and identification as precursors of union certification. *Organization Science, 18*(1), 108–126.

Berdahl, J. L., & Raver, J. L. (2011). Sexual harassment. In S. Zedeck, S. Zedeck (Eds.), *APA handbook of industrial and organizational psychology, vol. 3: Maintaining, expanding, and contracting the organization* (pp. 641–669). Washington, DC: American Psychological Association.

Berdahl, J. L. (2007). Harassment based on sex: Protecting social status in the context of gender hierarchy. *Academy of Management Review, 32*(2), 641–658.

Carson, P., Carson, K. D., Birkenmeier, B., & Toma, A. G. (2006). Looking for loyalty in all the wrong places: A study of union and organization commitments. *Public Personnel Management, 35*(2), 137–151.

Collings, D. (2008). Multinational corporations and industrial relations research: A road less travelled. *International Journal of Management Reviews, 10*(2), 173–193.

Cortina, L. M., & Wasti, S. (2005). Profiles in Coping: Responses to Sexual Harassment across Persons, Organizations, and Cultures. *Journal of Applied Psychology, 90*(1), 182–192.

Cropanzano, R., Bowen, D., & Gilliland, S. (2007). The management of organizational justice. *The Academy of Management Perspectives, 21*(4), 34–48.

De Dreu, C. (2011). Conflict at work: Basic principles and applied issues. In S. Zedeck, S. Zedeck (Eds.), *APA handbook of industrial and organizational psychology, vol. 3: Maintaining, expanding, and contracting the organization* (pp. 461–494). Washington, DC: American Psychological Association.

Dimotakis, N., Conlon, D. E., & Ilies, R. (2012). The mind and heart (literally) of the negotiator: Personality and contextual determinants of experiential reactions and economic outcomes in negotiation. *Journal of Applied Psychology, 97*(1), 183–193.

Dollard, J., Doob, L., Miller, N. E., Mowrer, O. H., & Sears, R. R. (1939). *Frustration and aggression.* New Haven: Yale University Press.

Equal Employment Opportunity Commission. (2005). *Sexual harassment charges: EEOC & fair employment practice agencies combined: FY 1992–FY 2004.* Available at: http://www.eeoc.gov/stats/harassment.html

Equal Employment Opportunity Commission. (2005). *Trends in harassment charges filed with the EEOC.* Available at: http://www.eeoc.gov/stats/harassment.html

Gelfand, M. J., Fulmer, C., & Severance, L. (2011). The psychology of negotiation and mediation. In S. Zedeck, S. Zedeck (Eds.), *APA handbook of industrial and organizational psychology, vol. 3: Maintaining, expanding, and contracting the organization* (pp. 495–554). Washington, DC: American Psychological Association.

Ilies, R., Hauserman, N., Schwochau, S., & Stibal, J. (2003). Reported incidence rates of work-related sexual harassment in the United States: Using meta-analysis to explain reported rate disparities. *Personnel Psychology*, *56*(3), 607–631.

Judge, T. A., Thoresen, C. J., Bono, J. E., & Patton, G. K. (2001). The job satisfaction-job performance relationship: A qualitative and quantitative review. *Psychological Bulletin, 127*, 376–407.

Kish-Gephart, J. J., Harrison, D. A., & Trevino, L. K. (2010). Bad apples, bad cases, and bad barrels: Meta-analytic evidence about sources of unethical decisions at work. *Journal of Applied Psychology, 95*, 1–31.

McKersie, R., Sharpe, T., Kochan, T., Eaton, A., Strauss, G., & Morgenstern, M. (2008). Bargaining theory meets interest-based negotiations: A case study. *Industrial Relations: A Journal of Economy & Society,47*, 66–96.

Meyer, J. P., & Allen, N. J. (1997). *Commitment in the workplace: Theory, research, and application.* Thousand Oaks, CA: Sage.

Olson-Buchanan, J. B., & Boswell, W. R. (2008). Organizational dispute resolution systems. In C. W. De Dreu, M. J. Gelfand (Eds.), *The psychology of conflict and conflict management in organizations* (pp. 321–352). New York: Taylor & Francis Group/Lawrence Erlbaum Associates.

Ospina, S., & Yaroni, A. (2003). Understanding cooperative behavior in labor management cooperation: A theory-building exercise. *Public Administration Review, 63*, 455–471.

Panagopoulos, C., & Francia, P. L. (2008). The polls—trends: Labor unions in the United States. *Public Opinion Quarterly, 72*(1), 134–159.

Rau, B. L. (2012). The diffusion of HR practices in unions. *Human Resource Management Review, 22*, 27–42.

Raver, J. L., & Barling, J. (2008). Workplace aggression and conflict: Constructs, commonalities, and challenges for future inquiry. In C. W. De

Dreu, M. J. Gelfand (Eds.), *The psychology of conflict and conflict management in organizations* (pp. 211–244). New York: Taylor & Francis Group/Lawrence Erlbaum Associates.

United States Department of Justice, Special Report on Workplace Violence, 1993–2009. http://www.bjs.gov/index.

van Knippenberg, D., De Dreu, C. W., & Homan, A. C. (2004). Work Group Diversity and Group Performance: An Integrative Model and Research Agenda. *Journal of Applied Psychology, 89*, 1008–1022.

Wade-Benzoni, R. (2002). Barriers to resolution in ideologically based negotiations: The role of values and institutions. *Academy of Management Review, 27*, 41–57.

Weber, J., Kopelman, S., & Messick, D. M. (2004). A conceptual review of decision making in social dilemmas: Applying a logic of appropriateness. *Personality and Social Psychology Review, 8*, 281–307.

Western, B., & Rosenfeld, J. (2011). Unions, norms, and the rise in U.S. wage inequality. *American Sociological Review, 76*, 513–537.

Whitman, D., Van Rooy, D., & Viswesvaran, C. (2010). Satisfaction, citizenship behaviors, and performance in work units: A meta-analysis of collective construct relations. *Personnel Psychology,63*, 41–81.

Willness, C. R., Steel, P., & Lee, K. (2007). A meta-analysis of the antecedents and consequences of workplace sexual harassment. *Personnel Psychology, 60*, 127–162.

Yukl, G., & Mahsud, R. (2010). Why flexible and adaptive leadership is essential. *Consulting Psychology Journal: Practice and Research, 62*, 81–93.

Glossary

360 Degree feedback = collecting subjective appraisal data from a variety of different raters

4/5th rule = the selection rate for a protected class must be at least 80% that of a comparison group

Active listening = a communication technique of reflecting meaning back to a speaker to ensure that understanding has taken place

Adverse impact = a result of a selection procedure, even if inadvertent, that results in disproportionate exclusion of members of a protected class

Adverse treatment = treating people differently as a function of their membership in a protected class

Affirmative Action Programs = an emphasis of casting a broad net during recruitment to have a workforce that is representative of the local labor pool

After Event Review = providing immediate feedback about performance events on the job

Alternative Dispute Resolution (ADR) = a formal approach to resolving conflict by bringing in a neutral third party for fact-finding and proposing solutions

Anchoring = a cognitive effect during rating in which some preliminary information is used to base subsequent ratings

Andragogy = the study of how learning best occurs for adults

Annotated bibliography = a document that contains a summary of information and referencing material for all sources used during a literature review

anonymity = 'without names'; no names are ever collected

Anxiety = a distressing psychological state characterized by a pervasive sense of dread and unease

APA-Style = the technical writing style requirements for publications in the field of psychology

Applicants = people who are interested in being considered for employment

Arbitration = a dispute resolution tactic in which a neutral third party gathers relevant information from all viewpoints and makes a legally binding decision

Assessment center = a series of job-related activities and simulations that can be used for employee development or personnel selection

At-will employment = either the employer or employee may end the working relationship for any lawful reason

Authorization cards = a signed document that indicates whether an employee is interested in being represented by a labor union

Automatic stage, or automaticity = a cognitive stage of learning related to task expertise

Automation= use of robotics, computers, and other machinery to provide goods and services

Balanced Scorecard = a performance management system that incorporates financial and nonfinancial metrics

Behavior Description Interview = the inclusion of questions that ask for specific behavioral examples of past performance instances

Behavioral psychology = a branch of psychology that emphasizes observable behaviors as a function of the environment

Behaviorally Anchored Rating Scale = a rating format that provides detailed descriptions of all ratings on a performance dimension

Big Five = a model of personality traits that includes Emotional Stability, Openness to Experience, Extraversion, Conscientiousness, and Agreeableness

Blind research = a methodological feature in which any person handling the data is unaware of the purpose of the study or its hypotheses

Bullying =the deliberate use of intimidation tactics to make another person feel threatened or vulnerable

Burnout = a type of job strain characterized by extreme exhaustion, depersonalization, and cynicism

Catastrophic thinking = Exaggerating a problem by imagining the worst-case scenarios

Coaching = a method of employee development in which a specialist provides career and life guidance to help employees achieve professional goals

Cognitive psychology = a branch of psychology that emphasizes sensation and perception

Collective bargaining= the process of negotiating employment conditions for members of a bargaining unit in a union

Compa-ratio = the ratio of an employees' salary to the midpoint of the salary range

Compensable factors = job requirements that are deemed valuable to the organization

Conciliation = a type of dispute resolution strategy based on meetings with peers with a goal to smoothing the conflict

Concurrent criterion-related validity = the extent to which job incumbents' scores on the selection test correlate with their job performance

confidentiality = names and information are kept separate to ensure privacy

Conflict = the state when a group or individual inhibits the goals of another group or individual

Conscientious = a personal trait associated with punctuality, reliability and strong attention to detail

Construct validity = the extent to which scores on the selection test correlate with a previously validated test of a similar concept

Constructive confrontation = a resolution strategy to agree on smaller items of dispute prior to addressing the more complex items

Constructive discharge = an unlawful end to the employment relationship that is based on a manager creating intolerable working conditions for an employee

Continuing Education = A strategy to maintain professional currency by seeking out professional development opportunities

Continuous learning organization = an organizational culture that places an emphasis on skills currency and the sharing of new knowledge

Control = the extent to which an employee has autonomy at work

Corporate universities = formal education that is specific to the requirements and culture of the trainees' organization

Criterion = an acceptable standard, or agreed upon yardstick, for measuring something; oftentimes performance is the criterion of interest in Workplace Psychology

Criterion Contamination = things that are measured that are unrelated to true performance.

Criterion Deficiency = real aspects of performance that are not measured.

Criterion Relevance = the correct measurement of real performance; measurement will be useful to organization and employee

Criterion-related validity = the extent to which scores on the selection test correlate with job performance

Cross training = a method of teaching employees the jobs typically done by other employees (coworkers) in the organization

Cross-cultural psychology=a branch of psychology that studies the extent to which cultures are the same and different from each other

Daily Hassles = annoying tasks that have to be endured on a regular basis

Deductive method = ideas are generated based upon their logical derivation from existing theories

Defamation = verbal communication of information that provides a negative image of a person and is false

Dependent variable (aka the criterion) = the one that is hypothesized to change as a function of changes to the independent variable

Depression = a distressing psychological state characterized by negative mood, hopelessness, and despair

Descriptive statistics = values that are calculated to provide a summary of the basic nature of data

Devil's advocate = a person who is appointed the role of taking an opposing viewpoint to provide feedback

Dissemination (of findings) = sharing the findings of a study via written documents and/or professional presentations

Distributive bargaining = a type of negotiation that is based on a "win-lose" mentality

Due process = employment actions follow established procedures to ensure fairness

Duty of obedience = an employment expectation that employees will respect the chain of command within the organization

Emergency management plans = a risk management tool in which the organization prepares ahead of time for various types of emergency situations

Employee Assistance Programs (EAPs) = a progressive approach to improve the well-being of employees by providing a variety of coping resources

Employee development = discretionary activities to help specific employees prepare for future advancement in the organization

Employee diligence = an employment expectation that employees will work conscientiously in the best interest of the organization

Employee Handbook = a document made available to employees that includes a detailed description of the organization, its policies, benefits, and expectations of work behavior

Employee performance = individual contributions toward organizational goals

Entitlement philosophy = a system of distributing job outcomes (such as pay) on the basis of seniority

Equal Employment Opportunity = a philosophy that people should have fair access to desired employment outcomes (hiring, evaluation, and promotion)

Equal Employment Opportunity Commission = a government agency charged with overseeing fairness in employment and adherence to related legislation

Equity philosophy = a system of distributing job outcomes (such as pay) on the basis of merit

Equity Sensitivity = a characteristic that describes how some people pay more attention to equity cues than others

Ergonomic Analysis = an inspection of the workplace, with interviews and observations of job activities to identify and reduce injury risk factors

Ergonomics = the study of the interaction between worker and the workplace with a view to making improvements to equipment or processes

Error variance = effects on the dependent variable that are unaccounted for by the research; makes it difficult to address hypotheses

Ethics = rules of conduct recognized in the concepts of right and wrong behavior

Eustress = a positive stress reaction that is characterized by a heightened state of physical arousal and a perception of facing a challenge

Excelsior list = a list providing the names and addresses of all employees who are elibile that must be provided by the employer to the organizing union

Exchange relationship = employees contribute time, energy, and productivity in exchange for direct and indirect rewards from the organization

Exhaustion = the physical breakdown of the body's systems under prolonged exposure to stress

Expatriates = employees from one country who are sent to another and must adapt to the culture of the hosting country

Expectancy = a component of expectancy theory in which the employee links the probability of achieving a certain performance level if they give their effort to a particular task

Experimental control = the degree to which extraneous variables are held constant

External equity comparison = a process of comparing one's own outcome/input ratio with another person

External validity= the degree of confidence that a study's findings can be applied to other settings

Extraneous variable = a variable that is not specified by the research model, but nevertheless influences the variables of interest

Face validity = the extent to which there is a common sense association between a selection test and requirements of the job

Factor comparison method = a highly detailed method of job evaluation that assigns a dollar value to each level of compensable factors prior to considering each job

Featherbedding = an unlawful practice in which a labor union required wage payments to its members even if their work was not needed

Fight or Flight response = the physiological mobilization of the body when faced with a potentially threatening situation

Financial Performance Metrics = measurements that address the overall fiscal picture of the organization

Flexplace = providing a flexible working arrangement such that employees are free to work the regular working hours at off-site locations

Flextime = a benefit of allowing employees to choose their work hours around mandatory "core" hours

Flextime = providing a flexible working arrangement such that employees must be on-site for certain hours, but can make their own schedules for the remaining hours in the work week

Forced Distribution Method = a rating format where the rater uses a normal "bell" curve to rate the performance of employees

Formative evaluation = a type of training assessment that is conducted to improve the training

Functional Organizational Structure = a structure based on the fundamental purpose of the department

Fundamental Attribution Error = an error in social perception in which people over-estimate the impact of personal traits (internal traits) in guiding another person's behavior

Gainsharing = a type of group incentive in which bonuses are shared at the team level if certain performance goals are met

General Adaptation Syndrome = the body's sequence of reactions to a stressor, including the Alarm, Resistance, and Exhaustion stages

General Duty Standard = a mandate that organizations attempt to identify and eliminate serious hazards to employee safety and health

Generalize = the application of findings from one study to other situations

Geographic Organizational Structure = a structure based on physical location

Goal setting = the use of challenging, numeric goals to raise motivation an d performance

Graphic Rating Scale = a rating format that is anchored at either end of a performance dimension

Green circle = a pay rate for an employee that is above the median of a salary range

Hiring (or personnel selection) system = the entire set of techniques used to identify the job candidates that are best-suited to the organization

Hostile work environment = a type of sexual harassment in which an employee feels unable to perform job functions because of sex-based intimidation at work

Hot cargo agreements = an unlawful practice in which members of a labor union refused to handle goods produced by a non-unionized company

HR Audit = careful examinations of Human Resources practices and policies to insure that they are functioning well and not creating risks to the organization

Human Relations Movement = an emphasis to the psychological meaning constructed at work, and the impact of the social environment.

Human Resources Generalist = A job title which requires job responsibilities in all basic Human Resources functions

Human Resources Information Systems = software that allows for detailed documentation of a wide variety of personnel

Human Resources Performance Metrics = measurements that can be used to address the value of the HR department

Hybrid Entitlement/Equity Philosophy = a system of distributing job outcomes (such as pay) on the basis of seniority and merit based on future-oriented bonuses

Hypothesis = a statement of a potential relationship between the independent variable(s) and dependent variable(s)

Impasse = a negotiation breakdown in which the parties cannot collaborate to reach a mutually agreeable solution

Independent variable (aka the predictor) = the one that is hypothesized to lead to changes in another variable or variables

Inductive method = ideas are generated based on observations of a particular topic or problem

Inferential statistics = values that are calculated and tested using probability theory to address hypotheses

Institutional Review Board (IRB) = a committee of people who are responsible for ensuring the ethicality of research

Instrumentality = a component of expectancy theory in which the employee links the probability of getting an outcome if they reach a certain performance level on a particular task

Intangible compensation = rewards are derived from reasons related to the task itself such as achievement, enjoyment, and recognition

Integrative bargaining = a type of negotiation that is based on a "win-win" mentality

Integrity test = a set of questions to measure traits that may be related to counterproductive work behaviors

Internal equity comparison = evaluating fairness by comparing one's job outcomes to one's work inputs

Internal validity = the degree of confidence that extraneous variables have been controlled in a study

Job Bidding = an internal recruitment strategy that encourages current employees to express their interest for moving into other positions in the organization

Job classification = a system based on broad groupings of jobs with similar value to the organization

Job demands = work pressures that can burden the resources of employees

Job Description = a detailed description of the responsibilities and activities performed on the job; often delineates essential and non-essential functions

Job design = a technique to improve jobs by changing the number or responsibility level of tasks

Job enlargement = a job design strategy of increasing the number of tasks at the same level of responsibility

Job enrichment = a job design strategy of increasing the responsibility level associated with tasks

Job evaluation = the formal method for assessing jobs in terms of their value to the organization

Job Posting = an internal recruitment strategy that provides job vacancy announcements to current employees

Job Related = the connection between any measure of a job applicant and the actual requirements of the job

Job rotation = training and assigning employees to a variety of different jobs within the organization

Job satisfaction = the affective evaluation of the job and its components

Job sharing = a benefit of allowing two employees to share one job by splitting the work hours

Job slotting = a method of fitting new jobs into an existing salary structure

Job Specification = an explanation of specific knowledge, skills, education, or physical characteristics that an employee needs to have in order to do the job

Job Summary = an overall narrative description of the job, including job title, purpose, and reporting relationships

Labor relations = topics that involve working conditions, covering both employer and employee rights

Labor unions = formal groups of workers who are organized for purposes of collective bargaining

Learning criteria = a type of training evaluation that is based on trainees' knowledge, typically measured with a test

Learning objectives = the specification of what trainees need to know and/or be able to do at the conclusion of the training

Levels of Analysis = the recognition that workplace psychology can be studied in terms of individual, work team, or organizational variables

Libel = written communication of information that provides a negative image of a person and is false

Line of Sight = the extent to which something is clearly visible in the daily working world of employees

Lockout = a labor relations breakdown in which the organization bars employee access to the worksite

Management By Walking Around = a tactic to improve labor relations and leadership effectiveness by being available at employees' work sites

Mass layoff = one of the events that qualifies for the employer to fulfill obligations specified in the WARN Act in which 33% of employees or 500 employees are laid off within a month period

Mastery goal orientation = a type of achievement motivation that bases success on developing expertise at a task

Matrix-Style Organizational Structure = a structure that includes aspects of both traditional functional and product-based organizational structures

Mediation = a dispute resolution tactic in which a neutral third party gathers relevant information from all viewpoints and makes a nonbinding suggestion

Mediator variable = a variable that explains how or why the independent variable affects the dependent variable

Mentoring = the process in which an experienced employee (mentor) helps a newer employee (protégé) in organizational socialization and employee development

Mission = the basic purpose of the organization in terms of what it does and who it serves; the framework for guiding the strategy.

Model = a graphical representation of the variables under study that attempt to capture some phenomenon

Moderator variable = a variable that explains the conditions that are necessary for the independent variable to affect the dependent variable

Motivation = the internal process that serves to direct attention, energize, and sustain goal-directed behavior over time

Multitasking = attempting to work on more than one task at a time

National Institute for Occupational Safety and Health (NIOSH) = an agency created as part of the Occupational Safety and Health Act to research and provide safety recommendations for workplaces

Needs assessment = a formal planning method to determine organizational objectives and whether these can be met with training

Negligent hiring = failing to ensure the safety of customers, clients, or employees through inadequate hiring practices

Negotiation = the process of finding an agreeable solution to the needs of two or more parties

Non-compete agreement = a formal, legally binding document in which an employee agrees not to work for a competitor or solicit business away from the organization

Non-disclosure agreement = a formal, legally binding document in which an employee agrees not to discuss any trade secrets or other confidential material

Normality = a distribution of data that is shaped like a bell curve

Objective appraisal data = performance information that can be directly observed and/or counted

Occupational Safety and Health Act (OSHA) = federal legislation charged with ensuring safe workplaces for employees

Offshoring = moving a job from within the US to another location, either within the same company or another company

Ombudsman = a designated person in the organization who is typically well-known and talented at defusing conflict

Onboarding = a process of integrating new employees into the organization

Organization analysis = the use of business plans to identify the potential need and benefit of a training effort; includes organizational goals, resources, and environment

Organization development (OD) = a systematic method for improving the organization in terms of culture, technology, emphasis, and/or work processes

Organizational Chart = a graphical representation of the organizational structure

Organizational commitment = the extent to which an employee identifies with the organization and plans to remain there

Organizational culture = shared values, beliefs, and traditions that define organizations

Organizational Dispute Resolution (ODR) = the organizational system for managing complaints, grievances, and all manner of conflict

Organizational socialization = a process in which new employees are introduced to the organizational culture and the requirements for expected behaviors and attitudes in the organization

Organizational Structure = describes the formal reporting relationships among employees

Outsourcing = replacing in-house permanent employees with those who work on a contractual basis

Pay grades = groupings of jobs based on similarity of value to the organization

Pay range = the difference between the minimum and the maximum salary in a pay grade

Pay-for-Performance = a compensation system that is based on how much each employee produces

Pedagogy = the study of how learning best occurs for children

Peer review panel = an attempt at conflict resolution based on meetings, often with a group of coworkers

Performance Appraisal = a formal system through which employers assess their employees; including progress reports and feedback

Performance evaluation = the measurement and documentation of employee performance

Performance goal orientation = a type of achievement motivation that bases success on showing superior results or avoiding failure

Performance management = the process of setting and evaluating metrics for ensuring that work goals are met

Perils of participation = a decline in labor relations that occurs if employees feel that their input has been ignored

Person analysis = consideration of individual-level performance and training needs

Personnel selection = the set of technique used to make hiring decisions

PEST analysis = an environmental scanning technique that gathers information about political, economic, social, and technical factors

Picketing = a public relations strategy of informing the public about an organization's practices by marching with signs and/or chanting

Pilot testing = practicing data collection with a goal of ensuring that a procedure runs as intended

Plant closing = one of the events that qualifies for the employer to fulfill obligations specified in the WARN Act in which a facility closes for 6 months or more

Point factor method = a method of job evaluation that is based on how much the job requires performance on each compensable factor

Population = the entire group (of people, usually) that one would like to generalize findings to

Power analysis = a procedure for determining an appropriate sample size for detecting statistical significance

Predictive criterion-related validity = the extent to which job applicants' scores on the selection test at one time correlate with their job performance at another time

Prima facie = "on the face of"...the initial evidence that there is unfair discrimination

Primary appraisal = the first cognitive reaction to a potential stressor in which a person evaluates whether or not it is a threat

Primary prevention strategies = proactive approaches to stress management that involve minimizing the impact of stressors on employees

Product-based Structure = a structure based on the product line or service to be delivered

Professional Human Resources Certification = the national credential indicating professional competence in Human Resources

Progressive Discipline = a process of documenting performance-related problems and specific employee changes needed to address the problems

Protected Class = a group that is explicitly included in employment law to ensure that members of this class do not face unfair discrimination

Psychological Contract = the principle that employees give their time, energy, and work in exchange for outcomes from the organization, such as pay or job security

Psychological flow = a state of optimal motivation and immersion in an activity

Psychometrics = the study of measurement properties of psychological variables, with an emphasis on reliability and validity.

Qualifying event = the cause of a loss of health insurance benefits that gives eligibility for COBRA

Qualitative = an approach based on narrative descriptions of the phenomenon of interest

Quantitative = an approach based on numerical assessments of the phenomenon of interest

Quid pro quo harassment = a form of sexual harassment typically perpetrated by a supervisor who indicates that conditions of employment will be based on acquiescence to requests

Random assignment = a methods technique to reduce the impact of participant characteristics

Ranking Method = a rating format where the rater makes a list of employees in order of best performance to worst performance

Rater = someone who is asked to provide formal evaluations of someone else

Reaction criteria = a type of training evaluation that is based on trainees' opinions and beliefs, typically measured with a survey

Realism= the extent to which the study simulates a naturally occurring environment.

Realistic Job Preview = an attempt to increase fit and decrease turnover by explaining the positive and negative aspects of a job to an applicant

Recruitment = locating potential research participants and encouraging their participation

Recruitment = the identification and encouragement of qualified applicants to apply for a position

Red circle = a pay rate for an employee that is below the median of a salary range

Reference check = the process of confirming the accuracy of information provided on a resume or job application

Reliability = the consistency of a measure

Replacement chart = a succession planning tool to identify performance potential of employees

Request for Proposal = the initiation of the process for bidding on contractual work.

Response rate = the ratio of participants to the total number of people contacted during recruitment

Reverse discrimination = a claim that a person who is not a member of a protected class has been unfairly rejected in favor of a minority candidate

Right to Work = state laws that make it illegal to require employees to join a labor union or pay membership dues

Risk acceptance = choosing to take no actions to address a risk that has been identified

Risk assessment = the process of identifying potential risks and the likelihood that each will occur

Risk avoidance = deciding to eliminate a risk that has been identified by removing it from the workplace

Risk management = the identification of potential risks/costs to the organization and how to deal with them

Risk mitigation= trying to lessen the impact of a risk that has been identified

Risk Transfer = assigning an identified risk to another organization, typically an insurance company

Role = a set of behaviors that an employee is expected to perform

Role ambiguity = a job stressor where an employee is uncertain of what to do

Role conflict = a job stressor where an employee perceives incompatible demands

Role overload = a job stressor where an employee perceives too many demands

Rumination = the recreation of a stressor by thinking of it repeatedly

Safety climate = the extent to which the organization places a value on occupational safety and a work environment with a low risk to injuries or accidents

Safety compliance = a part of employee safety performance that consists of using protective equipment and following correct procedures

Safety participation = part of employee safety performance that consists of actively promoting a safe environment and reporting violations

Salary structure = the formal allocation of pay based upon position in the organization

Sample = a subset of the population that is chosen for inclusion in a study; should be representative of the population

Scientific management = an approach directed towards maximizing efficiency and minimizing work-related injuries.

Scientific Method = a systematic process of inquiry that is used to guide data collection and analysis to minimize bias and promote scientific development.

Scientist-Practitioner Model = the philosophy of workplace psychology to use science to address practical work issues

Seamless Structure = a structure based on autonomous work groups or teams; uses technology to enhance communication and performance management across formal reporting relationships

Secondary appraisal = a cognitive evaluation of whether available resources can adequately cope with a stressor

Secondary prevention strategies = stress management techniques directed towards reducing the impact of stress on the mind and body

Settlement range = a negotiation outcome that is less than the target point but acceptable

Sick building syndrome = a set of physical and psychological complaints wherein the employee feels ill at work and fine upon leaving the building

Similar-to-me effect = a rater preference for other people who share characteristics with the rater

Situational Interview = the inclusion of questions that ask about what job candidates would do in hypothetical situations

Skill Inventory = an information management system (often a database) for documenting specialized skills or training

SMART goals = an acronym to summarize features of goal setting that enhance their usefulness; the goals should be specific, measureable, achievable, relevant, and time-bound.

Social loafing = an occurrence where individuals in a group reduce their level of effort

Social Perception = the process of collecting information about another person and making judgments about him or her

Social support = the network of friends, family, or colleagues that provide assistance and help reduce negative effects of stress

Statutory bar = a year-long stay on union certification or decertification activities following a union election

Stereotyping = a type of social perception in which a rater believes that everyone in a group shares characteristics, regardless of whether or not this is the case

Strain = a physical, psychological, or behavioral breakdown that is the result of prolonged or acute exposure to stress

Strategic Management = an organization's process for defining its purposes and how it will achieve those purposes

Stress = the physical and psychological processes of perceiving that one cannot cope with a threat

Stress management = techniques that can be used to stop the process of stress from leading to strain

Stressors = aspects of the environment that may be perceived as a threat

Strike = a labor relations breakdown in which employees refuse to engage in work processes

Structured Interview = the use of standardized questions for each job candidate

Subjective Appraisal data = information that relies on the judgment of one employee by another

Substance abuse = a pattern of use of drugs or alcohol in a way that exceeds societal norms and creates financial, medical, or social problems for the user

Succession planning = a long-range hiring system

Summative evaluation = a type of training assessment that is conducted to determine the effectiveness of training

SWOT analysis = an information-gathering approach to assess the internal strengths and weaknesses, and the external environment in terms of opportunities and threats

Sympathy strike = an expansion of the impact of a strike by refusing to cross the picket line of another union engaged in a strike

Tangible compensation = rewards are derived from the environment, such as rewards

Target point = the desired outcome of negotiations

Task analysis = the examination of job requirements to address training needs

Tertiary prevention strategies = stress management techniques aimed at dealing with the existing experience stress by providing coping resources

Theories = organizing frameworks for explaining a phenomenon; theories evolve over time on the basis of the support they receive

Theory X = a managerial assumption that people are primarily motivated by tangible rewards

Theory Y = a managerial assumption that people are primarily motivated by intangible rewards

TIPS guidelines = employers must not Threaten, Interrogate, Promise, or Spy during a union organization drive or union campaign

Training = a formal, planned, organizational effort to help employees increase job-relevant knowledge and skills

Training transfer= the extent to which behaviors learned during training are subsequently used at the job site

Trait assessments = a method of substantive selection in which tests (such as personality, cognitive ability, and integrity tests) are given to predict job performance

Unbiased = not having a vested interest or personal preference for a particular outcome

Union Security Clauses = arrangements with employees in terms of their membership and paying dues to the union

Valence = the value that an employee places on the outcome associated with performance on a particular task

Validity = the appropriateness of a measure

Values = the guiding principles in terms of ideals, principles, and beliefs about business conduct

Variable = anything that can take on different variables; the cornerstone of psychological research

Vision = a future-oriented, inspirational statement of what the organization is striving towards.

Wage compression = a pay discrepancy wherein newer employees are paid more than senior employees due to changes in labor market conditions

WARN Act = Congressional legislation passed in 1988 that mandated communication with employees in the event of a mass layoff or plant closing

Whole job ranking = a method of ordering jobs in terms of their value to the organization

Work engagement = a high level of involvement with work, characterized by vigor, absorption, and dedication

Work sample = a method of substantive selection in which the applicant is asked to perform samples of job-related tasks

Workforce analysis = a component of an Affirmative Action Program that considers job titles in terms of the current workforce in terms of gender, race, and wages

Workforce planning = the proactive approach to ensuring that the performance needs of the organization can be met with a skilled workforce

Workplace investigation = a systematic, immediate, and unbiased study of alleged incidents at work

Workplace psychology = the study of thought, emotions, and behavior as they relate to organizational effectiveness and individual well-being

Workplace violence = an act of physical aggression against someone with a specific goal of trying to inflict harm

Wrongful termination = an unlawful end to the employment relationship that violates a contract or violates employment law

Yellow dog contract = an illegal employer tactic of requiring employees to promise not to join a labor union

Credits

Chapter 1 cartoon: www.cartoonstock.com. Copyright © 2010 by Cartoonstock.com. Reprinted with permission. • "Unemployment in the U.S." Copyright in the Public Domain. • "Earnings and Demographics in U.S." Copyright in the Public Domain. • Knapp and Knapp, "Table 48-1: Certification Benefits," The Business of Certification. Copyright © 2002 by American Society of Association Executives. Reprinted with permission. • "Career Paths in Workplace Psychology." Copyright in the Public Domain. • Chapter 2, opening image: Copyright in the Public Domain. • Chapter 2 cartoon: www.cartoonstock.com. Copyright © by Cartoonstock.com. Reprinted with permission. • "Job Analysis: Task Rating." Copyright in the Public Domain. • Suzanne Lucas, "How to Write Performance Appraisals," U.S.News.com. Copyright © 2008 by US News & World Report Inc. Reprinted with permission. • "Checklist: Preparing a Performance Review." Copyright in the Public Domain. • "Checklist: Conducting a Performance Review." Copyright in the Public Domain. • Dwayne Devonish and Dion Greenidge, International Journal of Selection and Assessment, vol. 18, no. 1, pp. 83. Copyright © 2010 by John Wiley & Sons, Inc. Reprinted with permission. • Table: Examples of Objectives and Indicators. Journal of Applied Psychology, vol. 93, no. 3. Copyright © 2008 by American Psychological Association. Reprinted with permission. • Chapter 3, opening image: Copyright © Depositphotos/Tom Schumucker. • Chapter 3 cartoon: www.cartoonstock.com. Copyright © by Cartoonstock.com. Reprinted with permission. • "Workplace Diversity Practices Used by Organizations," at: http://www.shrm.org/Research/SurveyFindings/Documents/10-DiversityFlier_FINAL_spotlight.pdf. Copyright © 2010 by Society for Human Resource Management. Reprinted with permission. • Equal Employment Opportunity table. Copyright in the Public Domain. • "JobAid: Diversity SWOT Analysis." Copyright in the Public Domain. • Alexandra Levit, "Figure 5-2: Background Check Authorization Form," Success for Hire. Copyright © 2008 by American Society for Training and Development. Reprinted with permission. • "SHRM Research: Credit Background Checks," at: http://www.shrm.org/Research/SurveyFindings/Articles/Documents/CCFlier_FINAL.pdf. Copyright © 2010 by Society for Human Resource Management. Reprinted with permission. • "Survey Findings: Onboarding Practices," at: http://www.shrm.org/Research/SurveyFindings/Articles/Pages/OnboardingPractices.aspx. Copyright © 2011 by Society for Human Resource Management. Reprinted with permission. • "Negligent Hiring Cases: Employer Found Guilty." Copyright in the Public Domain. • "A Quick Recap of the EEOC 2010 Stats." Copyright in the Public Domain. • "Equal Opportunity Employment." Copyright in the Public Domain. • "Employment and Median Usual Weekly Earnings of Women, by Industry, 2009." Copyright in the Public Domain. • "Facts About the Americans with Disabilities Act." Copyright in the Public Domain. • Chapter 4, opening image: Copyright © Depositphotos/Yuri Arcurs. • Monika Sieverding, "'Be Cool!': Emotional costs of hiding feelings in a job interview," International Journal of Selection and Assessment, vol. 17, no. 4, pp. 396. Copyright © 2009 by John Wiley & Sons, Inc. Reprinted with permission. • Chapter 4 cartoon: www.cartoonstock.com. Copyright © by Cartoonstock.com. Reprinted with permission. • Rex Davenport, "Table A: Perceived Skill Gap," T+D, pp. 26. Copyright © 2005 by American Society for Training and Development. Reprinted with permission. • Michael Allen, "Table 13-1: Attributes and Benefits of E-learning," ASTD Handbook for Workplace Learning Professionals. Copyright © 2008 by American Society for Training and Development. Reprinted with permission. • Clark Aldrich, "Minigames: Miller Brewing Company," ASTD Handbook for Workplace Learning Professionals. Copyright © 2008 by American Society for Training and Development. Reprinted with permission. • "Employee Level and Diversity Training," at: http://www.shrm.org/Research/SurveyFindings/Documents/10-DiversityFlier_FINAL_spotlight.pdf. Copyright © by Society for Human Resource Management. Reprinted with permission. • Maxine Kamin, "Handout 13-3: Governing Forces in Customer Service," Customer Service Training. Copyright © 2002 by American Society for Training and Development. Reprinted with permission. • "Figure 6-3: Performance Distribution Following Identification of Gaps and Implementation of Performance Architecture." Copyright © 2007 by Exemplary Performance, LLC. Reprinted with permission. • Nancy Kristiansen, "Table 28-2: Sample Evaluation Statements That Reflect Assessment and Design," ASTD Handbook for Workplace Learning Professionals. Copyright © 2008 by American Society for Training and Development. Reprinted with permission. • Barbara Carnes, "Figure 1-1: Training Transfer Process Model," Making Learning Stick. Copyright © 2010 by American Society for Training and Development. Reprinted with permission. • "Figure 5: What Percentage of Your Learning Programs is Evaluated at Each Level of the

CPSIA information can be obtained
at www.ICGtesting.com
Printed in the USA
FSOW03n1819040915
10725FS